AT&T

The KornShell
Command and Programming Language

Morris I. Bolsky, David G. Korn
AT&T Bell Laboratories
Murray Hill, New Jersey

PTR Prentice Hall
Englewood Cliffs, New Jersey 07632

Production Supervisor: Sophie Papanikolaou
Cover Design: Lundgren Graphics, Ltd.
Cover Photo: Courtesy of New England, Inc.
Manufacturing Buyer: Mary Ann Gloriande

The authors and publisher of this book have used their best efforts in preparing this book.
These efforts include the development, research, and testing of the theories and programs
to determine their effectiveness. The authors and publisher make no warranty of any
kind, expressed or implied, with regard to these programs or the documentation
contained in this book. The authors and publisher shall not be liable in any event for
incidental or consequential damages in connection with, or arising out of, the furnishing,
performance, or use of these programs.

20 19 18 17 16 15 14 13 12 11

ISBN 0-13-516972-0

Prentice Hall International (UK) Limited, *London*
Prentice Hall of Australia Pty. Limited, *Sydney*
Prentice Hall Canada Inc., *Toronto*
Prentice Hall Hispanoamericana, S.A., *Mexico*
Prentice Hall of India Private Limited, *New Delhi*
Prentice Hall of Japan, Inc., *Tokyo*
Simon & Schuster Asia Pte. Ltd., *Singapore*
Editora Prentice Hall do Brasil, Ltda., *Rio de Janeiro*

CONTENTS

ACKNOWLEDGEMENTS

Steven Bourne wrote the Bourne shell, from which the KornShell language is derived, while at Bell Laboratories. Bill Joy wrote the original version of the C shell while at the University of California, Berkeley, California.

Mike Veach of AT&T Bell Laboratories contributed the original code for the **emacs** built-in editor used in the KornShell language. Pat Sullivan, also of AT&T Bell Laboratories, contributed the original code for the **vi** built-in editor used in the KornShell language, and has continued to maintain it.

The **emacs** editor was developed by Richard Stallman at the Massachusetts Institute of Technology. The **emacs** program, from which the **emacs** built-in editor used in the KornShell language was adapted, was developed by Warren Montgomery of AT&T Bell Laboratories. The **vi** program, from which the **vi** built-in editor used in the KornShell language was adapted, was developed by Mark Horton and Bill Joy while at the University of California, Berkeley, California.

The Rand Corporation, and the Department of Information and Computer Science at the University of California, Irvine, developed software and documentation for the MH Message Handling System, now in the public domain. Bruce Borden, Stockton Gaines, and Norman Shapiro were the initial designers and developers of MH. (The *Complete Application* chapter uses the MH system as an example of how to write an application in **ksh**.)

We are grateful to Rosemary Simpson who prepared the index.

We are especially grateful to everyone who has reviewed the drafts of this book, has given us suggestions for improvement, and has helped to debug the examples. In particular, we want to thank Harold Bamford, III, Bill Brelsford, Larry Cipriani, Glenn Fowler, Judy Grass, Jeff Korn, Doug McIlroy, John Mocenigo, Arnold Robbins, Steve Sommars, Kevin Wall, and Robert Wantz.

PREFACE

This book is the ***specification*** of the KornShell language and a
reference handbook for **ksh**, the program that implements the
KornShell language. This book also contains a ***Tutorial*** that describes
both of the functions of **ksh**; as an interactive command language, and as a
programming language. It contains numerous examples illustrating the
features of **ksh**, and many chapters have exercises. It also contains a
Quick Reference summary of the KornShell language, including page
references to the book.

This book is intended both for new users with little computer or shell
experience, and for experienced computer users who are familiar with **ksh**
and/or other shells. For new users, it has considerable tutorial material.
For all users, it is a comprehensive reference handbook.

What is the KornShell Language?

The KornShell language was designed and developed by David G. Korn
at AT&T Bell Laboratories. It is an ***interactive command language***
that provides access to the UNIX system and to many other systems, on
many different computers and workstations on which it is implemented.
The KornShell language is also a complete, powerful, high-level
programming language for writing applications, often more easily and
quickly than with other high-level languages. This makes it especially
suitable for prototyping.

There are two other widely used shells, the Bourne shell developed by
Steven Bourne at AT&T Bell Laboratories, and the C shell developed by
Bill Joy at the University of California. **ksh** has the best features of both,
plus many new features of its own. Thus **ksh** can do much to enhance
your productivity and the quality of your work, both in interacting with the
system, and in programming. **ksh** programs are ***easier to write***, and are
more ***concise*** and ***readable***.

ksh is larger than the C shell or the Bourne shell programs. In spite of its increased size, **ksh** provides ***better performance***. Programs can be written to run faster with **ksh** than with either the Bourne shell or the C shell, sometimes an order of magnitude faster.

ksh has ***evolved*** and ***matured*** with extensive user feedback. It has been used by thousands of people at AT&T since 1982, and recently at many other companies and universities. A survey conducted at one of the largest AT&T Bell Laboratories computer centers showed that 80% of their customers, both programmers and non-programmers, use **ksh**.

ksh is ***compatible*** with the Bourne shell. Virtually all programs written for the Bourne shell run with **ksh**. If you are familiar with the Bourne shell, you can use **ksh** immediately, without retraining.

ksh is ***readily available***. It is sold (source and binary) by AT&T, and by other companies under license from AT&T both in the USA and abroad. It has been purchased by dozens of major corporations, and by many individuals for use on home computers.

ksh is ***extensible***. The KornShell language uses the same syntax for built-in commands as for non built-in commands. Therefore, system developers can add new commands "transparently" to the KornShell language; that is, with minimum effort and with no differences visible to users other than faster execution.

ksh is intended to conform to the final Shell Language Standard being developed by the IEEE POSIX1003.2 Shell and Utilities Language Committee. At the time the manuscript of this book was sent to the publisher, Draft 6 was the current version of the POSIX Standard. Draft 6 has been adopted as the interim U.S. Federal Information Processing Standard (FIPS). To the best of our knowledge, the description of **ksh** in this book is consistent with Draft 6.

Organization of this Book

Part I, Introduction, tells what a shell is and lists the benefits of the KornShell language. It tells how to obtain **ksh** and explains about different versions of **ksh**. It also specifies the notation used in this book.

Part II, Tutorial, has chapters on the key concepts of ***Files and Processes***, and on the use of the KornShell language as a ***Command Language*** and a ***Programming Language***. The ***Files and Processes*** chapter provides background information to help you understand the KornShell language. You do not have to understand everything in it to read the remaining chapters.

The **Command Language** chapter is intended as a guide through the language by giving step-by-step instructions for some of the typical uses of **ksh**. It is not intended to explain in detail all of the features of **ksh**, or all of the possible uses of the features that are discussed in this chapter. All of the features of the KornShell language are covered in detail elsewhere in this book.

The **Programming Language** chapter is intended for those who want to use the KornShell as a programming language.

Part II, **Tutorial**, also has a chapter on **Customizing Your Environment**, which describes how to set up your profile and environment files. It also suggests ways for optimizing the performance of shell scripts.

Part III, **The Built-In Editors**, is a detailed manual for the **emacs** and **vi** built-in editors. One of the major benefits of using **ksh** is that you can use **emacs** or **vi** directives to edit your current command line or to edit and reenter previous commands.

Part IV, **Programming Language**, is both a specification for the KornShell language and a detailed guide to using it. It contains chapters on **Syntax**, **Command Processing**, **Compound Commands**, **Parameters**, **Built-in Commands**, and **Invocation and Environment**. It also contains a chapter, **Other Commands**, which documents programs that are not part of **ksh**, but which are used in the examples in this book and may prove useful to many users. UNIX® systems and many other systems have these programs.

Part V, **Application Programming**, has a chapter on **Shell Functions and Programs**, with several functions and programs written in the KornShell language. They are included primarily for illustrative purposes. However, you may find some of these functions and/or programs useful. It also has the chapter, **A Complete Application**, with an example of how to use **ksh** as a high-level programming language, to program an application. The example that we use is a slightly modified version of the MH (Message Handling) system.

Part VI, **Appendix**, contains a **Glossary**. It also has a **Quick Reference**, with the formats, options, and page references for all **ksh** built-in, non-built-in, and editor commands, parameters, and other details.

The **Portability** chapter contains information to help write portable scripts, with sections listing Features of **ksh** not in the Bourne Shell, Features of **ksh** not in the System V, Release 3 Shell, Compatibility of **ksh** with the System V, Release 3 Bourne Shell, New Features in 11/16/88 Version of **ksh**, Obsolescent Features, Possible Extensions to **ksh**, and the ASCII *Character Set*.

There is also a detailed *Index*. The outside back cover has page references to all commands and parameters, and a brief summary of key **emacs** and **vi** directives.

PART I

INTRODUCTION

1 ABOUT THE KornShell LANGUAGE

WHAT IS A SHELL?

The term "shell" gets its name from the UNIX system. Many systems on which the KornShell language is implemented are designed in a way that is similar to the UNIX system.

One of the things that makes the UNIX system so flexible is its layered design. At the core is the hardware. The hardware is surrounded by system software that most users never directly interact with, called the kernel. The kernel is surrounded by programs (often called utilities) such as **cat**, **date**, etc., that perform specific tasks. A program that provides easy access to these utilities by the user is called a *shell*. It is called a shell primarily because it is, in a sense, an outer layer. Since the shell is an ordinary program, not a part of the operating system, each user can choose whichever shell they prefer.

A shell enables the user to interact with resources of the computer, such as programs, files, and devices. An interactive shell acts as a command interpreter. In its role as a command interpreter, the shell is the interface between the user and the system. The user types commands to the shell, and the shell carries them out, usually by running programs. This is the primary function of the shell for many users. Some interactive shells contain a built-in editor facility to make it easy and fast for the user to correct typing errors and to edit previous commands.

Most shells can also be used as a programming language. Users can combine command sequences to create new programs. These programs are known as shell scripts. Shell scripts automate use of the shell as a command interpreter. For instance, if you frequently use the same sequence of, say, five shell commands, you could write a file with these five commands to avoid having to retype them each time. When you reference this file, the shell will interpret the lines in it as though they were typed from a terminal.

Some shells, such as the KornShell, are, in effect, a complete high-level programming language. For instance, the KornShell language includes variables, functions, built-in commands, and control flow commands (for instance, conditional and iteration commands). Thus, KornShell scripts can be application programs such as those that can be written in any other high-level language as Basic, Fortran, or the C language (not to be confused with the C shell).

The KornShell language is described in the preface of this book. Because of the ease of programming in the KornShell language, it is especially useful for prototyping. A prototype for an application system may be written first in the KornShell language. Parts of the application can then be rewritten in a lower level language as the need arises.

HOW TO OBTAIN ksh

ksh will be included in UNIX System V Release 4.

The binary for **ksh** is provided by some vendors, including Apollo Computers with the DOMAIN/OS system, Hewlett-Packard with the HP-UX system, and Apple Computer on the Mac II with the A/UX system. Other vendors sell **ksh** as add-ons to their systems. For example, AT&T includes **ksh** as part of the 386 UNIX VAR/ISV Software Developer's Toolkit. Third party vendors such as Aspen Technologies in Parsippany, New Jersey, sell **ksh** for use on several systems. An MS-DOS version of the KornShell language is available from Mortice Kern Systems, Inc. of Waterloo, Ontario in Canada.

Source code for **ksh** is available through the AT&T UNIX System Toolchest software distribution system. In the USA, phone 1-201-522-6900 and log in as **guest**. In Europe, phone AT&T UNIX Europe in London at 44-1-567-7711. In the Far East, phone AT&T UNIX Pacific in Tokyo at 81-3-431-3670.

BENEFITS OF USING ksh

Compared to other shells, **ksh** has improvements for use as a command language and improvements for use as a programming language. These improvements are summarized here.

Improvements as a Command Language

Command line editing. A major benefit of **ksh** is that it has an **emacs**-like and a **vi**-like interface with which to edit the current command line. Thus with **ksh** it is not necessary to backspace to the point where a change is needed, or to start over. Retyping a command is tedious, time-consuming, and error-prone, especially if changes need to be made several times. Users of **ksh** tend to form the habit of editing their current command before pressing `RETURN`. The same interface can also be used to make changes to previous commands, which **ksh** keeps in a history file.

Command history mechanism. ksh keeps a history file that stores the commands you enter. The history file can be accessed via **emacs** or **vi** editor directives, or via the built-in command **fc**. The history file is maintained across login sessions, and can be shared by several simultaneous instances of **ksh**. Thus a previous command can be modified and reentered with minimal overhead.

Command name aliasing. Command name and option combinations can be customized by defining shorthand names, called aliases, for commands that you use frequently.

Job control. ksh can display a completion message at the prompt after a background job terminates. On some systems, jobs can be stopped and moved to and from the background.

New cd capabilities. You can return to the previous directory without having to type the name of the directory. The working directory can be changed to a similarly named directory without having to type the complete name. **ksh** allows you to extend the functionality of the **cd** command by replacing it with a user defined function.

Tilde expansion. The home directory of any user, and the last directory that you were in, can be referred to symbolically. It is not necessary to type, or even to know, the name of the directory.

Improvements as a Programming Language

More general I/O mechanism. More than one file can be simultaneously opened and read. The number of columns printed for each item of information can be specified in a program.

Menu selection primitive. **ksh** provides a structured way to write programs that query the user via menus. **ksh** adjusts the menu display to the size of the terminal screen display.

Built-in integer arithmetic. **ksh** can perform integer arithmetic in any base from 2 through 36 using constants and **ksh** variables.

Substring operators. **ksh** can generate substrings from the values of shell variables.

Array variables and attributes. Strings can be converted to uppercase or lowercase. One-dimensional arrays of strings or numbers can be used.

More general function facility. Local variables within functions can be defined and, therefore, recursive procedures can be written. Code can be specified to be executed whenever the function terminates.

Co-process facility. **ksh** provides the capability to run one or more programs in the background, and to send and receive queries from it. This makes it easy to use shell scripts as a front end to a database management system, or to an editor.

Easier to debug. **ksh** displays better error diagnostics when it encounters an error. Thus the cause of the error can be located more easily. The execution of each function can be traced separately.

Better performance. **ksh** scripts can often be written to run an order of magnitude faster.

Better security. **ksh** allows a system administrator to log and/or disable all privileged scripts. On current UNIX systems, users need read permission to execute a script. With **ksh**, a system administrator can allow **ksh** to read and execute a script without giving a user permission to read it.

International. **ksh** has full 8-bit transparency so that it can be used with extended character sets. **ksh** can be compiled to support multibyte and multiwidth character sets as found in several Asian countries.

VERSION TO WHICH THIS BOOK APPLIES

ksh has evolved and matured with extensive user feedback. Thus there are several versions of **ksh**.

This book specifies the version of **ksh** dated 11/16/88. New features in this version are listed in the *Appendix* on page 322. This book also describes the older version of **ksh** dated 06/03/86 and named **ksh-i**, sold by the AT&T UNIX System Toolchest.

New features or changes in the 11/16/88 version are noted in this book by the word "*Version*," followed by a statement such as, "This feature is available only on versions of **ksh** newer than the 06/03/86 version." Note that examples do not use the 11/16/88 features, except where indicated. Differences between the 06/03/86 version and earlier versions are not noted in this book; however, most of this book is still applicable.

You can find out the date of the version of **ksh** you are using by:
• Looking in your system documentation.
• Using the **what** command with the appropriate pathname. (However, your system may not have the **what** command.)
  Example
  ```
  what /bin/ksh    # Or whatever pathname of ksh is.
  /bin/ksh:
              Version 06/03/86a
  ```
• Using the CONTROL v directive of the **emacs** built-in editor.

A suffix (a in the above example) following a date indicates minor and/or local modifications to the code. However, the features are the same for all releases of **ksh** with the same date, regardless of the suffix.

As with many other programs, **ksh** is implemented on many different systems, and on many different multiuser and single user (personal) computers. There inevitably are differences between implementations, usually minor, and presumably documented by the supplier of the program. Features of **ksh** that are most likely to differ on different implementations are noted in this book by the words "*Implementation-dependent*," followed by an explanation.

On some systems, the organization that built or installed **ksh** may have replaced the original date by another means of indicating the version, such as numbers and/or letters, or even by a date that has no relation to the dates mentioned above. In this case, you have to determine what you have from the documentation, by experimenting, and/or by asking others. However, the fact remains that most, if not quite all, of the information in this book will almost certainly be applicable to the implementation of **ksh** that you have.

For those readers who are familiar with the Bourne shell, subtle differences between the Bourne shell and **ksh** are noted in this book by the words, *"Bourne shell,"* followed by an explanation of the differences. Also, the chapter on *Portability* lists differences.

2 NOTATION USED IN THIS BOOK

GENERAL

For conciseness, we refer to:
- The program that implements the KornShell language, as **ksh**.
- The **emacs** and **vi** built-in editors, as **emacs** and **vi**. When we mean the complete programs, we say the **emacs** program or the **vi** program.
- Commands, just by their names. The names are in **bold** type, for instance, **alias** and **date**.
- The person providing input to **ksh**, as "you." Depending on the context, this would mean the person using **ksh** as an interactive command language, or as a programming language.

Usual pronunciation:
- **emacs**. *ee-macks* (*ee* as in *beet*).
- **ksh**. Pronounce each letter separately.
- MH. Pronounce each letter separately.
- UNIX. *u-nix* (*u* pronounced like *you*).
- **vi**. Pronounce each letter separately.

KEYS ON TERMINAL

Special keys that you press, such as CONTROL, are in uppercase Helvetica bold type in a box. Individual letter or symbol keys that you press, such as **h** or **]**, are also in **bold** type but are in Times font and are not in a box. Uppercase and lowercase characters are equivalent when you use the CONTROL key; for instance, CONTROL **h** or CONTROL **H**.

Some of these special keys may be labeled differently on different terminals. Some possible alternate labels are shown below. If your keyboard doesn't have any of these alternate labels, you can try the `CONTROL` key plus the individual letter or symbol key shown below. If necessary, see the **Character Set** for further clarification, plus the manual for your keyboard.

`BACKSPACE`	Press the key labeled BACKSPACE, or else `CONTROL` **h**.
`CONTROL`	Always use this key in conjunction with an individual letter or symbol key. While holding down the key labeled CONTROL or CTRL, press whatever individual letter or symbol key is appropriate.
`DELETE`	Press the key labeled DEL or DELETE, or RUB or RUBOUT, or `CONTROL` **?**, or else `CONTROL` `BACKSPACE`.
`ESCAPE`	Press the key labeled ESCAPE or ESC, or else `CONTROL` **[**.
`RETURN`	Press the key labeled RETURN or NEWLINE or ENTER, or else `CONTROL` **m**.
`SPACE`	Press the space bar.
`TAB`	Press TAB, or else `CONTROL` **i**.

TYPE FONTS USED IN THIS BOOK

Bold type indicates anything that you type exactly as shown, such as command and option names.

Lowercase *italics* are used for generic terms that represent values, including:

file	A pathname for a file.
string	One or more characters.
c	Any single character (letter, digit, or special character), as specified. For instance, on page 112, **f***c* means that you can type **f** followed by any character to move the cursor right to the next occurrence of the character defined by *c*.
n	Any single- or multi-digit number.
motion	A text region from the current cursor position to the cursor position defined by the **vi** built-in editor **Moving the Cursor** or **Moving To Character** directives.

Italics with Initial Caps is used for terminal control characters that you can define if you don't want to use the following defaults:

End-of-file	`CONTROL` d
Erase	# or `CONTROL` h
Interrupt	`DELETE` or `CONTROL` c
Kill	@ or `CONTROL` u or `CONTROL` x
Quit	`CONTROL` \
Restart	`CONTROL` q
Stop	`CONTROL` s
Suspend	`CONTROL` z

Courier Font Used in Examples. Most of this book is in the Times font. However, examples are in the Courier font to distinguish the examples from the rest of the text, and because Courier is a constant width font, which is closer to most computer displays than is the proportionally spaced Times font. The following Courier typefaces are used:

- **Bold** is what you type, or what you have in your **ksh** script; that is, what **ksh** reads and processes.
- *Oblique* is input that you type when a **ksh** command asks for input from you; that is, what your shell script reads and processes.
- Plain is output to you.

___(squiggly underline) In examples in the chapters on **emacs** and **vi**, we indicate the current cursor position by a squiggly underline.

Example

`abcdefg`

SYMBOLIC NAMES FOR CONSTANTS

Symbolic names are in Helvetica font with initial caps. If any of these names is followed by the letter s in Times font, it means that one or more are allowed. For instance, Spaces means that one or more spaces are allowed. The following symbolic constants are used:

True	Represents a return value of 0 (zero). This means that a command has completed successfully.
False	Represents a non-zero return value. This means that a command has not completed successfully. A number enclosed in parentheses after False indicates the value.
Null	Represents an empty string; that is, a string with no characters.
Space	Represents the ASCII character decimal 32.
Tab	Represents the ASCII character decimal 9.
Newline	Represents the ASCII character decimal 10.
Return	Represents the ASCII character decimal 13.
Bell	Represents the ASCII character decimal 7.

COMMAND SYNTAX NOTATION

[ ] (brackets) indicate an optional argument. For instance,

   [**a**] means **a** or no argument

   a[**b**] means **a** or **ab**

   [**a**[**b**]] means **a**, **ab**, or no argument

   [**a**] [**b**] means **a**, **b**, **ab**, or no argument

... (ellipsis) indicates that you can repeat the preceding argument, separating repetitions by either of:

- Spaces or Tabs.
- Newlines, as indicated in the format by the ellipsis appearing alone on a line.

If the ellipsis follows a closing bracket, you can repeat everything within the bracket.

PART II

TUTORIAL

3 FILES AND PROCESSES

ksh provides you with an interface to your system. To make the best use of **ksh,** you need to understand two basic concepts, files and processes.

This chapter describes what you should know about files and processes to use **ksh** to its fullest extent. It gives you background information that will help you to understand the following two chapters on the KornShell, *Command Language* and *Programming Language*. New users may find this chapter difficult because it introduces many unfamiliar concepts with little explanation. However, you do not have to understand everything in this chapter to read the following two chapters. Refer to the *Glossary* in the Appendix for terms that you do not understand. If you have difficulty with this chapter, return to it later. Experienced KornShell users may want to skim over this chapter and the following chapter.

THE FILE SYSTEM MODEL

ksh uses the UNIX system model of file system organization. Some readers will be using **ksh** with a non-UNIX system that has a different file system organization. In this case, either your operating system has a translation service to map UNIX system filenames and permissions to and from the operating system filenames, or else some of the features of **ksh** will not work.

Naming Conventions

The overall structure of the UNIX file system is that of a rooted tree (as illustrated on page 17) that is composed of directories and files, with these naming conventions:
- The name of the root is /.
- Each directory name or filename can be a sequence of characters other than /. Uppercase and lowercase characters are distinct. Some systems limit a filename to 14 characters, and some systems limit the set of characters that can be used in a filename.

- A pathname is a sequence of directory name(s), or a sequence of directory names followed by a filename, each separated from the other by one or more **/**. A pathname beginning with a **/** is called an absolute pathname.
- On most systems, filenames that begin with **.** (dot) are not listed when you list the contents of a directory, unless you specifically request it.
- Each special device, such as a terminal or a tape drive, has one or more pathname(s) associated with it. The convention on UNIX systems is to put special files under a directory named **/dev**.
- The pathname **/dev/null** is a special file that is always empty.

A pathname for a file is referred to as a link to the file. Each file can have several links to it.

Special Directories

Each process has a working directory. Each pathname that does not begin with a **/** begins at the working directory.

Each user is assigned a home directory by the system administrator. The working directory is set to your home directory when you log in.

The directory name:
- **.** (dot) is a synonym for the working directory.
- **..** (dotdot) is a synonym for the parent directory. The parent directory is the directory that contains the working directory. The parent of the root directory **/** is **/** itself.

On UNIX systems and many other systems, frequently used system programs are stored in a directory named **/bin**. Users often create a subdirectory of their home directory named **bin** to store their own programs. Also, by convention, temporary files are created in the **/tmp** directory.

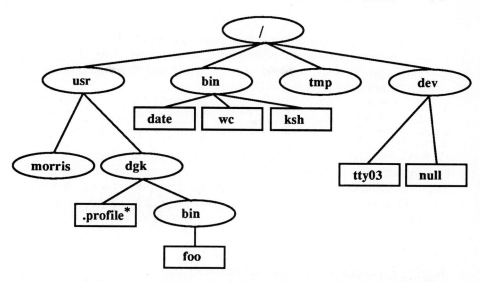

A sample file tree. Directories are ellipses, files are rectangles.
* pathname for .profile is /usr/dgk/.profile

File Permissions

Each file has an owner id and a group id. Whenever you create a file, the effective user id of the process that creates it becomes the owner id of the file, and the effective group id of the process that creates it becomes the group id of the file. Effective user ids are discussed on page 21.

A file can have any combination of the following permissions:
- Read permission by the owner, the group, and/or others.
- Write permission by the owner, the group, and/or others.
- Execute permission by the owner, the group, and/or others. You must have execute permission on a program to run it. You must have execute permission on a directory to find any file or executable program in the directory or any of its directories.
- Setuid and/or setgid permission. When you execute a program that has setuid and/or setgid permission, the effective user id and/or effective group id of the process is set by the system to the owner id and/or group id of the program. *Caution*: There are important security issues associated with setuid and setgid programs. Do not specify either of these permissions unless you understand the ramifications. Some systems remove this permission whenever you write to a file.

You specify permissions with a 4-digit octal number:
- 1st: Setuid and/or setgid permissions. Use this digit only if you wish to give a program special permissions. Setuid and setgid permissions often do not exist on non-UNIX systems.
- 2nd: Owner.
- 3rd: Group.
- 4th: Others.

Each octal digit, except the first, is the sum of all of the values corresponding to the permissions of the owner, group, and/or others. Thus, for instance, if the owner has read and write permissions, then the 2nd digit would be the sum of 4 and 2, which is 6. The values are:
- Read: 4
- Write: 2
- Execute or Search: 1

As a complete example, the permission **4751** means:
- Setuid
- Read, write, and execute for owner
- Read and execute for group
- Execute for others

Access permissions are sometimes represented by a permission string of 10 characters. The first character is **d** for a directory and – for a file. The other nine characters, in groups of three, represent the owner, group, and other permissions. An **r** indicates read permission and a **w** indicates write permission. An **x** indicates execute permission for a file and search permission for a directory. A – in any location indicates that it lacks the corresponding permission. An **s** in place of an **x** indicates setuid or setgid permission. As an example, **–rwsr–x-– x** represents the file permission **4751** described above.

Each process has a file creation mask to disable permissions whenever a file is created. The file creation mask is a 3-digit octal number; its digits represent the permissions to be disabled when a file is created. For instance, a file creation mask value of **022** disables write permission by group and others.

File Descriptors

A process associates a number with each file that it has opened. This number is called the file descriptor. When you log in, your first process has the following three open files connected to your terminal:
- Standard input: File descriptor 0 is open for reading.
- Standard output: File descriptor 1 is open for writing.
- Standard error: File descriptor 2 is open for reading and writing.

Special Files

Pathnames or file descriptors that refer to things other than disk files are called special files. Many special files refer to physical devices such as tape drives and terminals. By convention, filenames in the **/dev** directory refer to special files.

A pipe is a special file that is designed to pass data from one process to another. See interprocess communication on page 22.

PROCESSES

ksh uses the UNIX system model of processes. If you are using **ksh** with an operating system other than the UNIX system, and if the operating system has a different computing model than does the UNIX system, then the operating system must have special code to make it appear as if it has processes with the properties described below. If it has this special code, all of the features of **ksh** should work. Otherwise, some of the features of **ksh** will not work, as documented in this chapter. As an example, the MS-DOS system does not allow multitasking; thus it cannot run programs in the background as described on page 42.

You can think of a process as a program that has been launched but has not completed. It is an object created and controlled by the UNIX system and other similar systems. It consists of a program to execute, and of its own memory area that it can read and write.

Each process has a single thread of control. In theory, several processes can be running at the same time, even with the same program. On a computer that has as many processors as processes, this might actually be possible. However, on a computer with only one processor, processes take turns sharing the processor. This is called time-sharing. Even when the computer has as many processors as processes, the processes may not all be running at the same time because some of them might be waiting for data from a terminal, or waiting for data from another process.

Creating and Destroying Processes

The operating system that **ksh** runs on must provide a means of creating and destroying processes. **ksh** provides you with a simplified interface to the system for creating, destroying, and managing processes.

When a process is created, it is allocated resources such as a memory area and open files. When a process finishes executing a program, the system destroys the process and recovers its resources so that they may be reallocated to other processes.

Each process has a unique number associated with it called the process id. This number distinguishes the process from all other processes that have been created but have not yet been destroyed.

The system assigns a priority to each process. When there are more processes than there are processors, those processes with a higher priority are given preference over those with a lower priority. Programs such as **ksh** can influence the priority of a process that it creates.

Process Relationships

A process that creates another process is called the parent process. The created process is called the child process.

In the UNIX system, a process creates a child process by making a copy of itself. Except for the process id, these processes are initially identical. To run a new program, a process overwrites the code and data for the old program with the code and initial data of the new program. The program then begins execution. A property of this method is that the new process has a copy of all the resources of the one which created it. **ksh** can use, but does not require, the UNIX system method of process creation.

The term process environment refers to all the information associated with a process that affects how the process will behave (see page 23). When a child process is created, it inherits a copy of most of the environment of the parent. As a process runs, it may modify its copy of the environment. The parent process environment is not affected by changes made by the child, except by side effects through shared files.

A parent process can suspend its execution until one or more of its child processes exit. For example, **ksh** normally runs programs by creating a child process and waiting for it to complete before prompting the user for the next command. When a child process exits, it returns a number to its parent that indicates whether it encountered any errors. We call this number the return value. By convention, processes that run successfully have a zero return value.

Each process also has a number called the process group id. Processes with the same process group id form a process group. Only one process group can be associated with your terminal at a time; this group is called the foreground process group. If a process of yours is not in the process group associated with your terminal, it is called a background process.

Process Permissions

Each process has a real user id and one or more real group ids. These are set when you log in, and are inherited by all processes you create.

Each process also has an effective user id and an effective group id that determine what permissions that process has to read, write, and/or execute files. These ids are set to the real user id and real group id when you log in, and are inherited from the parent process.

If a file that contains a program has setuid and/or setgid permission, then when the system runs that program, the system sets the effective user and/or group id of the process to the owner and/or group of the file.

Signals

A signal is a message (a number represented by a symbolic name) that can be sent to a process or a process group by either the system or another process. Also, pressing certain keys on your terminal causes a signal to be sent to all processes in the foreground process group.

Different systems support different signals. A process must either explicitly ignore these signals, or must specify what actions to take when it receives them; otherwise, the process terminates. **ksh** requires that the system support at least these signals:

INT   Interrupt. This signal is sent to the foreground process group by pressing the *Interrupt* key. The default *Interrupt* key is usually `DELETE` or `CONTROL` c.

QUIT   Quit. This signal is sent to the foreground process group by pressing the *Quit* key, normally `CONTROL` \. Use this key when the program ignores the *Interrupt* key. Some systems create a file containing the memory contents of the receiving process (often called a core dump) when a program terminates due to this signal.

HUP   Hangup. This signal is sent by the system to the foreground process group when you disconnect from the system. Some systems also send **HUP** to background process groups associated with your terminal when you log out.

TERM   Termination. This signal is sent by a process to one or more processes owned by the same user to request termination.

KILL   Kill. This signal is sent by a process to one or more processes owned by a user to cause them to terminate. This signal cannot be ignored by the receiving process; also, the receiving process cannot specify any action to take when it receives this signal. Therefore, the process will exit. *Caution*: Do not confuse the **KILL** signal with the *Kill* character described later.

The job control feature described in the **Command Language** chapter supports these signals:

TSTP   Keyboard stop. This signal is sent to the foreground process group when you press the *Suspend* character, normally `CONTROL` z. By default, a process stops if it receives this signal.

TTIN   Tty input. This signal is sent to each process in the background process group that tries to read from the terminal. By default, a process stops if it receives this signal.

CONT   Continue. This signal causes a stopped process to resume execution.

STOP   Stop. This signal causes the receiving process to stop. A stopped process continues when it receives the **CONT** signal. This signal cannot be ignored by the receiving process.

Keys that cause the foreground process group to receive a signal can be altered by any process that has access to the terminal. However, these settings are associated with the terminal (not the process environment), so that all processes sharing the terminal are affected.

A process can send a signal to another process only if it has appropriate permission. For most signals, this means that the receiving process must have the same effective user id as the sending process. Some systems are less restrictive on sending signals.

Interprocess Communication

Processes can communicate with each other by reading from and writing to an ordinary disk file, or by using a special file called a pipe. A pipe is designed to be shared by more than one process. When a process tries to read from a pipe, the process performs one of these actions:
- Returns the data if a process has written to the file.
- Returns with an end of file indication if no other process has the pipe open for writing.
- Suspends execution until a process writes data to it.

A process can also send a signal to another process. Additionally, a child process also uses the return value when it exits, to communicate to its parent process.

Process Environment

The environment of a process consists of all information within a process that affects the process. This includes:

- Process and process group ids.
- Open files.
- Working directory.
- File creation mask.
- Real and effective user and group ids.
- Resource limits such as the size of the largest file that the process can create and the maximum amount of memory that it can use.
- The signal action settings.
- A set of named variables.

Each process has a separate environment that is initialized from its parent. A process can change its environment by using several of the **ksh** commands. However, changes made in the environment of programs that **ksh** runs do not change the environment of **ksh**.

Open files are inherited by child processes unless they are specified close-on-exec.

EXERCISES

1. When do path **bar** and path **/foo/bar** refer to the same file?

2. Can standard error and standard output be the same file? What file descriptor number is standard error? What number is standard input?

3. What is the absolute pathname for file **foo** in the sample file tree on page 17?

4. Which of the following are legal filenames on your system? Which are legal pathnames?
   a. **foo**
   b. **foo/bar**
   c. **foo***
   d. **/foo/bar**
   e. **//foo///bar**
   f. ***/***
   g. **foo.@#()bar**

5. What does a file creation mask of 024 mean?

6. What does the file permission 751 mean? Represent this permission as a permission string.

7. Under what circumstances can two processes have the same:
    a. Process id?
    b. Parent process id?
    c. Process group id?

8. Why should you never specify setuid permission and write permission for others on the same file?

9. Can a file have more than one owner id? Can a file have more than one group id?

10. In what ways can the actions of a child process affect its parent?

11. What is the purpose of **/bin**, **/tmp**, and **/dev**?

12. Can you execute a program that is in a directory for which you do not have read permission?

4 COMMAND LANGUAGE

This chapter is a tutorial for the KornShell command language. It is intended to guide you through the language by giving you step-by-step instructions for some of the typical uses of **ksh**. It is not intended to explain in detail all of the features of **ksh**, or all of the possible uses of the features that are discussed in this chapter. All of the features of the KornShell language are covered in detail in *Part IV* of this book.

This chapter is intended both for new users with relatively little computer or shell experience, and for experienced computer users who are familiar with other shells. For this reason, some material may appear not detailed enough to new users, while other material may appear too detailed to experienced users. New users who are not familiar with these commands may want to practice using them as they are introduced. However, new users should note that the intent of this chapter is to help you to learn how to use **ksh** as a whole, not how to use each command in detail. Experienced KornShell users may want to skim over or to skip this chapter.

There is only one KornShell language. The division between command language and programming language into separate chapters is for tutorial purposes only. We use the term *commands* to indicate what you type at your terminal for immediate execution. We use the term *scripts* to indicate what you put into a file for later execution. Scripts are programs that are written in the KornShell programming language. Learning **ksh** as a command language is one of the best ways of easing your way into writing scripts. On the other hand, you can use the features described in the *Programming Language* chapter when you are using **ksh** as a command language.

If you are not familiar with the **emacs** editor or the **vi** editor, and your terminal does not have local line editing, you will benefit by learning one of these editors before using **ksh**. You should first read the *Built-in Editors* part of this book.

The examples in this chapter use **ksh** built-in commands, which are described in the **Built-in Commands** chapter; they are a part of **ksh**. The examples also use programs, described in the **Other Commands** chapter, which are common UNIX system commands. These programs may behave differently than documented in this book, or may not be on your system at all.

The back cover of this book is a quick index to more detail about each of the commands in the examples, as well as to all of the other commands in this book. Use it to locate more complete descriptions of a command if you have difficulty with any of the examples. In addition, the **Quick Reference** chapter has detailed information on the commands and other aspects of **ksh**, as well as page references. Also see the **Glossary** starting on page 293 for terms with which you are not familiar.

Run **ksh** by typing its name, **ksh** (on some systems it may be **sh**), and then pressing RETURN. To make it even easier, on most systems your system administrator can arrange to have **ksh** be your default shell when you turn on your computer or when you log in. On some systems you yourself can make **ksh** your default shell by typing **chsh ksh** RETURN.

ksh displays a prompt when it is ready to read a command. This prompt is called the primary prompt. The default primary prompt string is **$** (dollar followed by Space).

To see the commands numbered as in this tutorial, type **PS1='!$ '**. Numbering commands in your prompt is explained on page 78.

EXECUTING SIMPLE COMMANDS

Enter a **ksh** command by typing a sequence of words. The first word in the line is the command name*. The following word(s) are mandatory or optional items of information used by the command, called command arguments. Press SPACE and/or TAB one or more times to separate the command name word from the command argument word(s), and to separate each of the command argument words. Uppercase and lowercase characters, such as **A** and **a**, are distinct. By convention, most command names and arguments are in lowercase.

---

* This description is an oversimplification. The words you type are processed as described in the **Command Processing** chapter to yield the command name and arguments.

ksh does not begin to process the command until you press RETURN . If the command refers to a program, then **ksh** creates a child process to run the program and waits for the child process to complete. Otherwise, **ksh** itself executes the command.

To continue a command onto another line, type \ as the last character of the line before pressing RETURN . **ksh** then displays a secondary prompt, normally > . The \ and the RETURN are discarded by **ksh**.

ksh redisplays the primary prompt if you press RETURN without entering a command. **ksh** displays the next primary prompt when it completes processing your preceding command. On some systems you can start typing your next command as soon as you press RETURN , without waiting for the prompt. This is useful for commands that take several seconds to complete. Output from the command may be intermixed with the keys that you type, but this does not interfere with your input.

To abort a program before it completes, press the *Interrupt* key. This causes the process to receive an **INT** signal, which causes most programs to terminate. This also causes any typeahead characters to be discarded. On some systems, the BREAK key may also cause the process to receive an **INT** signal. A few commands ignore the **INT** signal; in this case, use the *Quit* key, normally CONTROL \, to send the **QUIT** signal.

On systems that support stopping output (flow control), press the *Stop* key, usually CONTROL s, to stop the display of output to your terminal. Resume the output by pressing the *Restart* key, usually CONTROL q. On some systems, you can resume output by pressing any key.

The examples below use the following commands:
date   To display the date and time.
print   To display its arguments.
cat   To display the contents of the files you specify as arguments.

Examples
```
1$ date
Mon May  9 09:57:08 1988
2$ print hello world
hello world
3$ cat file1 file2
This is what is in file1.
You are now reading the second line.
This is the last line.
This is what is in file2.
You are now reading the second line.
This is the last line.
```

You can specify options to many commands. By convention, option arguments follow the command name; they consist of a single letter preceded by a – (minus). Some options have a value associated with them. The value is given by the argument that follows the option. Many commands allow you to group options without values associated with them into a single word preceded by a –. For example, the options **–x** **–v**, can be written as **–xv**. Arguments such as pathnames for files usually come last. A – or –– by itself is often used to signify that there are no more options. This allows you to enter other command arguments that begin with –, without their being mistaken for an option.

However, not all commands use the – convention. Some use a + rather than a –, often to reverse the normal meaning of the option.

If you enter a command incorrectly by providing unknown options, or too many or too few arguments, an error message is usually displayed. Error messages often display the correct usage for the program.

The **ls** command displays the names of files in your working directory. The **–l** option of **ls** causes a long listing for each file containing:
• The access permission string (see page 18).
• The number of names that refer to the same file.
• The owner.
• The group.
• The size in bytes.
• The time it was last modified.
• The filename.

Example
```
4$ ls -l
drwxr-xr-x    2 dgk      user       128 May   8 23:41 bin
-rw-rw-r--    1 dgk      user        86 Apr  14 10:04 file1
-rw-r--r--    1 dgk      user        86 Apr  14 10:11 file2
-rwxr-xr-x    1 dgk      user      4786 Apr  30 20:32 prog
-rw-r--r--    1 dgk      user       674 Apr  30 20:31 prog.c
-rw-r--r--    1 dgk      user       526 May   9 09:13 todo
-rw-rw-r--    1 dgk      user     29386 May   4 15:48 wishlist
```

SETTING AND DISPLAYING OPTIONS

ksh is itself a program. Thus **ksh** has several options that you can specify either when you invoke **ksh**, or with the **set** command. This tutorial describes many of these options. All of the options and their meanings are defined on page 197.

Several options affect how **ksh** processes commands. **ksh** turns on some options automatically, and you can specify some options. For instance, **ksh** automatically turns on the **interactive** option when you invoke **ksh** interactively. **ksh** issues prompts only when this option is on. **ksh** assigns default values to options, but you can change most of them. Use **set** to turn on, turn off, and display options.

You usually specify default options in your profile file (see page 77), which **ksh** executes when you log in, and/or in your environment file, which **ksh** executes when it begins execution. These files are described in more detail in the *Customizing Your Environment* chapter. For example, the **ignoreeof** option is customarily set in your profile file. It prevents you from being logged off if you inadvertently press the *End-of-file* character. With **ignoreeof** set, you must type the command **exit** to log out. The examples below use **set** to turn on the **ignoreeof** option and to display all the option settings.

Examples

```
5$ set -o ignoreeof
6$ set -o
Current option settings
allexport       off
bgnice          off
emacs           off
errexit         off
gmacs           off
ignoreeof       on
interactive     on
keyword         off
markdirs        off
monitor         on
noclobber       off
noexec          off
noglob          off
nolog           off
nounset         off
privileged      off
restricted      off
trackall        on
verbose         off
vi              on
viraw           off
xtrace          off
```

Version: The **nolog** option and the **noclobber** option are available only on versions of **ksh** newer than the 06/03/86 version.

CORRECTING YOUR TYPING

The **stty** command defines terminal control settings. In particular, you can use it to set the backspace character (referred to as the *Erase* character), and the line erase character (referred to as the *Kill* character). The default for *Erase* on some systems is #, and for *Kill* it is often @. You can change the *Erase* and *Kill* characters so that you can use the # and @ keys normally. Use **stty** as shown in the following example to set the *Erase* character to [BACKSPACE] and the *Kill* character to [CONTROL]x. **stty** affects the terminal settings for all processes that access your terminal. **stty** interprets the ^ in front of a character as meaning [CONTROL]. **stty** is normally placed in your profile file. On many systems you can enter a terminal control character as a regular character by preceding it with a \.

Example
```
7$ stty erase ^h kill ^x
```

If you make an error before typing [RETURN], there are several ways that you can make corrections:

- Press the *Erase* character to back up to the error, and correct the line from that point on.
- Press the *Kill* character to erase the entire line, and then type it over.
- If the **emacs** or **vi** option is on, you can move to earlier parts of the command line and correct mistakes by issuing editing commands called directives to distinguish them from shell commands. Issuing editing directives is referred to as command editing. A list of available editing directives for each of the edit options is in the ***Built-in Editors*** part of this book. You can also use command editing to make corrections to commands that you previously entered, and then to reenter them.

USING ALIASES AS SHORTHAND

An alias is a name that you can use as a shorthand for a command. As an example of how to use aliases, suppose that you always want to see long listings with the **ls** command. By defining an alias for **ls -l**, you do not have to type the **-l** each time that you list the contents of a directory.

You define an alias with the **alias** command, followed by a word of the form *name=value*. Do not press [SPACE] or [TAB] before or after the =; if you do, **ksh** will read what you typed as two or three words, not as the one word that it should be. If *value* has any Spaces or Tabs in it, then you must quote them using any of the mechanisms described briefly in this chapter on page 39, and in detail on page 133. ***Note***: You can use the name of the alias inside its value. For instance, in the example below, the alias for **ls** will be set to **ls -l**. The **ls** within the quotes will not be replaced again by **ls -l**.

To display the value of one or more aliases, specify the names of these aliases as arguments to the **alias** command. To display the complete list of aliases, run **alias** without arguments. Several aliases have been preset; they are listed on page 146.

ksh checks each command name to see if you have defined an alias for it. If you have, **ksh** replaces the command with the value of the alias.

Examples
```
8$ alias ls='ls -l'
9$ alias ls
ls -l
10$ ls
drwxr-xr-x   2 dgk      user       128 May  8 23:41 bin
-rw-rw-r--   1 dgk      user        86 Apr 14 10:04 file1
-rw-r--r--   1 dgk      user        86 Apr 14 10:11 file2
-rwxr-xr-x   1 dgk      user      4786 Apr 30 20:32 prog
-rw-r--r--   1 dgk      user       674 Apr 30 20:31 prog.c
-rw-r--r--   1 dgk      user       526 May  9 09:13 todo
-rw-rw-r--   1 dgk      user     29386 May  4 15:48 wishlist
```

REENTERING PREVIOUS COMMANDS

ksh keeps a log of commands that you enter from your terminal in a history file. Type **history** to display the most recent commands that you typed. **history** by itself displays at most 16 commands. However, you can specify, for instance:
   history −11 to limit the display to the last 11 commands.
   history 3 7 to display commands 3 through 7.
   history 11 to display commands starting at 11.
The indicated commands must still be accessible in the history file or **history** displays an error message.

To reenter the previous **ksh** command, run the **r** command with no arguments. **ksh** displays the command, and then executes it. To reexecute command 4, type **r 4**. To reexecute the last command that starts with **d**, type **r d**.

Examples
```
11$ r d
date
Mon May  9 10:03:13 1988
12$ history
1        date
2        print hello world
3        cat file1
4        ls -l
5        set -o ignoreeof
```

```
6          set -o
7          stty erase ^h kill ^x
8          alias ls='ls -l'
9          alias ls
10         ls
11         date
12         history
```

Use **emacs** or **vi** directives to access and edit commands in the history file. Any editor directive that would move you to a previous line if you were using the editor program, causes that previous line of the history file to be copied onto the line with your cursor so that you can edit and reenter the command.

EXERCISES

1. Practice the basics by doing each of the following in order:
   a. Press [RETURN] without entering a command.
   b. Turn on the **ignoreeof** option.
   c. Use the **stty** command to set the *Erase* character and the *Kill* character to whatever you choose.
   d. Use the **print** command to display your first and last name. Practice using the *Erase* character and the *Kill* character as you type your name.
   e. Repeat this command using the **r** command.
   f. Define an alias named **d** that displays the date.
   g. Use **d** to display the date and time.
   h. Use **r** to reexecute the **print** command.
   i. Display your option settings.
   j. Display the last six commands that you entered.
   k. Display the value of the aliases **d** and **r**.
   l. Display names and value of all the aliases.
   m. List the filenames in your working directory.
   n. Use the **print** command to enter a command and continue it onto another line.
   o. Use one of the built-in editors to fetch the command that printed your name. Delete your last name and enter the command.
   p. Practice using one of the built-in editors to change the arguments to the preceding command and then to reenter it. Do this until you feel comfortable with using the built-in editor to make corrections to the previous command.

2. Which of these input lines adhere to the normal command syntax conventions:
   a. `print`
   b. `PRINT`

    c. **date=time**
    d. **c128 is a computer**
    e. **ls foobar -1**
    f. **-c foobar**
    g. **foobar -option**

REDIRECTING INPUT AND OUTPUT

By convention, most commands write their normal output to standard output (file descriptor 1), and error messages to standard error (file descriptor 2). By default, **ksh** directs both standard output and standard error to be displayed on your terminal.

You can redirect the standard output of a command to a file instead of to your terminal by typing the redirection operator, >, followed by the name of the file.

You can put the > anywhere on the line; by convention, the > is normally placed at the end of the command after its arguments. Spaces and/or Tabs before and after the > are optional, unless the argument that precedes the > is a single digit. *Note*: This paragraph applies to all redirection operators, not just to >.

If the file already exists, and if the **noclobber** option is on, then **ksh** displays an error message. However, you can use >| instead of > to redirect to a file that already exists even if **noclobber** is on. If **noclobber** is off, or if you specify >|, then **ksh** deletes the contents of the old file. *Version*: noclobber and >| are available only on versions of **ksh** newer than the 06/03/86 version.

Examples
```
13$ date > savedate
14$ cat savedate
Mon May  9 10:07:34 1988
```

If the file does not already exist, then **ksh** creates it. **ksh** sets permissions to read and write by everyone, minus any permissions specified by the value of the file creation mask.

Use the **umask** command to set and/or display the file creation mask. Use the **chmod** command if it is necessary to change the access permissions.

Use > without specifying a command to create an empty file. Use **rm** to remove a file that you have created.

Examples
```
15$ umask
002
16$ umask 022
```

```
17$ > tempfile
18$ rm tempfile
```

If you want to discard the standard output from a command, you can do so by redirecting it to the special file, **/dev/null**. Any character written to this file will be thrown away.

You can append the standard output of a command to a file by typing the redirection operator >> followed by the name of the file. If the file does not already exist, then **ksh** creates it for you.

Example
```
19$ date >> savedate
20$ cat savedate
Mon May  9 10:07:34 1988
Mon May  9 10:07:57 1988
```

You can also redirect the standard input of a command so that it reads from a file instead of from your terminal. Type the redirection operator < followed by the name of the file.

Example
```
21$ mail morris < savedate
```

The **cat** command reads from standard input if you do not specify any file. Therefore, both **cat savedate** and **cat < savedate** yield the same result. However, in the former, **savedate** is an argument to **cat**, and in the latter, **cat** reads from standard input where **ksh** has opened **savedate** for use by **cat**. If **savedate** does not exist, you will get different error messages depending on whether you typed **cat savedate** or **cat < savedate**. This is because the error message is originated by **cat** in the former case, and by **ksh** in the latter.

You can redirect any file descriptor from **0** through **9** by specifying the file descriptor number immediately before the redirection operators <, >, and >>. For instance, to redirect standard error, specify **2>**. You can discard the output on both standard output and standard error by redirecting them both to **/dev/null**.

Example
```
22$ date > /dev/null 2> /dev/null
```

You can also specify that a file descriptor be redirected to the same place as another file descriptor. To cause file descriptor 2 to be redirected to the same file as file descriptor 1, specify **2>&1**. You can think of **>&** as meaning "redirect a copy of."

The order in which you specify redirection is important because the redirection operators are processed from left to right. In the following example, standard output is first redirected to **/dev/null** and then standard error is redirected there also so that both will be discarded. If the order of redirection were reversed, standard error would be redirected to wherever standard output is currently directed, and then standard output would be redirected to **/dev/null**.

Example

```
23$ date > /dev/null 2>&1
```

PIPELINES AND FILTERS

You can connect the standard output of one command into the standard input of another command by using the pipeline operator | between the commands. This is nearly equivalent to running the first command with its output redirected to a temporary file, then running the second command with its input redirected from the temporary file, and then removing the temporary file. However, **ksh** uses the pipe special file on systems that have them, rather than creating an intermediate file. In this case, the first command can produce more output than the largest permissible file size.

You can connect a sequence of commands together with | to create a pipeline. The number of commands you can connect may be limited by the number of processes the system allows you to create. You can continue pipelines onto more than one line by typing RETURN after the |.

A command that reads from its standard input and writes on its standard output is called a filter. You can use the | operator to connect one or more filters to preprocess and/or postprocess the output of any command.

As with many commands that process files, **grep** reads from standard input if you do not specify the name of a file as an argument. Therefore, **grep** can be used as a filter. **grep** displays the lines in one or more files that contain a specified sequence of characters. Use **grep** when you want to limit the output to only those lines that you need to see. The example below displays only those lines from the output of **set −o** that contain **ignoreeof**.

Example

```
24$ set -o | grep ignoreeof
ignoreeof          on
```

ksh redirects standard output to the pipe before any I/O redirections for the individual commands. Therefore you can use **2>&1** to direct standard error into the pipeline.

Use **tee** to capture, in a file, the data passing through any pipe in a pipeline. **tee** does not alter the data that passes through it. In the example below, the file **users** will contain the list of users logged onto your system as generated by the **who** command. Both standard output and standard error are written to the pipe.

The **wc** command displays the number of lines, words, and characters in the specified file(s). If no files are specified, **wc** uses its standard input.

Example
```
25$ who 2>&1 | tee users |wc
159       318      4077
```

On some terminals you cannot scroll back to earlier pages of output to the display. In this case you may want the output to stop whenever the screen fills up, until you indicate that you are ready to view the next page. A program that does this is called a pager, and **pg** is a commonly used pager program. You can cause the output of any command to be paged by running **pg** as the last command in a pipeline. Systems that do not have **pg** often have a command named **more** to perform this function.

TILDE EXPANSION

You can reduce your typing time by using ~ at the start of any word. **ksh** checks for expansion of each word you type that begins with a ~. Use the tilde expansion mechanism as a shorthand for:
- Your home directory. Use ~ by itself.
- Home directory of any user on the system. Follow ~ by the login name of the desired user (yourself or anyone else).
- Absolute pathname of the working directory. Use ~+.
- Previous working directory. Use ~-.

Tilde expansion characters extend up to the first **/**, if any. If there is no **/**, **ksh** processes the entire word. **ksh** leaves the word you typed as is, if the ~ is not followed by one of the above.

Example
```
26$ print ~morris/reminders
/usr/morris/reminders
```

PATHNAME EXPANSION

Many commands take a list of files as arguments. You can cause **ksh** to generate a list of pathname arguments by typing a word that consists of a pattern rather than typing each individual name. Patterns are used in other contexts by **ksh**, and are described more fully on page 126. If you use any of the following characters unquoted in a command word (see page 39 about quoting), then **ksh** processes that word as a pattern and expands it as follows:

*   Matches any string of characters, including Null.
?   Matches any single character.
[...]   Matches any character(s) between the brackets.

When you specify a pattern as a command word, **ksh** expands the pattern to the complete list of pathnames that match this pattern. If there are no matching pathnames, then **ksh** leaves the pattern unchanged.

When patterns are used to match pathnames, a **.** as the first character of a filename, and/or a **/**, must match explicitly. If the **markdirs** option is on, then a trailing **/** is added to each directory name that matches the pattern.

The pathnames that match the pattern become arguments to the command. Because the matching is done by **ksh**, pathname expansion applies to all commands.

If you specify a pattern as the pathname associated with an I/O redirection operator, **ksh** expands the pattern only if it matches a single pathname.

Examples

```
27$ print *
file1 file2 foobar prog prog.c todo wishlist
28$ ls file?
-rw-rw-r--   1 dgk    user    86 Apr 14 10:04 file1
-rw-r--r--   1 dgk    user    86 Apr 14 10:11 file2
```

TIMING COMMANDS

You can find out how long it takes to process a command or a pipeline, as with the example below, by using the **time** command. **time** is a reserved word in **ksh** and is processed specially. It applies to pipeline, not just to a single command.

After the command or pipeline completes, **ksh** displays on standard error three lines that specify in minutes and seconds:
• The clock time that has elapsed.
• The processor time used by the program.
• The processor time used by the system in running the command or pipeline.

I/O redirections apply to the command that you time, not to **time** itself.

Example
```
29$ time ls -l /bin | wc
98        875      5715

real 0m4.31
user 0m0.80
sys  0m1.36
```

The **sleep** command in the following example suspends execution for the number of seconds specified by its arguments. It is usually used within one of the compound commands described in the *Programming Language* chapter.

Example
```
30$ time sleep 10

real 0m10.94
user 0m0.04
sys  0m0.10
```

EXERCISES

1. Explain what each of the following commands does. Assume that they are run in the order shown.
   a. `print Keep track of everything > file1.out`
   b. `print Be careful  >> file1.out`
   c. `set -o | tee tee.out | grep ignoreeof`
   d. `cat tee.out | grep monitor`
   e. `grep monitor < tee.out`
   f. `print ~joe | grep joe | cat >> file1.out`
   g. `print *.out`
   h. `grep track *.out  | wc`
   i. `grep track < f*out | wc`
   j. `time sleep 20 > /dev/null 2>&1`

2. Write a command to do each of the following:
   a. Display the names of files in your directory ending in **out**.
   b. Display all the lines in files in the directory **/usr/include** that contain the string **FILE**.
   c. Display the time it takes to sleep for 5 seconds.
   d. Display the contents of your home directory.
   e. Create a file named **junk** that contains the date and time.
   f. Append to **junk** the lines from all files in your working directory that contain the word **bar**.

    g. Count the number of lines in **junk**.
    h. Remove the file **junk**.

SHELL PARAMETERS

ksh uses parameters to hold information that you can access. A parameter name can be one of the following:
- An identifier. These are called variables.
- A number. These are called positional parameters and are used mainly in scripts.
- One of the following characters: *   @   #   ?   – $!. These are called special parameters and are also used mainly in scripts.

You access the value of a parameter by preceding its name with a **$** and surrounding the parameter with {}. You can think of the **$** as meaning, "the value of." For instance, **${PWD}** means "the value of the **PWD** parameter."

Parameters whose names are identifiers are called variables. Assign values to variables with variable assignment commands. Variable assignment commands are of the form *name=value ... .* You cannot put any Spaces or Tabs before or after the =. You must quote any Spaces or Tabs in the value of a variable assignment. **ksh** performs tilde expansion on *value* if its first character is a **~**.

Some variables are initialized or inherited by **ksh** when you log in. For instance, the value of **HOME** is set to the absolute pathname of your login directory.

You can specify a parameter to be expanded anywhere, even as part of a word. The {} are optional when the name is a single digit or if the name is an identifier or a special symbol, unless the parameter is followed by characters that could be considered part of the parameter name.

Example
```
31$ d=$HOME/.profile s=~morris
32$ print ${d}_file $s/bin
/usr/dgk/.profile_file /usr/morris/bin
```

QUOTING SPECIAL CHARACTERS

Suppose that you want to display the character |. If you type **print** |, then **ksh** will prompt you with the secondary prompt **PS2** (normally >), indicating that it is waiting for you to type the remainder of the pipeline.

To remove the normal meaning that **ksh** places on |, or on any other special character, you must quote it. You can quote a single character by preceding it with a \. You can quote a string of characters by enclosing them in:

- Literal (single) quotes, '...', to remove the special meaning of all characters except '.
- Grouping (double) quotes, "...", to remove the special meaning of all characters except $, \ and `.

ksh normally splits the results of parameter expansion and command substitution of command words into fields, by using as field separators the characters in the value of a variable named **IFS**. By default, the value of **IFS** is Space, Tab, and Newline. **ksh** generates the arguments by performing pathname expansion on the fields. Use grouping (double) quotes to prevent both word splitting and pathname expansion. The quoting characters are removed after each command word is expanded.

In the following example we use the **–r** option to prevent the character \ from being processed specially by **print**.

Example
```
33$ print -r \\foo \~ '<$HOME>' "<$HOME>"
\foo ~ <$HOME> </usr/dgk>
```

WORKING DIRECTORY

Whenever a command uses a pathname that does not begin with a /, the system looks for the file relative to your current working directory.

To find the name of the working directory, use **pwd**. To change the working directory, use **cd** followed by the pathname of the new directory. You can use the **CDPATH** variable to specify a list of directories for **cd** to search through when you specify a pathname not beginning with a /. **pwd** displays the name of the new working directory when it uses the **CDPATH** variable to find it.

To return to the previous working directory that you were in, use **cd –**. **ksh** displays the name of the new working directory.

ksh sets the **PWD** variable to the working directory whenever you use **cd**. **ksh** also sets the **OLDPWD** variable to your previous working directory.

If you want to change to a directory whose pathname differs slightly from that of your working directory, you can do so by using **cd** with two arguments. The first specifies the part of the pathname that you want to change, and the second specifies what you want to change it to. **ksh** displays the new working directory.

Examples
```
34$ pwd
/usr/dgk
35$ cd /usr/morris
36$ cd -
/usr/dgk
37$ cd -
/usr/morris
38$ cd morris dgk
/usr/dgk
```

HOW ksh *FINDS A COMMAND*

If the command name is an alias, then **ksh** replaces the command name with the value of the alias and begins the search again.

If the command name contains a **/**, then, if possible, **ksh** executes the program whose pathname is the command name.

If the command name does not contain a **/**, then **ksh** checks the command name for one of the following, in the order shown:

- Reserved word (see page 125). If the reserved word begins a compound command, then **ksh** reads as many lines as necessary until it reads the complete command or it encounters an error, or until you press the *Interrupt* key. If the reserved word is invalid, then **ksh** displays a message on standard error.
- Built-in command. **ksh** executes the built-in command in the current environment.
- Function. **ksh** executes the function in the current environment.
- Tracked alias (see next bullet). **ksh** searches for the command only in directories in the **PATH** variable whose names do not start with a **/** and that precede the directory containing the tracked alias; and also in the directory containing the tracked alias.
- Otherwise. **ksh** uses the value of the **PATH** variable to construct a list of directories to search for the command name. The search occurs in the order that the directories are listed in the **PATH** variable. If the **trackall** option is on, **ksh** creates what is called a tracked alias. The name of the tracked alias is the command name; the value is the absolute pathname of the program corresponding to the command name. A tracked alias reduces the time **ksh** takes to find the command when it is subsequently referenced.

ksh displays a message on standard error if it cannot find the command, or if you do not have execute permission for the file.

Use the **type** preset alias to find out what a given name refers to. **type** tells you what type of item the specified name refers to. If the name corresponds to a program, **type** displays a pathname for the program. **whence** is similar to **type** except that **whence** displays only the absolute pathname for the command, if any.

Examples
```
39$ type ls date print r
ls is an alias for ls -l
date is a tracked alias for /bin/date
print is a builtin
r is an alias for fc -e -
40$ whence date
/bin/date
```

COMMAND SUBSTITUTION

You may want the output of a command to become the value of a variable. Or you may want the argument(s) to a command to be generated by another command. You can tell **ksh** to do either of these things by putting the command whose output you want inside **$(...)**. In addition, **$(<** *file*) expands to the contents of *file*.

Bourne shell: The Bourne shell syntax `...`, defined on page 134, is recognized by **ksh** but is considered obsolescent. All the examples in this book use **$(...)** instead of `...`. **$(...)** has simpler quoting rules and it nests easily.

Examples
```
41$ print dgk > foobar
42$ foo=$(< foobar)
43$ print $foo: "$(date)"
dgk: Mon May  9 11:02:28 1988
44$ d=$(whence date)
```

RUNNING COMMANDS IN BACKGROUND

By default, **ksh** waits for commands to finish executing before it issues the next prompt. The command that **ksh** waits for is called a foreground command.

Some commands take a long time to execute. You can type an **&** at the end of a command or a pipeline, just before you press `RETURN`, to cause it to execute in the background.

Before **ksh** starts a background command, it displays a message with a job number inside brackets, [ ], followed by the process id. If you did not redirect the output of the background command, then the output of the background command is displayed at your terminal.

The **find** command performs specified actions on every file in one or more specified directories, and also in subdirectories of these directories that satisfy specified conditions. It often takes a long time to complete. In the next example, the root directory is specified, and the action is to display the pathnames of all files with filename **foobar** as their last component. No conditions are specified, so all such pathnames will be displayed.

Example
```
45$ find / -name foobar -print &
[1] 2345
```

ksh dissociates background commands from your terminal. Therefore, you cannot use the *Interrupt* key to terminate a background command.

If the **monitor** option is on, **ksh** runs each background job in a separate process group that is not associated with your terminal. Otherwise, if you have not redirected the standard input, **ksh** sets the standard input for the command to the empty file **/dev/null**, preventing it from trying to read from the terminal at the same time that the shell does.

ksh ordinarily runs background jobs at the same priority as foreground jobs. If you turn on the **bgnice** option, then **ksh** runs background jobs at a lower priority.

Use the **nohup** command to cause a job to continue running even after you log out. The standard output and standard error are redirected to be appended to the file named **nohup.out** in the working directory. **nohup** takes as its arguments, the command name and arguments of the command you wish to run.

Example
```
46$ nohup find /usr/morris -name foobar -print &
[2] 2348
```

Use **tail –f nohup.out** to keep track of the progress of a command run in the background with **nohup**. **tail** displays the last few lines of the specified file. The **–f** option causes **tail** to keep checking for additional output when it reaches the end of the **nohup.out** file. Use the *Interrupt* key to cause **tail –f** to terminate. This will not affect the **nohup** command since it is running in the background. The following example reports on the progress of the preceding example.

Example
```
47$ alias chup='tail -f nohup.out'
48$ chup
/usr/dgk/shell/book/foobar
```

JOB CONTROL

Job control allows you to manage the execution of foreground and background jobs. **ksh** provides complete job control on systems that support it. On other systems, **ksh** provides a subset of the job control features.

The **monitor** option must be set for job control to be active. *Implementation-dependent*:

- On systems that allow complete job control, the **monitor** option is implicitly turned on for interactive invocations of **ksh**.
- On other systems, you must specify this option with **set –o monitor**. You would normally do this in your environment file.

Each pipeline that you run is called a job. **ksh** assigns each job a small number. If the **monitor** option is on, then **ksh** displays the job number enclosed in [ ] when each background job is started. Before issuing a prompt, **ksh** displays a status message for each background job that completes whenever the **monitor** option is on.

You can refer to a job by process id or by name with **wait**, **kill**, **fg**, and **bg**. To refer to a job by name, use:

%number	To refer to the job by *number*.
%string	To refer to the job whose name begins with *string*.
%?string	To refer to the job whose name contains *string*. **Version**: This is only available on versions of **ksh** newer than the 06/03/86 version.
%+ or *%%*	To refer to the current job.
%–	To refer to the previous job.

Use **jobs** to display the list of background jobs and their status.

You can cause **ksh** to wait for a specific background job to complete, or to wait for all background jobs to complete, with **wait**.

You can cause a foreground job to receive an interrupt signal, **INT**, by pressing *Interrupt*. Most programs terminate when they receive this signal. You can cause a foreground job to receive the **QUIT** signal by pressing *Quit*. You can terminate a background job or process by sending it a **TERM** signal with the **kill** command. Some systems generate a core dump when you do this. You may be able to use the core dump for debugging.

Systems that have full job control allow you to stop a process and to reestablish the association with your terminal. On these systems, you can use **ksh** to stop jobs and to move commands to and from the background. The following three paragraphs and the examples apply to systems that have this capability.

Press *Suspend*, normally [CONTROL] z, to stop the job that is running in the foreground. **ksh** displays a message when the job stops, and issues a prompt. However, you cannot stop functions or compound commands which are discussed in the next chapter.

A background job will stop whenever it tries to read from your terminal. Use **stty tostop** to specify that a background job is to stop whenever it tries to output to your terminal. Use **kill** to send a **STOP** signal, to stop a background job. The alias **stop='kill –STOP'** is useful if you frequently stop background jobs.

Use **fg** to move a background job into the foreground, or to restart a job that you have stopped and run it in the foreground. Use **bg** to restart a job that you stopped, and to run it in the background.

Examples

```
49$ sleep 60
CONTROL z
^Z[1] + Stopped            sleep 60
50$ bg
sleep 60&
51$ jobs
[1] + Running              sleep 60
52$ kill %s
[1] + Terminated           sleep 60
```

COMPOUND COMMANDS

Compound commands are introduced in the *Programming Language* chapter below, and are presented in more detail in the *Compound Commands* chapter. You ordinarily use compound commands such as **if**, **while**, **select**, and **for** when writing scripts. However, once you become familiar with these commands, you can enter any compound command interactively as well.

Most compound commands are normally entered on more than one line. Type [RETURN] following any command within a compound command to cause the command to be continued onto another line; in this case, **ksh** displays the secondary prompt (the value of the **PS2** variable). *Note*: **ksh** does not begin execution until you enter the entire command.

The following example uses the **for** compound command introduced in the next section. The *[0–9] is a pattern that matches all filenames in the current directory ending in a digit. For each file, this example creates a new file whose name is the same as the old name but with **.new** appended. The **tr** command, as specified, converts lowercase characters from the original file to uppercase in the new file.

Example
```
53$ for i in *[0-9]
> do  print $i
>       tr "[a-z]" "[A-Z]" < $i > $i.new
> done
file1
file2
```

EXERCISES

1. Explain what each of the following commands does. Assume that they are run in the order shown.
   a. `type type time print cat whence`
   b. `d=/dev b=/bin h=~ s=$PWD`
   c. `print $d \$d '$d' '$'d "$d" $PWD/bin`
   d. `cd $h`
   e. `type date`
   f. `x=$(whence date)`
   g. `ls $d | grep tty > ~/foo`
   h. `rm ~/foo`
   i. `cd -`
   j. `cd ~-`
   k. `> bar`
   l. `rm ~/bar ~-/foo`
   m. `nohup ls -l /bin &`

2. Write a command to do each of the following:
   a. Display all the directories named **bin** on your system.
   b. Run a job in the background.
   c. Wait for the last **nohup** command to complete.
   d. Assign the number of users logged into your system to a variable named **nusers**.
   e. Display the absolute pathname of the **grep** command.
   f. Remove a file that has a ∗ in its name.
   g. Change directory to the last directory that you were in.
   h. Change directory from **/usr/src/cmd/shell** to **/usr/home/src/cmd/shell**.

5 PROGRAMMING LANGUAGE

This chapter is a tutorial for the KornShell programming language. As stated earlier, there is only one KornShell language. The division of command language and programming language into separate chapters is for tutorial purposes only. Use **ksh** as a programming language by grouping commands together into programs that are called scripts. Scripts can consist of a sequential list of commands. Also, you can write **ksh** scripts using control flow commands to perform tasks usually written in a more traditional programming language, such as the C language or the BASIC language.

CREATING AND RUNNING A SHELL SCRIPT

Use any editor to put a group of **ksh** commands into a file to create a new command. A file that contains **ksh** commands is called a shell script, or just a script. Run a script by typing its name followed by its arguments, separated by Spaces and Tabs, as you do for any other command. This is referred to as invoking a script by name. You can also run a script by running **ksh** with the name of the script and the arguments to the script as arguments to **ksh**. This causes a separate invocation of **ksh**. On some systems these two methods may not yield identical results in all cases. See page 237 for more details.

You do not have to compile your script after you write it, but you do have to make the file executable with **chmod +x** to run the command by name. If you write scripts frequently, you could define an alias such as **cx='chmod +x'**.

Use the **#** comment syntax defined on page 124 to make your script easier to read. *Caution*: Some systems process **#!** specially (as described on page 237) when they are used as the first two characters of the first line of a script.

Also, indent the code in your script to make it easier to read. See examples in the *Application Programming* chapter for a useful indentation style.

ksh reads, expands, and runs the commands in your script sequentially until requested to terminate or until there are no more commands. See *Command Processing* for a description of how commands are read and expanded. See page 237 for a list of conditions that cause a script to terminate.

Example
```
54$ alias cx='chmod +x'
55$ print 'print hello world' > world
56$ cx world
57$ world
hello world
58$ ksh world
hello world
```

POSITIONAL PARAMETERS

Parameters denoted by numbers are called positional parameters.

When you invoke a script, **ksh** stores the arguments to the script as positional parameters. **ksh** sets positional parameter **0** to the name of the script, and sets the other positional parameters, from **1** on, to the other arguments that you supply.

Reference positional parameters with any of the following:

$4   The fourth argument. Braces around the parameter number are required with a positional parameter greater than **9**, for example, **${20}**.

$#   The number of positional parameters, not counting **0**.

"$*"   One argument consisting of all positional parameters from **1** on.

"$@"**   **$# arguments consisting of all positional parameters from **1** on. The double quotes prevent parameter values with Spaces or Tabs from being split up into separate arguments and prevent Null arguments from being removed.

Use **set** to assign new values to the positional parameters beginning with **1**. You cannot assign values to positional parameters individually. You can only replace one set of positional parameters with another.

Use **set – –** without arguments to unset the positional parameters.

Use **set –s** to sort the positional parameters based on their position in the ASCII character set (see *Character Set* in the Appendix).

Use **shift** to shift positional parameter(s) to the left. **ksh** discards as many old parameter(s) as it shifts, beginning with parameter **1**.

Example
```
59$ print 'print hello $1' > hi
60$ cx hi
61$ hi there world
hello there
```

MORE ABOUT PARAMETERS

Shell parameters and variables (named parameters) were introduced in the last chapter. Since parameters and variables are used primarily when writing scripts, many aspects of their use were not discussed. The **Parameters** chapter describes in detail each parameter and variable that **ksh** uses.

ksh does not limit the length of the name of a variable or limit the length of its value. Choose names for variables that make your script easier to read. We recommend using lowercase for variables that are local to your script. To concatenate the value of two or more parameters together, reference them one after the other, for instance, **foo1**.

When you reference a parameter, you can modify the value of its expansion by following the parameter with one of the following modifiers and a word. If the word following the parameter modifier is needed to complete the parameter expansion, **ksh** performs command substitution and parameter expansion on it before using it. Use the parameter modifier:

-      To specify a value to be used if the parameter is not set; for example, **${1–*default*}**. Use a **:** in front of the **–**, if *default* is to be used if the parameter is Null or is not set.

?   To specify a message to be displayed on standard error if the parameter is not set. Use a **:** in front of the **?**, to cause the message to be displayed if the parameter is Null or is not set.

To specify that the smallest leading portion of the value that matches the pattern that follows # be discarded.

To specify that the largest leading portion of the value that matches the pattern that follows ## be discarded.

%   To specify that the smallest trailing portion of the value that matches the pattern that follows % be discarded.

%%   To specify that the largest trailing portion of the value that matches the pattern that follows %% be discarded.

Examples
```
${foo%??}   # Expands foo and deletes last two
            # characters.
${0##*/}    # Expands pathname of script to a
            # filename.
${d-$(date)} # Expands to value of d if set;
            # otherwise expands to output of date.
```

Caution: Unless a reference to a parameter is inside double quotes, leading and trailing Spaces are discarded when the parameter is used as a command argument.

The value of **${#***parameter***}** is the number of characters in the value of *parameter*.

Each variable can be given one or more of the attributes listed on pages 165-169. Some attributes affect the value of the variable. Assign or change any attribute for a variable with **typeset**. For example, to control the width and justification of its value, use:

typeset –L [*width*]

> To specify a left-justified fixed-width variable. When you assign a value that is wider than the width, **ksh** discards excess trailing characters from the end of the value. If the value is narrower than the width, **ksh** adds Spaces at the end.

typeset –R [*width*]

> To specify a right-justified fixed-width variable. When you assign a value that is wider than the width, **ksh** discards excess leading characters from the beginning of the value. If the value is narrower than the width, **ksh** inserts Spaces at the beginning.

typeset –Z [*width*]

> To specify a fixed-width field that behaves like the right-justified attribute, except that if you assign a value beginning with a digit that is narrower than the width, zero(s) are inserted at the beginning to fill up the field.

Examples
```
typeset -L4 x    # x is 4 characters, left-justified.
typeset -R5 y=7 # y is 5 characters, right-justified.
typeset -L1 z    # z will be the first character only.
typeset -Z3 n=7 # n will be 007.
```

To specify that the values of variables be uppercase or lowercase, use:

typeset –u

> To cause all lowercase characters to be changed to uppercase.

typeset –l

> To cause all uppercase characters to be changed to lowercase.

Examples
```
typeset -u x=abc      # x will have value ABC.
typeset -L2 -l y=ABC  # y will have value ab.
```

MORE ON QUOTING

Quoting restores the literal meaning to characters that are processed specially by **ksh**. Literal (single) quotes, '...', cause all the characters between them to acquire their literal meaning. The literal quotes are not passed on to the command.

Grouping (double) quotes, "...", allow parameter expansion and/or command substitution to take place, but process the rest of the characters literally. Only the characters $, `, and \ are special with "...". When you use "...", **ksh**:
- Expands parameters and commands within them.
- Treats literally the characters in the resulting expansion.
- Removes the grouping (double) quotes.

Use the escape character, \, to quote the next character. Inside double quotes, \ is processed as an escape character only if it precedes a $, `, ", or \.

Caution: Use double quotes around command words that contain parameter references, to prevent the value from being split into separate arguments and to prevent pathname expansion from being done on its value. Also, if a command word expands to Null and it is not enclosed in "...", **ksh** does not create a command argument. Therefore, use "..." to specify a mandatory command argument as a parameter that might expand to Null. The double quotes are not needed for parameter references within the value of variable assignments because, as noted in the table on page 147, word splitting and pathname expansion are not performed.

Examples
```
x='foo bar'    # Variable x has a space in its value.
"|$x|"         # Expands to single argument, |foo bar|.
*foo\ bar\**   # Matches anything containing foo bar*.
y=             # Sets y to null string.
set -- $y "$y" # Expands to one argument.  The first $y
               # is discarded.
```

OPENING AND CLOSING FILES

Use **exec** without arguments to open and close files in the current environment. Use the I/O redirection syntax defined on page 136 to specify the files that you want to open or close. You can open and/or close file descriptors from **0** to **9**. **ksh** sets file descriptors from **3** to **9** close-on-exec.

Use I/O redirection without a command name to create a file or to remove the contents of an existing file. **ksh** opens or creates the file and then closes it.

The parameter **$** expands to the process id which is a number that is unique to all scripts running at the same time. Use **$$**, the value of parameter **$**, within a pathname to generate the name of a temporary file.

Examples

```
exec 3< foo       # Opens foo for reading, as file
                  # descriptor 3.
exec 3<&-         # Closes file descriptor 3.
>/tmp/foo$$       # Creates a temporary file.
exec 3<> foo      # Opens foo for reading and writing,
                  # as file descriptor 3.
```

READING FROM TERMINALS AND FILES

Input to **ksh** is line oriented. **ksh** does not process its input until it reads the Newline character. Use **read** to read from any open file. **read** reads one line at a time. Use **read –u***n* to specify file descriptor *n*. If you omit **–u**, the default is **0**, standard input.

You normally specify **read –r**. If you do not specify **–r** and the last character on the line is \, then **ksh** discards the \ and Newline character, and reads the next line.

read assigns the characters that it reads to the variable(s) that you specify as arguments. If you specify:
- No variable, **ksh** assigns the characters it reads to the **REPLY** variable.
- One variable, **ksh** assigns the characters it reads to the variable that you specify.
- More than one variable, **ksh** splits the line it reads into fields using the characters in the **IFS** variable as follows:
  - Each character of **IFS** terminates a field. Each field is assigned to the next variable.
  - Two adjacent separators, neither of which is a Space or a Tab, denote a Null string.
  - **ksh** assigns leftover characters to the last variable.
  - **ksh** sets excess variables to Null if you specify more variables than needed.

To specify a prompt that is displayed when you read from a terminal, follow the first variable with a **?** and the prompt.

If the input to **read** comes from a terminal and an editor option is on, then editor directives can be used when entering lines. The **–s** option causes each line that is read to be saved into the history file (see page 76).

Examples
```
read -r                # Reads a line into variable REPLY.
read -rs               # Also copies line into history file.
read -r line           # Reads a line into variable line.
read -u3 line          # Reads from file descriptor 3.
read -r line?"Enter foo "
                       # First displays "Enter foo ".
```

WRITING TO TERMINALS AND FILES

Use **print** or **echo** to display lines on a terminal and to write lines to a file. *Caution*: The behavior of **echo** is system-dependent and is intended for compatibility with the Bourne shell. We use **print** in all the programs and examples in this book.

Ordinarily **ksh** replaces certain sequences beginning with \ as described on page 206, and then displays each of the arguments to **print** on standard output followed by a Newline. *Caution*: You must quote the escape sequences to prevent **ksh** from removing the \ when it expands the arguments to **print**.

Specify:

−r To prevent escape sequences from being replaced. Use **−r** to display a parameter whose value can contain an escape sequence.

−u *n* To direct the output to file descriptor *n*. If omitted, **ksh** uses file descriptor **1**.

−n To prevent a Newline from being appended.

−s To direct the output to be appended to the history file as a command.

− To indicate that subsequent arguments are not **print** options. Use − to display anything that might begin with a −. The examples in this book use − whenever the next argument is a parameter reference, to avoid problems that arise when the parameter expands to a string beginning with −.

Examples
```
print -r - "$foo"      # Displays line with value of foo.
print -u2  -r - "$foo" # As above, except
                       # file descriptor 2.
print -rs - "$foo"     # Appends line with value of foo
                       # to the history file.
print -n "\t\t"        # Displays two tabs and stays on
                       # the line.
```

HERE-DOCUMENTS

You can specify that one or more commands in your script read its input from lines within your script, rather than from your terminal or a file. Use the I/O redirection operator <<, followed by an arbitrary delimiter-word. The lines starting after the next Newline and continuing until a line containing only the delimiter-word, are called a here-document.

Ordinarily, **ksh** performs parameter expansions and command substitutions on the here-document before the contents are passed to the specified command. The characters $, `, and \ are special and should always be preceded by a \ if you want them to have their literal meaning. However, if you quote any character of the delimiter-word in any way, then the here-document is passed to the command without any expansions.

If you specify the operator <<- instead of <<, then **ksh** deletes leading Tabs from each line of the here-document before passing it on to the command. As illustrated in the next example, Tabs that precede the delimiter-word are also ignored. Tabs can make your script easier to read.

You can use a here-document as the basis for a form letter generator or program generator. Specify **cat** with the template for the form or program you want to generate. Use parameter expansion and/or command substitution to generate the variable information in the form or program.

Example
```
name=Morris
cat <<- EOF    # Deletes leading tabs, quits at EOF.
        Dear $name,

        I am writing this on $(date).
        Remember to go to the dentist at two-thirty.
        EOF
Dear Morris,

I am writing this on Thu May 19 12:03:13 1988.
Remember to go to the dentist at two-thirty.
```

RETURN VALUES

Each command has a return value. The return value of a command is used with conditional commands and iteration commands discussed later in this chapter. The return value is a number from 0 to 255. A value of:
- 0 indicates a normal exit. When used in a conditional or iteration command, this value represents True. Any other value means that the command returns False.
- 1 indicates failure.

- 129-160 indicate that a command has exited because of the receipt of a signal. Subtract 128 to determine the number of the signal that caused the command to exit.

ksh sets the parameter **?** to the return value of the last command. The return value is documented with each command in this book.

Make sure that each script or function you write has sensible return values. The return value should be True if it ran successfully. The return value of a script or function is the value of the last command it executes.

Use **return** within a function to specify the return value. Use **exit** within a script to cause the script to exit with the return value that you specify.

GROUPING COMMANDS

A Newline separates commands. However, you can put several commands on the same line by separating them with a ;. Since ; is an operator, you do not need Spaces or Tabs before or after it.
Example

```
print -n '\t'; print -r - "$HOME"
        /usr/dgk
```

Use braces { } to group several commands together. For historical reasons, { and } are reserved words, not operators. A Space, Tab, Newline, or control operator (see page 124), is required before and after the { and }. Otherwise **ksh** will read them as part of the next word. Both { and } are reserved words and must appear in the position of a command name. The ; (or a Newline) just before the } in the example below is required; if you omit the ;, the } would be processed as a command argument rather than a reserved word. You can specify I/O redirection after the }. Any redirection you specify applies to all commands within the group except those that are explicitly redirected. The next example reads the first two lines of file **foobar** into variables **line1** and **line2** and then displays the rest of the file on standard output.
Example

```
{ read -r line1; read -r line2; cat;} < foobar
```

You can also use ( ) to group several commands together. Since (and)
are operators, you do not have to separate them with Spaces or Tabs;
however, the (must appear in the position of a command name. ( ) creates
a subshell environment (see page 238) to run the enclosed commands.
Therefore, there can be no side effects, except on files. Because it runs in
a subshell environment, it is slower than { }, unless the group of
commands would run in a subshell environment anyway; for example, a
brace group followed by **&**. You can specify I/O redirection after the).
Any redirection that you specify applies to each command within the
group, unless it is explicitly redirected.

Example
```
( date; who ) | wc
```

COMPOUND COMMANDS

A compound command is a sequence of two or more commands separated
by an operator, a grouping command, or a command that begins with one
of the reserved words listed on page 143. The pipeline command
described earlier, is an example of a compound command. See the
Compound Commands chapter for a more detailed description of each of
the compound commands described here.

Use pipelines to perform complex programming tasks. Each element of a
pipeline can be any command, including any of the compound commands.
The pipeline in the following example reads its input and displays on
standard output each word in alphabetical order, preceded by a count of the
number of times it appears in its input. It does this with the following
sequence of filters, which performs each of the following steps in order:

- Creates a list of all words in the input, one per line. The **−c** option of **tr**
  causes all characters that are not alphabetic to be replaced by the Newline
  character. The **−s** option causes multiple Newlines to be squeezed into a
  single Newline.
- Makes all characters lowercase.
- Sorts the lines.
- Displays each distinct line preceded by a count of how many times it
  occurs.

Example
```
tr -cs '[A-Za-z]' '\n' < file  |  tr '[A-Z]' '[a-z]' |
     sort | uniq -c
```

ksh does not recognize words such as **if** as reserved words, unless they
appear as the first word of a command. It is customary to put most
reserved words as the first word on a line. Use indentation to improve
readability.

Use **if** to cause conditional execution. **ksh** executes the **then** command part only if the return value of the conditional command is True. **ksh** executes the **else** command part only if the return value of the conditional command is False. The **if** command ends with the reserved word **fi**. The conditional command can itself be a compound command. In the example below, note that **read** returns True if it has successfully read a line of data.

Example

```
if   print 'Please enter your name: \c'
     read -r name
then if   mail "$name" < mailfile
     then :
     else print "Cannot mail to $name"
     fi
else print 'end-of-file'
     exit 1
fi
```

ksh provides two other operators for combining commands more compactly than with the **if** command. The binary operator:

		Runs the command following the		only if the command preceding the		returns False.
&&	Runs the command following the **&&** only if the command preceding the **&&** returns True.

Examples

```
read -r line || exit
cd foobar && echo $PWD
```

Use **case** for a multiway branch. **case** finds which specified pattern, if any, matches a given word, and executes the command sequence associated with that pattern. Use **;;** to terminate each command sequence. You can specify a list of patterns for the same command sequence by separating them with **|**. The following example tries to match the value of positional parameter **1** in order with strings beginning with **–d** or **–D**, strings beginning with **–e**, or anything else. It is not necessary to use double quotes around **$1** because **ksh** does not perform word splitting or pathname expansion in this context.

Example

```
case  $1 in
-d*|-D*)   dflag=1;;
-e*)     eflag=1;;
*)       print 'You must specify -d, D, or -e';;
esac
```

Parameters in the **case** pattern words are expanded to form the pattern. This makes it easy to construct patterns within a script. The following example reads a line and checks if the line begins with any character found in the value of positional parameter **1**.

Example
```
read -r line
case  $line in
[$1]*)  ;; # ok
*)      print "Line must begin with one of: $1"
        exit 1;;
esac
```

Use **while** to execute a group of commands repeatedly as long as the conditional command has a True return value.

Example
```
while read -r line        # read a line
do    print -r - "$line"   # print the line
done
```

until is like **while**, except that the body of the loop is executed until the conditional command has a return value of True. The example below uses the return value of a pipeline command. The return value of a pipeline is the return value of the last command in the pipeline.

Example
```
until who | grep morris   # until morris logs in
do    sleep 60             # try again in 60 seconds
done
```

Use **for** to repeat a sequence of commands once for each item in a specified list. Before the loop begins, **ksh** expands the list of words that you specify following the reserved word **in**. These words are expanded just as **ksh** expands command words. The body of the **for** command is executed once for each argument in the expanded list. **ksh** assigns the loop index variable, **i** in the following example, the value of each argument in turn.

Example
```
for i in *  # For each file in the working directory.
do  if    test -d "$i"
    then  print -r - "$i"  # Print subdirectory names.
    fi
done
```

TESTING FILES AND STRINGS

ksh has conditional expressions to check for the existence of a file, its access permissions, and/or its type; to test whether two pathnames refer to the same file; and/or to test whether one file is older than another. Conditional expressions can also be used to compare two strings or to compare two arithmetic expressions. See ***Conditional Expression Primitives*** on page 131 for a list of conditions to test.

Version: On versions of **ksh** newer than the 06/03/86 version, use the compound command [[...]] to specify conditional expressions. On the 06/03/86 and earlier versions of **ksh**, you must use the **test** or [command. Since words inside [[...]] do not undergo word splitting and pathname expansion, many of the errors associated with **test** and [are eliminated. Also, since **ksh** determines the operators within [[...]] before the words are expanded, no problem arises when a parameter expands to a value that starts with –. Finally, **&&** and | | are used as logical connective operators, and unquoted parentheses can be used for grouping.

Use **test X**"$*parameter*" = **X** to test whether parameter *parameter* is Null. You need:

- Spaces and/or Tabs before and after the =, since = is a separate argument to the **test** command.
- Grouping (double) quotes, in case the value contains Spaces, Tabs, or pattern characters.
- The **X** or any other letter or number, in case the value begins with –. You can eliminate the need for **X** by reversing the order, for example, **test "" = "$***parameter*".

To specify more complex tests, use the logical connective operators (listed here in decreasing order of precedence):

!   Not.
–a   And. Use **&&** within [[...]].
–o   Or. Use | | within [[...]].

Use parentheses to override normal precedence. For **test** and [, parentheses are separate arguments and must be quoted. For [[...]], parentheses are part of the grammar and must not be quoted.

Note: Each operator and operand must be a separate argument.

Examples

```
test -x file -a ! -d file  # True if file is executable
                           # but is not a directory.
test "X$1" = Xabc          # True if $1 expands to abc.
[ "X$1" = Xabc ]           # Same as above.
[[ $1 = abc ]]             # Same as above in versions
                           # of ksh newer than 06/03/88.
test "$1" -ef .            # True if $1 is the working
                           # directory.
test foo -nt bar           # True if foo is newer than
                           # bar.
test ! \(-w file -o -x file \)
                           # True if file is neither
                           # writable nor executable.
```

```
[[ ! (-w file || -x file ) ]]
                            # Same as above in versions
                            # of ksh newer than 06/03/88.
```

ARÍTHMETIC

Use **let** to do integer arithmetic in any arithmetic base from 2 through 36.
Use the format *base#number* for constants in any base other than 10.
Caution: Each argument to **let** is a string that it evaluates as an arithmetic
expression. Therefore you cannot use Spaces or Tabs without using
quotes.

See *Arithmetic Expressions* on page 129 for a list of operators and
precedences.

Whenever **ksh** encounters an identifier within an expression, it replaces it
with the value of the variable with this name.

You can specify the integer attribute and an arithmetic base for any variable
with **typeset –i** or with the preset alias **integer**. The value of an integer
variable is evaluated when you specify a value with a variable assignment
command. You do not need to use **let**.

Many of the arithmetic operators have special meaning to **ksh**, and must be
quoted.

The construct ((*expression*)) is equivalent to **let** "*expression*". You
normally use this as the conditional command for **if**, **while**, and **until**.

Use the **RANDOM** variable to generate a uniformly distributed sequence
of random numbers. Each time **RANDOM** is referenced, it expands to a
different random number.

Examples
```
integer even=0 count=0
while ((count < 100))
do      if      ((RANDOM%2==0))
        then    even=even+1
        else    odd=odd+1
        fi
        count=count+1
done
let odd=count-even
print even=$even odd=$odd
even=47 odd=53
```

ARRAYS

You can specify a subscript with any variable to define an array using the array syntax *identifier*[*subscript*]. You do not have to declare that a variable is an array to use it with a subscript. The subscript can be any arithmetic expression that evaluates between 0 and some implementation-defined value that is at least 511.

Each attribute that you specify applies to all elements of an array.

Assign values to array elements individually with variable assignment commands. Use **set –A** *name* to assign a list of values to an array sequentially. *Version*: **set –A** is available only on versions of **ksh** newer than the 06/03/86 version.

Use braces around the array name and subscript when referencing an array element, for instance **${foo[bar]}**. If you omit the braces, **ksh** would expand **$foo**, concatenate it with the pattern **[bar]**, and replace it with pathnames that match this pattern. When you reference an array variable without specifying a subscript, then **ksh** uses element **0**. Use subscript **@** or * to refer to all the elements of an array.

Example
```
# The following prints a random card from a card deck.
integer i=0
typeset -u card
for suit in clubs diamonds hearts spades
do   for n in ace 2 3 4 5 6 7 8 9 10 jack queen king
     do   card[i]="$n of $suit"
          i=i+1  # The let keyword is not required with
                 # integer variables.
     done
done
print - ${card[RANDOM%52]}
QUEEN OF DIAMONDS
```

CREATING AND USING MENUS

Use **select** to display a list of alternatives for a user to select from. **select** displays the list of items you specify in rows and columns, with each item preceded by a number and a right parenthesis. **select** uses the variables **COLUMNS** and **LINES** to help format the menu selections.

select displays the **PS3** variable as a prompt when it is ready to read the user selection. The user's reply is saved in the **REPLY** variable. If the user enters a number corresponding to one of the choices, the **select** index variable is assigned the corresponding value. Otherwise, the **select** index variable is set to Null. If the user enters RETURN by itself, **ksh** redisplays the choices and the **PS3** prompt and reads the selection again.

You usually use a **case** within the body of **select** to specify the appropriate action to take.

Example
```
PS3='Pick one of the above:
select i in list edit quit
do    case $i in
      list)    cat "$foo";;
      edit)    vi "$foo";;
      quit)    break;;
      "")      print you must select one of the above;;
      esac
done
1) list
2) edit
3) quit
Pick one of the above: 3
```

USING eval

The *Command Processing* chapter explains the order in which **ksh** processes a command to construct the command name and arguments. Use **eval** when you want results from expansions to be applied to earlier stages of the expansion, or when you want a stage of the processing repeated again. **ksh** expands the arguments to **eval** with the normal processing rules. **ksh** then forms a string by concatenating the arguments of **eval**, separating each by a Space. **ksh** reads and processes the resulting string as a command.

Use **eval** to:
- Process the result of an expansion or substitution by a step that precedes it during command processing.
- Find the value of a parameter whose name is the value of another parameter.
- Execute a line you read.

The return value of **eval** is the return value of the command formed by its arguments.

Examples
```
eval last='$'{$#}        # Last positional parameter.
eval print '$'$name      # Displays variable named $name.

cmd='date | wc'
eval $cmd                # Causes | to mean pipeline.

read -r line
eval "$line"             # Processes line as a command line.

if    eval [ ! -d \${$#} ]
then  print -r - "${0}: Last argument is not a directory."
      exit 1
fi
```

EXERCISES

1. Explain what each of the following commands does. Assume that they are run in the order shown.
   a. **typeset -L1 x; typeset -R1 y**
   b. **x=foobar y=foobar**
   c. **print x=$x y=$y ${#x}**
   d. **{ integer i=3 j=2; i=i*2; print $i+$j ; }**
   e. **(i=i+j; print $i)**
   f. **a[1]=foo a[3]=bar; print "${a[@]}"**
   g. **((i>j)) && i=j**

2. Write a command to do each of the following:
   a. Assign the value **foo** to a variable whose name is stored in variable **bar**.
   b. Open a here-document on file descriptor 3.
   c. Read 50 lines of a file (or until the end of the file if the file is less than 50 lines) looking for a line containing the string **foobar**.
   d. Display the sum of two random numbers in the range 1 to 6, 100 times.
   e. Read a line and execute:
      date if user types **d**.
      who if user types **w**.
      exit if user types **e**.
   f. Open a here-document on file descriptor 3.

SETTING TRAPS TO CATCH INTERRUPTS

Use **trap** to specify actions to be executed when any one of a specified set of asynchronous conditions arises. A condition arises when your script receives a signal.

The action you specify is expanded when **trap** is processed, and again just before **ksh** executes the action. Therefore, use literal (single) quotes rather than grouping (double) quotes to avoid expansion when you specify the action.

A trap on **EXIT** is executed when the script completes. Use this trap to specify cleanup actions such as removing temporary files.

If you specify a trap on **EXIT** within a function, then the trap executes right after the function completes. A trap on **DEBUG** is executed after each command completes. Use this trap to aid debugging functions and/or scripts. *Version*: The **DEBUG** trap is available only on versions of **ksh** newer than the 06/03/86 version.

Examples
```
trap 'rm -f /tmp/file$$' EXIT      # Remove /tmp files
                                   # before exit.
trap 'mail morris <<\!
The program aborted
!
'  HUP TERM
```

PROCESSING ARGUMENTS

It is a good practice to follow the command syntax conventions described on page 28 when designing shell programs.

All arguments, both option and non-option, are stored as positional parameters when the script begins. Process options by reading each of the option arguments and creating variables for each of the specified options. Shift the positional parameters so that after option processing is complete, they contain only non-option arguments.

Version: Use the **getopts** command to process option arguments on versions of **ksh** newer than the 06/03/86 version. Otherwise, use the method illustrated in the next example. This example illustrates how to process a script that allows options, ±**a**, ±**b**, and −**o**. The −**o** option requires a value. The same example appears on page 216 using the **getopts** command.

Example

```
c=$1
typeset -L1 sign     # sign holds one character
while true
do   case $c in
     -a*)    aflag=1;;
     +a*)    aflag=;;
     -b*)    bflag=1;;
     +b*)    bflag=;;
     -o)     shift; c=
             if     [ $# -gt 0]
             then   oflag=$1
             else   print "$0: -o requires a value:
                    exit 2
             fi;;
     --)     break;;
     [+-]*)  print -u2 "$0: unknown option $c"
             print -u2 "USAGE: $0 [ -a -b -o value] file ..."
             exit 2;;
     *)      break;;
      esac
      sign=$c
      c=${c#[+-]?}                   # compute next arg
      case $c in
      "")   shift; c=$1;;
      *)    c=$sign$c;;
      esac
done
```

CO-PROCESSES

From within a script, you can run a command or a pipeline in the background that can communicate with your program. This is particularly useful when you want to provide a new interface to an existing program, or write a program to interface to a transaction-oriented program such as a database manager.

To run a co-process in the background, put the operator |& after the command. The standard input and the standard output of the command will each be connected to your script with a pipe.

Use **print –p** to write to the co-process, and use **read –p** to read from the co-process.

Caution: The co-process must:
• Send each output message to standard output.
• Have a Newline at the end of each message.
• Flush its standard output whenever it writes a message.

Example
```
ed - foobar |&
print -p /morris/
read -r -p line
print -r - "$line"
This line in file foobar contains morris.
```

Version: The remainder of this section on co-processes applies only to versions of **ksh** newer than the 06/03/86 version. The 06/03/86 and earlier versions of **ksh** allowed only one co-process at a time.

Use I/O redirection to move the input and/or output pipes of the co-process to a numbered file descriptor. Use **exec 3>&p** to move the input of the co-process to file descriptor **3**. Once you connect the input of a co-process to a numbered descriptor, you can redirect the output of any command to the co-process with the usual redirection syntax. For instance, **date >&3** directs the output of date to the co-process that has been moved to file descriptor **3**. You can invoke another co-process once you move the co-process input to a numbered descriptor. The output of both co-processes will be connected to the same pipe. Use **read –p** to read from this pipe. Use **exec 3<&–** to close the connection to the first co-process.

Use **exec 4<&p** to move the connection from the output of the co-process to file descriptor **4**. Use **read –u4** to read from the co-process after you move the connection to file descriptor **4**.

Example
```
(read; print -r "$$: $REPLY") |& # Begin co-process 1.
[1]   258
exec 5>&p                        # Move to descriptor 5.
(read; print -r "$$: $REPLY") |& # Begin co-process 2.
[2]   261
exec 6>&p                        # Move to descriptor 6.
date >&6                         # Date to co-process 2.
print -u5 foobar                 # Print to co-process 1.
exec 3<&p                        # Move input of both
                                 # co-processes to 3.
read -ru3 line                   # Read from co-process.
print -r "$line"                 # Display the line.
261: Mon May  9 12:13:05 1988
read -ru3 line                   # Read another line.
print -r "$line"                 # Display it.
258: foobar
```

DOT SCRIPTS

ksh runs a script in a separate environment whether you invoke a script by name or by running **ksh** with the name of the script as an argument. In either case, changes made to the environment of the script, such as changing the value of any variable, will not affect the environment of the calling program.

Use the **.** (dot) command to cause the script to execute in the current environment. The arguments to the **.** command are the name of the script and its arguments. Arguments to the script replace the positional parameters.

A script invoked by the **.** command is called a dot script. A dot script is normally used to initialize the environment of a program. An application can read a **.** script to create a default environment prior to processing command arguments.

Example
```
cat foo.init
# This file sets default values.
Logfile=$HOME/foo.log
Tmpdir=/usr/tmp
Prompt='feed me! '
. foo.init
```

PATTERN MATCHING

Patterns were introduced briefly in connection with pathname expansion on page 37. In addition to pathname expansion, **ksh** uses patterns in **case** and [[...]] compound commands, and for substring expansions. The rules for forming patterns can be found starting on page 126.

Version: The remainder of this section on patterns applies only to versions of **ksh** newer than the 06/03/86 version. The 06/03/86 and earlier versions of **ksh** allowed patterns with *, ? and [.

In addition to *, ? and [, patterns can be formed with any of the following:

?(*pattern* [|*pattern*] ...)	To optionally match any of the given patterns.
*(*pattern* [|*pattern*] ...)	To match zero or more of the given patterns.
+(*pattern* [|*pattern*] ...)	To match one or more of the given patterns.
@(*pattern* [|*pattern*] ...)	To match exactly one of the given patterns.
!(*pattern* [|*pattern*] ...)	To match anything except the given patterns.

Examples
```
@(foo|bar|bam)          # Matches foo, bar, or bam.
?(foo|bar|bam)          # Matches foo, bar, or bam or null.
+([0-9])?(.)*([0-9])    # Matches one or more digits,
                        # optionally followed by a decimal
                        # point and any number of digits.
!(*.o)                  # Matches any string not ending in .o.
```

DEFINING AND USING FUNCTIONS

Functions provide an efficient vehicle for writing relatively simple commands that execute in the current environment. They also provide a means of breaking a script into smaller, well-defined pieces that are easier to write.

Use the **function** compound command to define new functions, or to redefine existing functions. A function must be defined, or at least declared to be a function, before it is referenced.

A function differs from a script in that it runs in the current environment and, therefore, can share variables with the script that invokes it. A function differs from a dot script in that positional parameters are saved and restored, and local variables can be defined. A function executes faster than a dot script because **ksh** reads a function when it is defined and does not read it each time that it is referenced.

Use **typeset** within a function definition to declare local variables. Changing the value of a local variable has no effect on a variable of the same name in the script that calls the function. If you do not declare a variable to be local, then any change that you make to the variable remains in effect after the function returns to the calling script.

Use **return** to return to the calling script. If you do not use **return**, the function returns after **ksh** processes the last command in it. Do not use **exit** unless you really want to terminate the current script.

Invoke a function in the same way you invoke a built-in command, a script, or a program. Specify the function name followed by its arguments, if any. These arguments become the positional parameters inside the function, but do not change the current positional parameters for the invoking script. The value of positional parameter **0** is set to the name of the function.

After expanding all the words of a command, **ksh** first checks the command name to see if it is a built-in, then to see if it is a function, and finally to see if it is a program. Therefore, it is meaningless to define a function whose name is the same as that of a built-in command. You must use a combination of aliases and functions, as described on page 70, to replace a built-in command with a function.

When you write functions, try to avoid producing side effects with each of the following:

- Variables. Alter global variables only when essential. Do not change their values or their attributes.
- Functions. Create, delete, or export functions only when essential.
- Aliases. Create, delete, or export aliases only when essential.
- Traps. **Version**: On the 06/03/86 and earlier versions of **ksh**, traps other than **EXIT** were shared between a function and its caller. Thus, setting traps could cause side effects. On versions of **ksh** newer than the 06/03/86 version, **ksh** restores traps after returning from a function call.
- Working directory. Because functions execute as part of the same process, it is possible to change the working directory. The calling script should not unexpectedly be left in another directory.
- Temporary files. Before it returns to its caller, a function should remove any temporary files that are created for its exclusive use. Take special care when creating temporary pathnames formed using the **$** parameter, which evaluates to the current process id, because both the function and its caller run in the same process. Use the function name, or an abbreviation, as part of the pathname.

Function names and definitions are not inherited across separate invocations of **ksh**. You should put function definitions in your environment file if you want them to be defined whenever **ksh** is invoked.

To export a function, you must both define the function in your environment file and use **typeset –xf** on its name. Functions defined in your environment file are not inherited by scripts run by **ksh,** unless you specify the **–x** attribute on the function.

Use the preset alias, **functions**, to display the definition of one or more functions. To remove a function, use **unset –f** followed by the name of the function.

Example
```
# isnum returns True if its argument is all digits.
function isnum # string
{
    typeset str=$1 num=1
    while true
    do    case $str in
          [0-9]*)   str=${str#?}
                    num=0;;
          "")       return $num;;
          *)        return 1;;
          esac
    done
    # Not reached.
}
```

AUTO-LOAD FUNCTIONS

A function that becomes defined the first time it is referenced is called an auto-loaded function. Its primary advantage is better performance, since **ksh** does not have to read the function definition if you never reference the function.

Version: On versions of **ksh** newer than the 06/03/86 version, you can specify that a function auto-load with the **autoload** preset alias. When **ksh** first encounters an auto-loaded function, it uses the **FPATH** variable to search for a filename whose name matches that of the function. This file must contain the definition of this function. **ksh** reads and executes this file in the current environment and then executes the function.

Example
```
FPATH=$HOME/funlib
                   # Directories to search for functions.
autoload foobar    # Specifies that foobar be auto-loaded.
foobar *.c         # Executes foobar with files ending
                   # in .c.
```

Version: On the 06/03/86 and earlier versions of **ksh**, you must define an alias whose name is the name of the function. The value of this alias must be the dot command with an argument which is the name of the file that contains the function definition, followed by a ; and the function name. Inside the function definition file, you must unalias and define the function.

Example

```
alias foobar='. $HOME/funlib/foobar; foobar'
            # Specifies that foobar be auto-loaded.
            # You must specify unalias foobar in
            # $HOME/funlib/foobar.
foobar *.c # Executes foobar with files ending in .c.
```

Note: You can load a library of related functions with the first reference to any of its members, by putting them all in one file. For each function defined, you can use **ln** to create a filename with the name of the function that refers to this file.

FUNCTIONS AND ALIASES

Aliases can also be used inside scripts. However, you must understand how **ksh** reads commands if you define or unset an alias within a compound command. See the **Command Processing** chapter for a description of when aliases are read and how they are processed.

Use the combination of aliases and functions to do things that you cannot do with either one of them individually.

To write a function to replace a built-in command, define an alias whose name is that of the built-in command you want to replace, and whose value is the name of the function that defines the code to replace the built-in command. If you want to refer to the built-in command from within the function, quote the name to prevent alias substitution. See **\cd** in the example below.

Example

```
# Redefinition of cd.
alias cd=_cd
function _cd
{
    \cd "$@"     # Prevents recursive call.
    print "Directory changed from $OLDPWD to $PWD"
}
```

ksh performs pathname expansion on the arguments to each command prior to running it unless the **noglob** option is on. To write a function that is called without pathname expansion on its arguments, define an alias whose value is **'set -o noglob;** *name*'. Inside function *name* put the command **trap 'set +o noglob' EXIT**.

Example
```
alias printargs='set -o noglob; _printargs'
function _printargs
{
    trap 'set +o noglob' EXIT
    print -r - "$@"
}
printargs * ???
* ???
```

Use aliases and functions to add new constructs to the language.

Example
```
alias repeat='function _repeat {  '  from='}; _from'
function _from # var=start to finish [by incr]
{
    typeset var="${1%%=*}"
    integer incr="${5:-1}" "$1"
    while (( $var <= $3 ))
    do      _repeat
            let $var=$var+incr
    done
}
# The following is an example of how to use this.
repeat
{
    let x="i*i"
    print "$i   $x"
}
from i=1 to 13 by 3
1   1
4   16
7   49
10  100
13  169
```

DEBUGGING

You can check the syntax of a script without actually executing it, by invoking **ksh** with the **noexec** option. You can often catch errors that you will not find when running the script, because certain portions of a script may be skipped when you run it without **noexec**.

You can cause **ksh** to display its input as it reads it, with the **verbose** option.

The best method of debugging a script is by having **ksh** display an execution trace. An execution trace is a listing of each command after **ksh** has expanded it, but before it has run the command. To cause **ksh** to display an execution trace of each command in a:

- Script. Invoke **ksh** with the **xtrace** option, or turn on the **xtrace** option with **set −x** (or **set −o xtrace**) within the script.
- Function. Specify **typeset −ft**.

The **PS4** prompt is evaluated for parameter expansion and displayed in front of each line of an execution trace. Use the **LINENO** variable within the **PS4** prompt to identify the line number in the script or function that corresponds to the line **ksh** displays. *Version*: The **PS4** and **LINENO** variables are available only on versions of **ksh** newer than the 06/03/86 version.

When **ksh** detects a syntax error while reading a script, it displays the name of the script, the line number within the script it was reading when it encountered the error, and the cause of the error. The line number that **ksh** displays for a mismatched quote is often not the line that caused the error because quoted strings can legally extend over any number of lines. Work your way back through the script or function until you find the quote you omitted, or the extra quote you inserted.

Example

```
# This is the file bar.
function badquote
{
    print "This is line 1   # This is the culprit.
    for i in *
    do      foo
    done
    print "Last line"
}
bar: syntax error on line 8 : `"' unmatched
```

When **ksh** detects an error while executing a function or script it displays an error message preceded by the function name or script name, and the line number of the error enclosed in [ ]. Line numbers are relative to the beginning of the file for a script, and relative to the first line of the function when inside a function.

Sometimes it is helpful to comment out portions of the code to locate an error. Insert a # at the beginning of each line that you want commented out.

You can insert a call to a function, such as the function defined in the following example, at any point in a script or function that allows you to interactively examine the environment at that point.

Example
```
function breakpoint
{
    while read -r line?">> "
    do      eval "$line"
    done
}
```

You can use the **DEBUG** trap to specify a command to execute after **ksh** executes each command. *Version*: The **DEBUG** trap is available only on versions of **ksh** newer than the 06/03/86 version.

EXERCISES

1. Write a function to do each of the following:
   a. Display its arguments on standard error and exit.
   b. Return True if its first argument is a number.
   c. Given an argument that is a number representing dollars and cents, display the value in words as you would write it on a check.
   d. Save the current trap settings in an array. Hint: You can use a here-document to avoid creating any processes.
   e. Read lines from the terminal and execute only commands whose names do not contain a /. The function should prompt the user with the **PS1** prompt when it is ready to read a command. Each command should be entered into the history file.

2. Write a script named **behead** that displays a file without the first few lines. You should be able to specify the number of lines to behead as an option *−n*.

3. Write a script named **bundle** that takes a list of pathnames, and creates a shell program which will restore the files if they are deleted. You do this by creating a here-document for each file whose pathname is the contents of the file. The script should also preserve the file permissions.

4. What is the output of the following program when called with an argument of 2, and when called with an argument of 3?
   ```
   function hanoi # n from to spare
   {
           integer nm1=$1-1
           ((nm1>0)) && hanoi $mn1 $2 $4 $3
           print "Move disc $2 to $3"
           ((nm1>0)) && hanoi $nm1 $4 $3 $2
   }
   case $1 in
   [1-9]|[1-9][0-9])
   ```

```
        hanoi $1 1 2 3;;
*)      print -u2 "Argument must be from 1 to 99"
        exit 1;;
esac
```

5. Write a program that draws a histogram of an array of integers. Each row of the histogram should represent the number in that array element. Scale using **COLUMNS** if necessary, so that the histogram fits across the page.

6. Write a program that takes a positive integer and does the following:
   a. If the number is 1, stops.
   b. If the number is even, divides by two and starts over.
   c. If the number is odd, displays the number in base 10 and in base 2. Then multiplies the number by 3, adds 1, and starts over.

---

6 CUSTOMIZING YOUR ENVIRONMENT

This chapter describes some files that **ksh** uses, and explains how you can customize your environment based on your own preferences.

You can specify actions for **ksh** to perform each time you log onto the system and run **ksh**.

You can specify functions and aliases that will be defined whenever you run **ksh** interactively and/or with shell scripts.

This chapter also gives you advice on how to decrease the time it takes **ksh** to start up. It also tells you how to write scripts that run faster.

HISTORY FILE

ksh uses a file to store the commands that you enter from your terminal. This file is called the history file. Both the **emacs** and **vi** built-in editors have editing directives that allow you to retrieve commands from the history file to edit them and reenter them. Use **history** to display commands in your history file.

If you do not specify the **nolog** option, then **ksh** also uses the history file to store function definitions. *Version*: The **nolog** option is available only on versions of **ksh** newer than the 06/03/86 version.

ksh opens the history file as soon as it encounters a function definition or after it finishes reading the environment file, whichever is first. The name of the history file will be the value of the **HISTFILE** variable at the time that **ksh** opens it. If the history file does not exist, or if **ksh** cannot open it for reading and appending, then **ksh** creates a new history file and sets its permissions so that only you can read and write it.

ksh always appends commands to the history file. You can also use **read –s** and **print –s** to add commands to the history file. For example, to change the value of the **PATH** variable, run **print –s PATH=$PATH** and then use one of the built-in editors to edit the previous command.

ksh imposes no limit to the size of the history file. However, the value of the **HISTSIZE** variable at the time that the history file is opened specifies a limit to the number of previous commands that **ksh** can access.

ksh does not delete the history file at the end of a login session. Each time you log in, **ksh** deletes commands from your history file older than the last **HISTSIZE** commands. *Caution*: On some systems, **ksh** does not delete old commands from the history file when you log in, and the history file may continue to grow. This causes **ksh** to take longer to begin execution and uses space on the file system. On some systems you can avoid this problem by specifying **ksh** as your login shell. On other systems you have to remove your history file periodically.

Separate invocations of **ksh** share the history file between all instances that specify the same name and have appropriate permission. Commands typed from one invocation are accessible by all the interactive instances of **ksh** that are running concurrently and sharing the same history file. On a terminal with multiple windows, you can type a command in one window and access it through another window.

LOGIN ENVIRONMENT (PROFILE)

Whenever you use **ksh** as your login shell, **ksh** executes the script **/etc/profile** if it exists, and then executes the file with the pathname that results from parameter expansion on **$HOME/.profile**. You can use this file to:

- Set and export values of variables that you want to have set for all the programs that you run, such as the **TERM** variable to specify the type of terminal that you are using.
- Set options such as **ignoreeof** that you want to apply to your login shell only.
- Specify a script to execute when you log out. Use **trap** on the **EXIT** condition.

The *Shell Functions and Programs* chapter contains a sample **.profile** suitable for most UNIX systems.

ENVIRONMENT FILE

Whenever **ksh** begins execution, it expands the **ENV** variable, and executes a script by this name if it exists. This file is called your environment file. Use this file to:
- Define aliases and functions that apply for interactive use only; or for both interactive use and scripts invoked from **ksh**.
- Set default options that you want to apply to all **ksh** invocations.
- Set variables that you want to apply to the current **ksh** invocation.

You may want certain commands in your environment file to be in effect only for interactive shells. The – parameter contains an **i** in its value when **ksh** runs interactively. You can check **$–** within the environment file.

If all the commands are for interactive use, you can specify a value for **ENV** that expands to Null when **ksh** is not interactive. The following example shows how to define a subscript that will evaluate to 0 or 1, depending on the value of parameter –. Use this to define a value for **ENV** that will expand to a file only when the **interactive** option is on.
Example
```
export FILE=$HOME/.envfile
# The subscript below evaluates to 0 when interactive.
ENV='${FILE[(_$-=0)+(_=1)-_${-%%*i*}]}'
```

Caution: For security reasons, your environment file is not processed when the **privileged** option is on.

The *Shell Functions and Programs* chapter contains a sample environment file suitable for most UNIX systems.

CUSTOMIZING YOUR PROMPT

ksh displays the primary prompt whenever the **interactive** option is on and **ksh** is ready to read a command.

The **PS1** variable determines your primary prompt. **ksh** performs parameter expansion on the value of **PS1** each time before displaying the prompt. After **PS1** is expanded, the character **!** is replaced by the current command number. Use **!!** if you want the prompt to contain **!**.

Use the parameter expansion **${PWD#$HOME/}** within your prompt to display your working directory relative to your home directory.

Use the **SECONDS** variable to put the time of day in your prompt. Use the fact that subscript evaluation occurs first and can have side effects, to generate the hour and minute of the day from the **SECONDS** variable. Put the following lines in your profile file:

```
# Set SECONDS to number of seconds since midnight.
export SECONDS="$(date '+3600*%H+60*%M+%S')"
# The following variables store hours and minutes.
typeset -Z2 _h _m          # Two columns, leading zeros.
# The following are formulas for hours and minutes.
_hh="(SECONDS/3600)%24" _mm="(SECONDS/60)%60"
# The following expression reformats SECONDS.
_time='${_x[(_m=_mm)==(_h=_hh)]}$_h:$_m'
# Use _time within PS1 to get the time of day.
PS1="($_time)"'!$ '
# Note that $_time gets replaced by above expression.
# Expression gets evaluated when PS1 is displayed.
```

CHANGING DIRECTORIES

ksh always remembers your previous working directory. Use **cd –** to return to the previous working directory.

You can set the **CDPATH** variable to a list of directory prefixes that **ksh** searches whenever you type a pathname that does not begin with a /. **ksh** displays the pathname of the new working directory when the new directory is not a subdirectory of your current working directory.

When you run interactively, you may want **ksh** to keep track of the directories you visit so that you can go back to a directory without typing its name again. You can write functions and put them in your environment file to do this. The *Shell Functions and Programs* chapter has the code for two different interfaces for directory manipulation. Refer to that chapter for details.

IMPROVING PERFORMANCE

Whenever **ksh** is invoked, it reads the environment file. To decrease the time it takes **ksh** to process the environment file, you should:
- Minimize the amount of information that you put into it.
- Auto-load functions that you use infrequently, instead of putting the definitions in your environment file.
- If you only need the environment file for interactive uses of **ksh**, define the **ENV** variable so that it evaluates to Null when non-interactive.
- Use **set –o nolog** to keep function definitions from being stored in the history file.
- Follow the guidelines on the next page for writing efficient scripts, when writing your environment file.

ksh also reads the history file whenever you begin an interactive execution. Therefore, you should:
- Remove the history file if it gets large.
- Use **set −o nolog** to keep function definitions from being stored in the history file.

To improve the interactive performance of **ksh**:
- Specify the **trackall** option in your environment file. This will reduce the time it takes to find some commands.
- If you use the **vi** built-in editor, do not use the **viraw** option unless you need to.
- Use aliases in place of functions where possible.
- Do not set the **MAILCHECK** variable to a value lower than its default.

To decrease the time it takes **ksh** to execute a script or function:
- Use built-in commands whenever possible. Built-in commands usually run more than an order of magnitude faster than do programs.
- Functions are slower than built-in commands but are still much faster than programs.
- Command substitution of built-in commands is much faster than command substitution of programs.
- Avoid command substitution altogether whenever you can use parameter expansion, arithmetic evaluation, or pattern matching to achieve the same result.
- Move loop invariants, especially command substitutions, to before the loop.
- Use the construct **$(** < *file*), rather than **$(cat** *file*) or `**cat** *file*`.
- It is faster to perform several variable assignments, alias definitions, attribute declarations, or arithmetic evaluations by using multiple arguments to one command, than by using individual commands for each assignment, etc.
- Use **set −f** (**set −o noglob**) when you don't want pathname expansion.
- On some systems, the time it takes to invoke a program will increase if you define many functions.
- Use { } rather than ( ) to group commands. ( ) always creates a subshell environment, whereas { } does so only when necessary.
- It is faster to specify redirection for a complete **for**, **while**, or **until** loop, rather than redirecting commands within the loop.
- Specify the integer attribute on numeric variables. If **foo** is an integer variable, it is faster to use **foo** rather than **$foo** within an arithmetic expression.
- Do not use the **exec** command to keep **ksh** from creating extra processes. **ksh** has been optimized to reduce the number of processes it creates. Using **exec** should never help and in some cases could cause scripts to run slower.

EXERCISES

1.   Write a shell script named **basename** that displays the last component of a specified pathname. The script should take an optional second argument that specifies a suffix to be removed from the resulting filename if it is present. For example, **basename /usr/include/stdio.h .h** should display **stdio**.

2.   Write and time a script that uses an integer variable and counts to 1000.

3.   Modify the above and time a script that takes two arguments and does the assignment **base=$(basename "$1" $2)** 1000 times.

4.   Rewrite **basename** as a function and time how long it now takes.

5.   Rewrite and time the script using the substring operators to write the assignment, without using command substitution or any other command.

PART III

THE BUILT-IN EDITORS

7   INTRODUCTION

One of the major benefits of using **ksh** is that you can use an **emacs**-like or a **vi**-like interface to edit your current command line. Thus with **ksh** you do not, as with other current shells, have to backspace to the point where you want to make a correction, or to just start over. Backspacing or starting over is tedious, time-consuming, and error-prone, not to mention that you may want to make changes or corrections several times. You can also use the same editor interface to make changes to your previous commands, which **ksh** keeps in a history file.

emacs and **vi** are single-line editors. That is, with the exception of **vi** search/edit directives (which allow you to copy previous commands from your **ksh** history file to become the current line), you can edit **ksh** commands one line at a time.

The rest of the KornShell language is independent of these editor interfaces. Therefore, you do not have to use either of the built-in editors to use **ksh**. Some systems provide an editing mechanism that you can use whenever you are entering text. In this case, you may wish to use the editor with which you are familiar and run **ksh** without a built-in editor. You can take advantage of the history feature of **ksh** without using a built-in editor.

TERMINAL REQUIREMENTS

Environment Variable Usage

ksh uses the **COLUMNS** variable to determine the width of your screen. **ksh** does not use the **TERM**, **TERMCAP**, or **TERMINFO** variables.

Non-Screen or Paper-Only Terminals

Most people will use **ksh** with screen terminals. However, you can also use **ksh** with non-screen or paper-only terminals in a very limited mode. Some points you should be aware of:

    emacs. Use *Kill Kill* (see page 94) to cause each line erase to advance to the next line.

    emacs and **vi**. Use the CONTROL l directive (see page 97) to cause a line to be redrawn.

Space, Backspace, and Return

The following requirements apply to what your terminal should do when it receives one of these three characters. These requirements do not apply when you yourself type one of these characters. If you do not have a problem using **ksh**, you need not concern yourself with these requirements. If you do have a problem, consult the system administrator if there is one. However, there are some terminals on which these requirements may not be met, and thus on which you may not be able to use **emacs** and **vi**.

ksh works on almost all terminals. The only requirements made by **ksh** on your terminal (or your terminal emulator, if you are using one) are that if the computer sends:

- Space character. Your terminal should erase the current position and move the cursor one position to the right. This is frequently referred to as a destructive space.
- Backspace character (decimal 8). Your terminal should move the cursor one position to the left, without erasing the character at the current position. This is frequently referred to as a non-destructive backspace.
- Return character. Your terminal should move the cursor to the very first character on the line without doing a linefeed, even if the first character is a Space or a Tab. If your terminal does not meet this requirement, you can get around it by putting a control character other than Bell , for instance CONTROL e, in your prompt.
- Users of some other terminals may require special settings. For instance, ADM terminal users should set the "Space-Advance" switch to "Space." Hewlett-Packard series 2621 terminal users should set the straps to "bcGHxZetX."

Escape Key

If your terminal does not have an ESCAPE key, then try using CONTROL [.

HOW TO USE THE BUILT-IN EDITORS

This section discusses how you communicate with **ksh** and how **ksh** communicates with you, when you are using the **emacs** or **vi** built-in editors. We use the term directives to describe actions that are to be processed by the built-in editors.

Entering ksh Commands

You enter commands by typing them and then pressing `RETURN`.

If you make a mistake while typing a command, use any of the edit directives described in this chapter to position the cursor to the place where you made a mistake. Then use any of the edit directives to correct the mistake. Press `RETURN` while the cursor is anywhere on the line if you want **ksh** to execute the command.

Use the directives described in this chapter to recall a command that you entered previously. These directives display a copy of the previously entered commands on your terminal for you to edit. Press `RETURN` when you have finished editing the command and **ksh** will execute it.

Typeahead

"Typeahead" is the term used for when you start to type a command before you get the prompt. When you do this, **ksh** will probably display the characters that you type both when you type them, and when the prompt appears, just prior to execution of the command.

Tabs

Tabs are located at every 8 columns, at columns 1, 9, 17, etc. **ksh** does this automatically. You cannot change this, unless you want to modify **ksh** itself.

How ksh Displays Characters

See **Character Set**, for information on control characters, octal codes, etc.

ksh displays letters, digits, and punctuation characters as you would expect.

`CONTROL` *c*. **ksh** displays this as ^, followed by a character or a symbol. This means that, for instance, if you press `CONTROL` **g**, the effect is not the same as if you type the character ^ followed by **G**, even though **ksh** displays both as **^G**:

- $\boxed{\text{CONTROL}}$ **g** is a control character with a special meaning.
- Your typing **^G** results in a literal **^** and a literal **G**, with no special meaning.

To tell, when you are reading the screen and you see a **^**, if it is a literal **^** or a control character, move the cursor one space to the left or the right in **emacs** or **vi**. If it is a:

- Literal **^**, **ksh** processes this as it does any other literal character. Thus the cursor moves just one space.
- Control character, **ksh** processes the **^** with the following character as a unit. For historical reasons, the result is that in **emacs**, it is not possible to position the cursor on the character following the **^**. And in **vi**, it is not possible to position the cursor on the **^**.

$\boxed{\text{DELETE}}$ (octal 177). **ksh** displays this as **^?**.

ksh *Lines Wider Than the Screen*

You can type a **ksh** line of 256 characters (more on some systems). This number is set when **ksh** is compiled, and may be different on your system. If a line comes from a file instead of being typed by you on your terminal, the line can be of unlimited size.

ksh has a one-line "window" through which you look at the current **ksh** line that you are inputting or editing. The window width is the value of the **COLUMNS** variable if you defined it (default is 80 columns). If the current line is wider than the window width minus 2 (for instance, wider than 78 columns if the width is 80 columns), **ksh** horizontally scrolls the line on your screen to the left or the right, so that you can see different segments of the line. **ksh** does this scrolling automatically when you move the cursor toward the edge of the screen. **ksh** uses the following notation in the last column displayed on the screen, on the right, to indicate that it is scrolling the line, and that there is more text to the:

- \>   Right.
- \<   Left.
- *   Right and left.

Caution: The width of the window is affected by the width of your prompt. **ksh** may miscalculate the width of your prompt, especially if it contains escape sequences. **ksh** calculates the width of your prompt by adding the number of characters that occur after the last Newline or Return. Therefore, if you use escape sequences in your prompt, follow them with a Newline or a Return to keep **ksh** from miscalculating the width of your prompt.

Alerting You to Disallowed Actions

ksh sends the Bell character when you try to do something that is not allowed, or a search fails, or you type ESCAPE from **vi** control mode.

Most terminals sound an audible alarm when they receive the Bell character. Others may flash the screen.

TURNING ON/OFF THE BUILT-IN EDITORS

We use the terms "turn on" and "turn off" for the **emacs** and **vi** built-in editors, rather than "invoking" and "exiting." This is because they are options, and thus they are not invoked or exited as a program would be.

You can turn on only one built-in editor at a time: **emacs**, or **vi**. The built-in editor that you want to turn on must have been compiled into **ksh** by the system administrator or whomever you obtained your system from. Your system might have **ksh** with both **emacs** and **vi**, or with just one of them, or with neither of them.

Since the editors are built into **ksh**, they take virtually no time to turn on.

Turning On for Just the Current Session

Substitute **emacs** or **gmacs** for **vi** in the following settings, if you want to turn on **emacs** or **gmacs** (see page 91), respectively.

You can turn on a built-in editor in any of the following three ways:
set −o vi
EDITOR=...**vi**
VISUAL=...**vi**
Note: With the last two ways, you can use any pathname (indicated here by ...) ending in **vi**. If you set the **EDITOR** and **VISUAL** variables differently, **VISUAL** overrides **EDITOR**.

Examples
VISUAL=/usr/bin/vi
VISUAL=/usr/ucb/vi

Turning On Automatically at Login

Do the same as above, but do it in your **.profile** file, or in your environment file.

Turning Off the Built-In Editors

set +o vi Turns off **vi** and puts you in **ksh**, without a built-in editor.

set −o emacs Turns off **vi** and turns on **emacs.**

DIFFERENCE BETWEEN BUILT-IN EDITORS

Caution: If you use both **emacs** and **vi**, keep in mind this basic difference between them:

emacs Works on **ksh** history file lines. That is, it works on just one line at a time.

vi Works on **ksh** history file commands, which may consist of more than one line.

8 emacs
BUILT-IN EDITOR

With **emacs**, you can edit your current **ksh** line as well as lines in your **ksh** history file.

For historical reasons, **emacs** comes in two versions, one named **emacs** and the other named **gmacs**. The only difference is that when you press CONTROL t :
> **emacs** transposes the current character with the next character.
> **gmacs** transposes the two previous characters.

The **emacs** built-in editor is a somewhat modified subset of the **emacs** program. It does not have all of the features of the **emacs** program. Directives sometimes differ from the **emacs** program directives, even though the directive names are the same. The **emacs** built-in editor has the following features that are not in the **emacs** program:

- Pathname listing. The ESCAPE = directive displays the list of pathnames that result from the expansion of the word under the cursor.
- Pathname completion. The ESCAPE ESCAPE directive appends characters to the word under the cursor to complete the pathname of an existing file. Characters are appended up to the point that they would match more than one pathname or until the filename is completed. If a complete pathname results, **ksh** appends a / if the pathname is a directory; otherwise a Space. *Version*: This feature is available only on versions of **ksh** newer than the 06/03/86 version. ESCAPE ESCAPE was equivalent to ESCAPE * on the 06/03/86 version of **ksh**.
- Pathname expansion. The ESCAPE * directive replaces the word under the cursor with the list of pathnames that results from expansion of word.
- Last argument. The ESCAPE _ directive inserts the last argument of the previous command.
- Version identification. The CONTROL v directive displays the current version of **ksh**.

- Operate and get next. The $\boxed{\text{CONTROL}}$ **o** directive causes **ksh** to operate on the current line and to fetch the next line from the history file. Use this to rerun multiline commands.

All **emacs** directives operate from any place on the line, not just at the beginning of the line. Press $\boxed{\text{RETURN}}$ only when you want to execute the **ksh** command.

Whenever you type a character that is not one of the **emacs** directives, **ksh** inserts the literal character at that point.

You need to use the $\boxed{\text{ESCAPE}}$ key with many **emacs** directives. In the usual **emacs** terminology, it is often called the "Meta" key.

In this chapter, we use the term emacs-word to indicate a string of characters consisting of only letters, digits, and underscores.

MOVING THE CURSOR

$\boxed{\text{CONTROL}}$**f** $\boxed{\text{ESCAPE}}$*n*$\boxed{\text{CONTROL}}$**f**

(**f**orward) Moves the cursor right 1 (or *n*) characters.

Example
Before   After
$ **print foobar** $\boxed{\text{CONTROL}}$**f** $ **print foobar**

$\boxed{\text{CONTROL}}$**b** $\boxed{\text{ESCAPE}}$*n*$\boxed{\text{CONTROL}}$**b**

(**b**ack) Moves the cursor left 1 (or *n*) characters.

Example
Before   After
$ **print foobar** $\boxed{\text{CONTROL}}$**b** $ **print foobar**

$\boxed{\text{ESCAPE}}$**f** $\boxed{\text{ESCAPE}}$*n*$\boxed{\text{ESCAPE}}$**f**

(**f**orward) Moves the cursor right to the first character past the end of the current emacs-word or *n* emacs-words.

Example
Before   After
$ **print foo bar** $\boxed{\text{ESCAPE}}$**f** $ **print foo bar**

$\boxed{\text{ESCAPE}}$**b** $\boxed{\text{ESCAPE}}$*n*$\boxed{\text{ESCAPE}}$**b**

(**b**ack) Moves the cursor left to the beginning of the emacs-word or *n* emacs-words.

Examples

Before		After
$ **print foo bar** [ESCAPE]b		$ **print foo bar**
$ **print foo bar** [ESCAPE]b		$ **print foo bar**

[CONTROL] a

Moves the cursor to the start of the line.

Example

Before		After
$ **print foo bar** [CONTROL]a		$ **print foo bar**

[CONTROL] e

(**end**) Moves the cursor to the end of the line.

Example

Before		After
$ **print foo bar** [CONTROL]e		$ **print foo bar**

[CONTROL]] *c*

(**character**) Moves the cursor to the next instance of *c* on the current line; repetitions of this directive step to the next *c*(s) on the line.

Implementation-dependent: In **ksh-i**, the international version of **ksh**, *c* can be a multibyte character.

Example

Before		After
$ **print foo bar** [CONTROL]]a		$ **print foo bar**

DELETING

Erase   [ESCAPE] *n Erase*

Deletes the preceding 1 (or *n*) characters. The default is often # or [CONTROL]**h**, depending on your system. You can set *Erase* with **stty**.

Example

Before		After
$ **print floo bar** [CONTROL]h		$ **print foo bar**

Kill

Deletes the entire line. If you type *Kill* two times in succession, all subsequent *Kill* characters cause the cursor to move to the beginning of the next line. This feature is useful with paper-only terminals. Typing *Kill* twice in succession a second time causes **emacs** to revert to its previous behavior.

The default is often **@** or $\boxed{\text{CONTROL}}$ **x**, depending on your system. You can set the *Kill* character with **stty**.

Example
Before   After
$ `print foo bar` $\boxed{\text{CONTROL}}$ **x** $ _

$\boxed{\text{CONTROL}}$ **k**

(**k**ill) Deletes from the cursor to the end of the current line.

Example
Before   After
$ `print foo bar` $\boxed{\text{CONTROL}}$ **k** $ `print f`_

$\boxed{\text{ESCAPE}}$ *n* $\boxed{\text{CONTROL}}$ **k**

(**k**ill) Deletes:
- If column *n* is to the left of the cursor, from *n* up to, but not including, the cursor.
- If column *n* is to the right of the cursor, from the cursor up to, but not including, column *n*.

Example
Before   After
$ `print foo bar` $\boxed{\text{ESCAPE}}$ 3 $\boxed{\text{CONTROL}}$ **k** $ `priar`

$\boxed{\text{CONTROL}}$ **d** $\boxed{\text{ESCAPE}}$ *n* $\boxed{\text{CONTROL}}$ **d**

(**d**elete) Deletes 1 (or *n*) characters. If $\boxed{\text{CONTROL}}$ **d** is your *End-of-file* character, and it is the first character on the line, then it is treated as an *End-of-file*.

Example
Before   After
$ `print foo bar` $\boxed{\text{CONTROL}}$ **d** $ `print fo bar`

$\boxed{\text{ESCAPE}}$ **d** $\boxed{\text{ESCAPE}}$ *n* $\boxed{\text{ESCAPE}}$ **d**

(**d**elete) Deletes from cursor to end of current (to right) 1 (or *n*) words.

Example
Before   After
$ `print foo bar` `ESCAPE`d $ `print f_bar`

`ESCAPE` `CONTROL`h   `ESCAPE`*n*`ESCAPE` `CONTROL`h
`ESCAPE` `CONTROL`?   `ESCAPE`*n*`ESCAPE` `CONTROL`?
`ESCAPE`h   `ESCAPE`*n*`ESCAPE`h

Deletes from the current cursor back to the beginning of the current
(to left) 1 (or *n*) words. When you press `BACKSPACE`, the terminal
generates `CONTROL`h. If your *Interrupt* character is the default
interrupt, `CONTROL`? (octal 177), then this directive does not work.
When you press `DELETE`, the terminal generates `CONTROL`?.

Examples
Before   After
$ `print foo bar` `ESCAPE` `CONTROL`h $ `print bar`
$ `print foo bar` `ESCAPE` `CONTROL`h $ `print foo ar`

`CONTROL`w

(wipe out) Deletes the line, from the cursor to the mark. The first line
of the following example sets a mark, as described in the next section.

Examples
Before   After
$ `print foo bar` `ESCAPE` `SPACE` $ `print foo bar`
$ `print foo bar` `ESCAPE`f $ `print foo_bar`
$ `print foo_bar` `CONTROL`w $ `print f_bar`

MARKING, YANKING, AND PUTTING

`ESCAPE` `SPACE`

Sets a mark at the location of the cursor. See the example above.

`CONTROL`x `CONTROL`x

(exchange) Interchanges the cursor and the mark. That is, the cursor
goes to where the mark is, and the mark is set to where the cursor
was. Thus you can go back to where the cursor was, by just repeating
the directive.

Examples

Before		After
$ `print foo bar`	`ESCAPE` `SPACE`	$ `print foo bar`
$ `print foo bar`	`ESCAPE` f	$ `print foo bar`
$ `print foo bar`	`CONTROL` x `CONTROL` x	$ `print foo bar`

`ESCAPE` **p**

(**p**ush) Selects the region from the cursor to the mark, and saves it into a buffer for subsequent use with `CONTROL` **y**. The previous contents of the buffer are deleted.

`CONTROL` **y**

Restores the last text deleted from the line, at the present location of the cursor.

Examples

Before		After
$ `print foo bar`	`ESCAPE` `SPACE`	$ `print foo bar`
$ `print foo bar`	`ESCAPE` f	$ `print foo bar`
$ `print foo bar`	`ESCAPE` p	$ `print foo bar`
$ `print foo bar`	`CONTROL` y	$ `print foooo bar`

MISCELLANEOUS

`CONTROL` **t**

(**t**ranspose) This is the only difference between **emacs** and **gmacs**:
* **emacs** transposes the current character with the next character.
* **gmacs** transposes the two previous characters.

Example

Before	emacs	After
$ `print foo bar`	`CONTROL` t	$ `pritn foo bar`

Example

Before	gmacs	After
$ `print foo bar`	`CONTROL` t	$ `pirnt foo bar`

`CONTROL` **c**   `ESCAPE` *n* `CONTROL` **c**

(**c**hange) Changes the current (or *n*) characters to uppercase and moves the cursor to the right 1 (or *n*) characters.

Example

Before   After
$ `print` `foo` `bar` CONTROL c $ `print` `fOo` `bar`

ESCAPE c   ESCAPE *n* ESCAPE c

(**c**hange) Changes from the current cursor to the end of the current (or
*n*th) emacs-word to uppercase, and moves the cursor to the beginning
of the next (or *n*th) word.

Example

Before   After
$ `print` `foo` `bar` ESCAPE c $ `print` `fOO bar`

ESCAPE l   ESCAPE *n* ESCAPE l

(**l**owercase) Changes from the cursor to the end of the current (or *n*th)
emacs-word to lowercase, and moves the cursor to the beginning of
the next (or *n*th) emacs-word.

Example

Before   After
$ `print` `FOO` `bar` ESCAPE l $ `print` `Foo bar`

CONTROL l

(**l**ine redraw) Moves to the next line, and displays the current line.

Use this to redraw the current line if the screen becomes garbled, or if
you are using **ksh** on a non-screen terminal.

End-of-file

Acts as *End-of-file* only if it is the first character on the line.
Otherwise, it acts as a normal character. The default is often
CONTROL d. You can set *End-of-file* with **stty**.

If you have the **ignoreeof** option set, **ksh** displays a message telling
you to type **exit** to log out. Otherwise, **ksh** terminates the current
shell. If this is your login shell, you are logged out.

Caution: We recommend that you set the **ignoreeof** option in your
login shell, so that you will not accidently log yourself out by pressing
End-of-file.

CONTROL j

CONTROL m

Executes the current line. When you press:
LINEFEED , the terminal generates CONTROL j.
RETURN , the terminal generates CONTROL m.

ESCAPE =

Lists pathnames that match the current emacs-word, as if an * were appended to the current emacs-word.

Example
Before
```
$ print foo bar   ESCAPE =
```
After
```
1) foo.c
2) fool
$ print foo bar
```

ESCAPE   ESCAPE

Pathname completion. The ESCAPE ESCAPE directive appends characters to the word under the cursor to complete the pathname of an existing file. Characters are appended up to the point that they would match more than one pathname or until they complete the filename. If a complete pathname results, **ksh** appends a / if the pathname is a directory; otherwise a Space. ***Version***: This feature is available only on versions of **ksh** newer than the 06/03/86 version. ESCAPE ESCAPE was equivalent to ESCAPE * on the 06/03/86 version of **ksh**.

Example
Before   After
```
$ print f             ESCAPE ESCAPE   $ print foo.c
```

ESCAPE *

Pathname expansion. Causes an * to be appended to the current emacs-word to form a pattern, and pathname expansion to be attempted. If any pathnames match the current emacs word, **ksh** replaces the emacs-word by the pathnames that match the pattern. Otherwise, **ksh** sends the Bell character.

Example
Before   After
```
$ print foo bar   ESCAPE *       $ print foo.c fool bar
```

boxed(CONTROL) u

Multiplies the count of the next directive by **4**.

Example
Before   After
$ `print` f̲o̲obar   boxed(CONTROL) u boxed(CONTROL) f $ `print foobar`̲

\

Escapes the next character. Editing characters, and the user's *Erase*,
Kill, and *Interrupt* (normally boxed(CONTROL) **?**) characters may be entered in
a command line or in a search string if preceded by a \. The \
removes the next character's editing features, if any.

Example
Before   After
$ `print` f̲o̲obar   \ boxed(CONTROL) h $ `print f^Hoobar`̲

boxed(CONTROL) v

(version) Displays the version date of **ksh**. Press any key to resume
entering commands.

Examples
Before   After
$ `print foobar`   boxed(CONTROL) v $ `Version 06/03/86a`̲
$ `Version 06/03/86a`̲   d $ `print foodbar`̲

boxed(ESCAPE) *letter*

(macro expander) Searches your alias list for an alias by the name
_ *letter*. If you have defined an alias by this name, **ksh** inserts its
value on the input queue.

letter must not be one of the letters used with boxed(ESCAPE) above
(**f, b, d, p, l, c, h**). *Caution*: Use uppercase letters to avoid
possible conflict with new features in future releases of **ksh**.

Example
If alias _Q has value,
`alias _Q='` boxed(ESCAPE) `b"` boxed(ESCAPE) `f"'`
Before   After
$ `print` f̲o̲o `bar`   boxed(ESCAPE) Q $ `print "foo"̲ bar`

| ESCAPE | . | | ESCAPE | *n* | ESCAPE | . |
| ESCAPE | _ | | ESCAPE | *n* | ESCAPE | _ |

. (dot) or _ (underscore).

ESCAPE . inserts on the line, the last emacs-word of your previous **ksh** command.

ESCAPE *n* ESCAPE . inserts on the line, the *n*th emacs-word of your previous **ksh** command.

Examples
Before
```
$ print foo bar          RETURN
```
After
```
foo bar
```
Before   After
```
$ print foo        ESCAPE _          $ print foobar
```

FETCHING OLD HISTORY FILE LINE

CONTROL p   ESCAPE *n* CONTROL p

(**previous**) Fetches your previous **ksh** line (or *n* lines back) in your **ksh** history file. Each time you subsequently press CONTROL p, **ksh** fetches the previous **ksh** line from the line that you last fetched.

If you use both **emacs** and **vi** at different times, keep in mind that:
- **emacs** works on **ksh** history file lines. That is, **emacs** works on one line at a time.
- **vi** works on **ksh** history file commands, which may consist of more than one line.

For multiline commands, use CONTROL o rather than RETURN to cause the first line to be processed by **ksh** and to fetch the second and subsequent lines.

ESCAPE <

Fetches your least recent (oldest) **ksh** history file line.

You cannot go back more commands than are defined by the **HISTSIZE** variable.

ESCAPE >

Fetches the most recent (the one that you input last) **ksh** line that you typed.

`CONTROL` **n**   `ESCAPE` *n* `CONTROL` **n**

(**n**ext) Moves down (forward) in your **ksh** history file. Fetches the next 1 (or *n*) lines forward from the most recent line you fetched.

`CONTROL` **r** [*string*] `RETURN`

`ESCAPE` **0** `CONTROL` **r** [*string*] `RETURN`

Searches the history file for the first occurrence of a command line containing *string*. If you specify:
- *string*, and specify a count of zero. Searches forward.
- *string*, and do not specify `ESCAPE` **0**. Searches in reverse order.
- No *string*, but do specify `ESCAPE` **0**. Searches in the reverse direction of the previous search.
- Neither *string* nor `ESCAPE` **0**. Fetches the next command line containing the most recent *string*.

`CONTROL` **r^***string* `RETURN`

`ESCAPE` **0** `CONTROL` **r^***string* `RETURN`

(**r**everse) Same as above, except matches *string* only if it is at the beginning of the line. ***Version***: This feature is available only on versions of **ksh** newer than the 06/03/86 version.

`CONTROL` **o**

(**o**perate) **ksh** processes the current line, and fetches the next line (relative to the current line) from the **ksh** history file. Do this repeatedly to execute multiline commands.

Examples

```
history -6
35     date
36     print foobar
37     cat foobar | wc
38     for i in *
       do  print $i
       done
39     find $HOME -name foobar -print
40     who | grep morris
```

Before		After	
41$	`ESCAPE` >	41$	who | grep morris
41$ who | grep	`CONTROL` rfoo	41$	cat foobar | wc
41$ cat foobar | wc	`CONTROL` r	41$	print foobar
41$ print foobar	`CONTROL` n	41$	cat foobar | wc
41$ cat foobar | wc	`CONTROL` n	41$	for i in *

```
41$ for i in *          CONTROL o    > do  print $i
> do  print $i          CONTROL o    > done
```

9 vi
BUILT-IN EDITOR

With **vi**, you can enter (in input mode) and edit (in control mode) the current command that you are typing, as well as commands in your **ksh** history file.

Press the ESCAPE key to enter control mode from input mode. If you press ESCAPE from control mode, **ksh** will send your terminal the Bell character and you will remain in control mode. On most terminals this will generate an audible sound like a bell or buzzer. Thus if you are not sure which mode you are in, you should press ESCAPE.

The **vi** built-in editor is a somewhat modified subset of the **vi** program. It does not have all of the features of the **vi** program. Directives sometimes differ from the **vi** program directives, even though the directive names are the same. The **vi** built-in editor has the following features that are not in the **vi** program:

- Comments. The # control mode directive enters the current command into the history file as a comment.
- Pathname listing. The = control mode directive displays the list of pathnames that result from the expansion of the word under the cursor.
- Pathname completion. The \ control mode directive appends characters to the word under the cursor to complete the pathname of an existing file. Characters are appended up to the point that they would match more than one pathname or until the end of the last filename. If a complete pathname results, **ksh** appends a / if the pathname is a directory; otherwise a Space. *Version*: This feature is available only on versions of **ksh** newer than the 06/03/86 version.
- Pathname expansion. The * control mode directive replaces the word under the cursor with the list of pathnames that result from expansion of word.
- Escape to **vi**. Type **v** from control mode to invoke the **vi** program from the **vi** built-in editor, on a file containing the current command. **ksh** executes the file when you leave **vi**.

We use the following special notation in this chapter:
- vi-WORD indicates a sequence of letters, digits, and/or punctuation marks delimited by Newline, Space, Tab, or the beginning of a line. Punctuation marks are counted as vi-WORDS only if they are surrounded by a Space or Tab on both sides.
- vi-word indicates a sequence of letters and/or digits delimited by Newline , Space, Tab, the beginning of a line, or a punctuation mark. A sequence of one or more punctuation marks on a line counts as one vi-WORD. For instance,) is one vi-word, while (") is also just one vi-WORD.

CHARACTER AND LINE INPUT

Terminology

The usual terminology for:
- Character-at-a-time input is raw (unprocessed) mode.
- Line-at-a-time input is canonical mode. It is also called "cooked" (processed) mode, which is the opposite of "raw" mode.

We use the terms character input and line input, because we feel that they are more descriptive.

Initial Status

When you get a **ksh** prompt, **ksh** puts you into line input. Then, when you press ESCAPE, **ksh** automatically puts you into character input for the remainder of the command, until you press RETURN.

To use character input at all times, type **set −o viraw**. Some systems may be configured in a way such that you are always in character input. You can type **set −o** to list all option settings, to see how the **viraw** option is set. Then, if you want to, you can type **set −o viraw**.

Response Time

Character input is the most reliable and full featured method, but it consumes more computer cycles. This may, under certain conditions, cause longer response times on multiuser computers, for you and/or for other users. On single user (personal) computers, character input does not cause longer response time; thus you can always use it.

Line input has fewer features, as listed below. It was created primarily for users of multiuser computers, because of the longer response time discussed above. ***Caution***: Some systems have been implemented in a way that, in combination with some terminal types, may cause line input to behave at times in unpredictable ways. If you experience problems, use character input by typing **set −o viraw**, as discussed above.

Display of Characters

Character input has horizontal scrolling, and Tabs are always expanded. When you type a control character, for instance, CONTROL a, **ksh** expands it immediately, so that you can immediately see ^A displayed on the screen.

Line input does not have horizontal scrolling. Depending on your system, when you type a control character or a Tab, you see it expanded immediately, after you press the RETURN or ESCAPE key, or, if transmission speed is under 1200 baud, you may not see it expanded at all if you press RETURN . You will see all expansions and you will enable horizontal scrolling if you press ESCAPE to enter control mode.

Character Input

Character input. On all systems, CONTROL v and CONTROL w work as documented in this chapter.

Line input. On some systems, CONTROL v and CONTROL w do not work as documented in this chapter.

INPUT MODE

vi has two modes; input mode, and control mode. By default, when you turn on **vi**, **ksh** puts you in input mode. ***Caution***: This is in contrast to what happens when you execute the **vi** program, where you are placed in control mode.

Press ESCAPE to exit input mode and enter control mode. In control mode, you can move the cursor wherever you want and edit what you have input, using the other **vi** directives in this chapter.

Erase

Deletes the preceding character. The default is often # or `BACKSPACE`, depending on your system. You can set *Erase* with **stty**.

Example
Before
$ `print foo bar`   `CONTROL`h

After
$ `print foo ba`

Kill

Deletes the entire line, and goes to the first character position after the prompt. The default is often **@** or `CONTROL`x, depending on your system. You can set *Kill* with **stty**.

Example
Before
$ `print foo bar`   `CONTROL`x

After
$

`CONTROL`v

Escapes the next character. That is, it enables you to insert in your **ksh** command line or in a search string, as a literal character, a non-printing or a special character such as *Erase* or *Kill* or `CONTROL`w. *Implementation-dependent:* May not work when using line input on some systems.

Examples
Before
$ `print foobar`   `CONTROL`v @
$ `print foobar`   `CONTROL`v `CONTROL`v

After
$ `print foobar@`
$ `print foobar^V`

\

Similar to `CONTROL`v, above, except that it escapes only the next *Erase* or *Kill* characters.

End-of-file

Acts as *End-of-file* character only if it is the first character on the line. Otherwise, acts as a normal character. The default is often `CONTROL`d, depending on your system. You can set *End-of-file* with **stty**.

If the **ignoreeof** option is on, **ksh** displays a message telling you to type **exit** to log out. Otherwise, **ksh** terminates the current shell. If this is your login shell, you are logged out.

Caution: We recommend that you turn on the **ignoreeof** option in your login shell, so that you will not accidently log yourself out by pressing *End-of-file*.

CONTROL W

(**word**) Deletes the previous input vi-word.
Implementation-dependent: May not work when using line input on some systems. Always works when using character input.

Example
Before

`$ print foo bar` CONTROL w

After

`$ print foo`

MISCELLANEOUS CONTROL MODE DIRECTIVES

Except for RETURN , you must be in control mode to enter any of the directives in this and the following sections. Press ESCAPE to enter control mode.

RETURN

Executes the **ksh** current line, regardless of whether you are in input mode or control mode.

Synonyms
- CONTROL **j** is equivalent to LINEFEED .
- CONTROL **m** is equivalent to RETURN .

Example
Before
`$ print foo bar` RETURN
After
`foo bar`
`$`

CONTROL l

(**line redraw**) Moves to the next line and displays the current line. Use this to redraw the current line if the screen becomes garbled, or if you are using **ksh** on a non-screen terminal.

Example
Before
`$ print foo bar` CONTROL l

After
`$ print foo bar`

# #

Comment. Inserts a # at the beginning of a command in order to put the command in your **ksh** history file as a comment. Useful for causing the current line to be inserted in your **ksh** history file as a comment so that it won't be executed, but can be referenced for editing in the future.

Example
Before
```
$ print foo bar        #
```
After
```
#print foo bar
$
```

=

Lists pathnames that match the current word, as if an * were appended to it.

Example
Before
```
$ print foo bar      =
```
After
```
1) foo.c
2) fool
$ print foo bar
```

\

Pathname completion. The \ directive appends characters to the vi-WORD under the cursor to complete the pathname of an existing file. Characters are appended up to the point that they would match more than one pathname or until the end of the last filename. If a complete pathname results, **ksh** appends a / if the pathname is a directory; otherwise a Space. *Version*: This feature is available only on versions of **ksh** newer than the 06/03/86 version.

Example
Before   After
```
$ print f                  \        $ print foo.c
```

*

Pathname expansion. Causes an * to be appended to the current vi-WORD, and pathname expansion to be attempted. If any pathnames match the current vi-WORD, **ksh** replaces the vi-WORD by the list of pathnames that match the matching pattern, and then enters input mode. Otherwise, **ksh** sends the Bell character.

Example

Before

```
$ print foo bar  *
```

After

```
$ print foo.c fool_bar
```

@*letter*

Macro expander. Searches your list of aliases for an alias by the name _ *letter*. If an alias of this name is defined, inserts its value on the input queue for processing.

Example

If alias _q has the value,

```
alias _q='1Bi"[CONTROL]v[ESCAPE]Ea"[CONTROL]v[ESCAPE]'
```

Before

```
$ print foo bar  @q
```

After

```
$ print "foo" bar
```

~   *n*~

Changes the single (or *n*) character(s) at the current cursor position to uppercase if it was lowercase, and vice-versa. Also moves the cursor 1 (or *n*) character(s) to the right. *Version*: You can specify *n* only with versions of **ksh** newer than the 06/03/86 version.

Example

Before

```
$ print foo bar  ~
```

After

```
$ print fOo bar
```

.   *n*.

(dot) Repeats 1 (or *n*) times, the most recent **vi** directive that changed the contents of the current command or a previous command.

Examples

Before

```
$ print foo bar  ~
$ print fOo bar  2 .
```

After

```
$ print fOo bar
$ print fOO Bar
```

v   *n*v

(vi) Returns the command:

```
fc -e ${VISUAL:-${EDITOR:-vi}}  n
```

This command invokes the **vi** program with a file that contains the designated command. The command is the **ksh** line that you were editing with the **vi** built-in editor if you omit *n*, or command *n* in the history file. When you exit the **vi** program, **ksh** displays and executes the command that you edited.

CONTROL MODE – MOVING THE CURSOR

l   *n***l**

SPACE   *n* SPACE

(lowercase letter **l**, or SPACE) Moves cursor right 1 (or *n*) characters.

Example
Before   After
$ print foo bar   3l $ print foo bar

w   *n***w**

(word) Moves the cursor right to the beginning of the next (or *n*th next) vi-word.

Example
Before   After
$ print foo.c bar   w $ print foo.c bar

W   *n***W**

(**W**ord) Same as above, but moves to the next (or *n*th next) vi-WORD.

Example
Before   After
$ print foo.c bar   W $ print foo.c bar

e   *n***e**

(end) Moves the cursor right to the next (or *n*th next) end of vi-word.

Example
Before   After
$ print foo.c bar   e $ print foo.c bar

E   *n***E**

(**E**nd) Same as above, but moves over vi-WORDS.

Example
Before   After
$ print foo.c bar   E $ print foo.c bar

h   *n***h**

Moves the cursor left 1 (or *n*) characters.

Synonyms
- *Erase*
- CONTROL h

Examples
Before		After
$ print foo.c bar	h	$ print foo.c bar
$ print foo.c bar	3h	$ print foo.c bar

b   *n***b**

(**b**ack) Moves the cursor left to the preceding (or *n*th preceding) beginning of vi-word.

Examples
Before		After
$ print foo.c bar	b	$ print foo.c bar
$ print foo.c bar	b	$ print foo.c bar
$ print foo.c bar	3b	$ print foo.c bar

B   *n***B**

(**B**ack) Same as above, but backs over vi-WORDS.

Examples
Before		After
$ print foo.c bar	B	$ print foo.c bar
$ print foo.c bar	2B	$ print foo.c bar

^

Moves the cursor left to the first character on the line that is not a Space or a Tab.

Example
Before		After
$ print foo.c bar	^	$ print foo.c bar

0

(zero) Moves the cursor left to the first character on the line.

Example
Before		After
$ print foo.c bar	0	$ print foo.c bar

$

Moves the cursor right to the last character on the line.

Example

Before	After
$ `print foo.c bar    $`	$ `print foo.c bar`

| *n* **|**

Moves the cursor to the *n*th character on the line. Default is 1. Moves to the last character on the line if *n* is greater than the line length.
Version: This directive is available only on versions of **ksh** newer than the 06/03/86 version.

Example

Before	After
$ `print foo.c bar    10|`	$ `print foo.c bar`

CONTROL MODE – MOVING TO CHARACTER

Implementation-dependent: In **ksh-i**, the international version of **ksh**, *c* can be a multibyte character.

f*c*   *n***f***c*

(**f**ind) Moves the cursor right to the next (or *n*th next) *c*.

Example

Before	After
$ `print foo.c bar    fa`	$ `print foo.c bar`

F*c*   *n***F***c*

(**F**ind) Moves the cursor left to the preceding (or *n*th preceding) *c*.

Example

Before	After
$ `print foo.c bar    2Fo`	$ `print foo.c bar`

t*c*   *n***t***c*

(**t**o) Moves the cursor right to the character before the next (or *n*th next) *c*.

Equivalent to **f** followed by the **h** directive.

Example

Before	After
$ `print foo.c bar    ta`	$ `print foo.c bar`

T*c*   *n***T***c*

> (Back **T**o) Moves the cursor left to the character following the
> preceding (or *n*th preceding) *c*.
>
> Equivalent to **F** followed by the **l** directive.
>
> ***Example***
> Before   After
> ```
> $ print foo.c bar    2To        $ print foo.c bar
> ```

;   *n***;**

> Repeats the most recent **f**, **F**, **t**, or **T** directive once (or *n* times). The **;**
> itself can, of course, be repeated. For instance, **;;;** is equivalent to **3;**.
>
> ***Examples***
> Before   After
> ```
> $ print go to togo  fo          $ print go to togo
> $ print go to togo  2;          $ print go to togo
> ```

,   *n***,**

> Same as above, but in the reverse direction to the original directive.
> Useful if you overshot the character that you wanted.
>
> ***Examples***
> Before   After
> ```
> $ print go to togo  fo          $ print go to togo
> $ print go to togo  2;          $ print go to togo
> $ print go to togo  ,           $ print go to togo
> ```

CONTROL MODE – ADDING AND CHANGING

How to Use These Directives

Type one of the following directives. **ksh** puts you into input mode. Next
type the text that you want to append or to insert. When you finish, press
ESCAPE to go back to control mode or press RETURN to execute the
command at once.

a

> (**append**) Appends text to the right of the current cursor position.
>
> ***Example***
> Before   After
> ```
> $ print foo bar  ad ESCAPE        $ print food bar
> ```

A

(**A**ppend) Appends text to the end of the current line.

Equivalent to **$a**.

Example
Before   After
$ `print foo bar Ad` `ESCAPE` $ `print foo bard`

i

(**i**nsert) Inserts text to the left of the current cursor position.

Example
Before   After
$ `print foo bar id` `ESCAPE` $ `print fodo bar`

I

(**I**nsert) Inserts text to the left of the first character on the line that is not a Space or a Tab. Equivalent to **^i**.

Example
Before   After
$ `print foo bar Id` `ESCAPE` $ `dprint foo bar`

R

(**R**eplace) Each character that you type replaces the character at the cursor, and moves the cursor right.

Examples
Before   After
$ `print fox bar Rod` `ESCAPE` $ `print foodbar`
Before
$ `print fox bar Rod` `RETURN`
After
`foodbar`
$ ___

c*motion*

c*n* *motion*   *n***c** *motion*

motion defines a region that consists of the text from the current cursor position to the cursor position defined by the ***Moving the Cursor*** or ***Moving to Character*** directives.

(**c**hange) Changes the characters starting at the current cursor position up to the cursor position defined by the specified directive *motion*, to the characters that you type. If the *motion* is **c**, the entire line is deleted and input mode is entered.

Notes
- **c***n* and *n***c** have the identical effect; use whichever form you prefer.
- If *motion* is **w** or **W**, the cursor must be at the beginning of the word if you want to change the entire word. If the cursor is within the word, only the remaining part of the word is changed.
- *Caution*: Unlike the **vi** program, the text is first deleted, and then you enter input mode.

Examples

Before		After
$ **print** s̲**and bar**	**cwfood** ESCAPE	$ **print food bar**
$ **print** s̲**and bar**	**clla** ESCAPE	$ **print sala̲d bar**
$ **print** s̲**and bar**	**cfatee** ESCAPE	$ **print stee̲r**
$ **print** s̲**and bar**	**c$alad** ESCAPE	$ **print sala̲d**

C

(**C**hange) Deletes the current character through the end of the line, and enters input mode. Equivalent to **c$**.

S

(**S**ubstitute) Deletes the entire line and enters input mode. Equivalent to **cc**.

CONTROL MODE – REPLACE

r*c*   *n***r***c*

(**r**eplace) Replaces with *c*, 1 or *n* character(s) starting at the current cursor position. The cursor is positioned at the last character changed. *Version*: You can specify *n* only on versions of **ksh** newer than the 06/03/86 version.

Example

Before		After
$ **print foo̲l bar**	**rd**	$ **print foo̲d bar**

_   *n_*

(underscore) Causes the last word (or *n*th vi-WORD from the beginning), of the previous **ksh** command to be appended, and then enters input mode.

Example
```
print foo.c bar
```
Before   After
$ `grep bar`   2_ ESCAPE $ `grep bar foo.c`

CONTROL MODE – X/DELETE

x   *n***x**
X   *n***X**

(**x**-, **X**-ing out) Deletes 1 (or *n*) characters.
- **x** *n***x**   Starts at the current cursor position and deletes to the right.
- **X** *n***X**   Starts immediately to the left of the current cursor position and deletes to the left.

Examples
Before   After
$ `print fool bar`   x $ `print foo bar`
$ `print fool bar`   X $ `print fol bar`
$ `print fool bar`   5x $ `print far`

d*motion*

d*n motion*   *n***d***motion*

motion defines a region that consists of the text from the current cursor position to the cursor position defined by the ***Moving the Cursor*** or ***Moving to Character*** directives.

(**delete**) Deletes characters starting at the current cursor position up to, and including, the other end of the specified *motion*. **ksh** saves the characters in a buffer. You can retrieve them with the **u**ndo or **p**ut directives. **d***n* and *n***d** have the identical effect; use whichever form you prefer.

If *motion* is **w** or **W**, the cursor must be at the beginning of the word if you want to delete the entire word. If the cursor is within the word, only the remaining part of the word is deleted.

Examples

Before		After
$ `print food bar` dw		$ `print fbar`
$ `print food bar` d2w		$ `print f`
$ `print food bar` d5l		$ `print far`
$ `print food bar` dta		$ `print far`
$ `print food bar` d$		$ `print f`

D

(**D**elete) Equivalent to **d$**, immediately above.

dd

(**d**elete) Deletes the entire command, no matter where the cursor is located on the line.

CONTROL MODE – YANK/PUT

y*motion*

y*n* *motion*   *n***y***motion*

motion defines a region that consists of the text from the current cursor position to the cursor position defined by the *Moving the Cursor* or *Moving to Character* directives.

(**y**ank) Yanks the current character through the character that *n motion* would move the cursor to, and stores the characters in a buffer for subsequent use with the **p** or **P** directive (see below). The previous contents of the buffer are deleted. The text and the cursor are not changed. **y***n* and *n***y** have the identical effect; use whichever form you prefer.

Y

(**Y**ank) Yanks from the current cursor position to the end of line. Equivalent to **y$**. *Caution*: This is different from the **vi** program.

yy

(**y**ank) Yanks (copies) the entire current line into the buffer, no matter where the cursor is located on the line.

p   *n***p**

(**p**ut) Puts the previously yanked or deleted text (or *n* copies of the yanked text) to the right of the cursor.

P   *n***P**

(**P**ut) Puts the previously yanked or deleted text (or *n* copies of the yanked text) to the left of the cursor.

Examples

Before	After
$ print food bar yw	$ print food bar
$ print food bar P	$ print food_food bar
$ print food_bar p	$ print food food_bar

CONTROL MODE — UNDO

u

(**u**ndo) Undoes the preceding text-modifying directive.

If you repeat the **u**, this undoes the first **u**. This is useful to compare two versions of text.

Examples

Before	After
$ print food bar dw	$ print f bar
$ print f bar u	$ print food bar
$ print food bar u	$ print f bar

U

(**U**ndo line) Undoes all of the text modifying directives made on the current line. Use **u**, if you want to undo **U**.

Examples

Before	After
$ print food bar dw	$ print fbar
$ print fbar x	$ print far
$ print far U	$ print food bar

FETCHING PREVIOUS COMMANDS

These **vi** directives fetch commands from your **ksh** history file. Thus they act on previously entered **ksh** commands, not just on the current **ksh** command. The **HISTSIZE** variable limits how far back you can search in your **ksh** history file.

A **ksh** command can be more than one line. If it is a multiline command, then Newline characters, except the last one (i.e., the ⬚RETURN at the end of the **ksh** command), are displayed as **^J**.

k   *n***k**

—   *n*—

> (minus) Moves up (back) to fetch the preceding (or *n*th preceding)
> **ksh** command. Each time that you enter **k**, the preceding **ksh**
> command back is fetched. If you specify a value for *n* that would
> move back more than you can access, **ksh** sends the Bell character and
> leaves you positioned at the command farthest up that you can access.

j   *n***j**

+   *n*+

> (plus) Moves down (forward) to fetch the next (or *n*th next) **ksh**
> command. Each time that you enter **j**, the next **ksh** command forward
> is fetched. If you specify a value for *n* that would move past the most
> recent command, **ksh** sends the Bell character and leaves you
> positioned at the most recent command.

G   *n***G**

> (**G**o back) Fetches your oldest accessible **ksh** command, or command
> *n* from your **ksh** history file.

/*string* RETURN

> Moves left and up (back) through your **ksh** history file to search for
> the most recent occurrence of *string*.

> Null *string*: The previous string that you specified is used.

> *Caution*: Differences between the **vi** built-in editor and the **vi**
> program:
> • You cannot specify regular expressions with the **vi** built-in editor.
> • **/** and **?** directives operate in the **vi** built-in editor in the opposite
>   direction to the way that they operate in the **vi** program.
> • You cannot specify a string with the format **/***string***/**+*n* in the **vi**
>   built-in editor, as you can in the **vi** program.
> • There is no wraparound in the **vi** built-in editor, as there is in the **vi**
>   program.
> • *string* can contain a **/** and/or a **?** without escaping them.

/ ^*string* RETURN

> Same as **/***string*, except matches *string* only if it is at the beginning of
> the line. *Version*: This feature is available only on versions of **ksh**
> newer than the 06/03/86 version.

?*string* RETURN

Same as **/***string*, above, but searches in the reverse direction, right and down (that is, forward).

? ^*string* RETURN

Same as **?***string*, except matches *string* only if it is at the beginning of the line. *Version*: This feature is available only on versions of **ksh** newer than the 06/03/86 version.

n

Repeats the most recent **/** or **?** directive. That is, searches for the next match of *string*.

N

Same as above, but in the reverse direction. Useful if you overshot the string that you wanted.

Examples

```
history -6
35    date
36    print foobar
37    cat foobar | wc
38    for i in *
      do  print $i
      done
39    find $HOME -name foobar -print
40    who | grep morris
```

Before		After
41$ _	ESCAPE k	41$ who	grep morris
41$ who	grep	/foo	41$ cat foobar	wc
41$ cat foobar	wc	n	41$ print foobar
41$ print foobar	j	41$ cat foobar	wc
41$ cat foobar	wc	38G	41$ for i in *^Jdo print >

PART IV

PROGRAMMING
LANGUAGE

10 SYNTAX

Lexical analysis is the process of splitting input into units called tokens. This chapter describes the lexical rules of the KornShell language.

See the *Quick Reference* chapter for a more concise description of the grammar for the language.

NEWLINES

A Newline is a token that is used both to terminate a simple command and to separate parts of a compound command. Press the RETURN key to enter a Newline. You can use multiple Newlines wherever a Newline is legal.

Except within a single quoted string, you can continue a command onto more than one line by immediately preceding the Newline with an unquoted \. The \ and the Newline are both removed.

FORMAT

A word is a token that consists of any number of characters considered as a unit, separated from words on the left- and right-hand side by:
- Any nonzero number of unquoted Spaces, Tabs, or Newline characters.
- Any one of the operators listed on the next page. An operator may immediately adjoin a word without any intervening Space or Tab or Newline, but it still is an operator token and not a part of the word.

We suggest that you indent code with Tabs and/or Spaces to improve readability. See the examples in the *Shell Functions and Programs* chapter for a recommended indentation style.

ksh reads a sequence of characters held together with one of the quoting mechanisms described on page 133 as a word, or a part of a word.

COMMENTS

Comments begin with an unquoted # sign, and go up to the next Newline. That is, nothing can follow a comment on the same line. A comment is legal anywhere that a token may begin. For a multiline comment, you have to start a new comment on each line.

Some systems use a comment of the form **#!** *pathname* in the first line of a shell script. The purpose of this is to define the name of the interpreter that will process your script if you invoke it by name, rather than specifying the script as a command argument to **ksh**.

Examples
```
# This is a comment line.
# You don't have to balance quotes in a comment.
ls -l # Displays long listing of the directory.
```

SPECIAL CHARACTERS

ksh processes the following characters specially (you must use one of the quoting mechanisms if you want them to represent themselves):
| & ; < > ( ) $ ` \ " ' Space Tab Newline

ksh processes the following pattern characters specially whenever patterns are processed: * ? [ ]

ksh processes the following characters specially when they begin a new word: # ~

ksh processes the following characters specially when processing variable assignments: = [ ]

OPERATORS

Operators are tokens. They are recognized everywhere, unless you quote them. Spaces are allowed, but not needed, before and after an operator, except when an adjacent character may be concatenated to form another operator token, for example, ((. Without the Spaces this would be processed as the single operator ((.

I/O redirection operators: > >> >& >| < << <<- <& <>

You can precede each I/O redirection operator by a single digit from 0 to 9, without any intervening Space or Tab . The digit applies to the operator. *Version*: The >| and <> operators are available only on versions of **ksh** newer than the 06/03/86 version.

Control operators: | & ; ( ) || && ;; (( )) |&

RESERVED WORDS

Reserved words are processed specially only in the contexts described below. If you use any of these reserved words elsewhere, **ksh** processes them as regular words. The reserved words are:

{   }   case   do   done   elif   else   esac   fi   for   function if   in   select   then   time   until   while   [[   ]]

Version: The words [[and]] are reserved words only on versions of **ksh** newer than the 06/03/86 version.

ksh recognizes reserved words only when they appear:
- As the first word on a line.
- After the operators: **; | || &   && |&   (   )**
- As the first word after a reserved word, except after **case**, **for**, **in**, **select**, and **[[**.
- As the second word after **case**, **for**, and **select**. In this case, **in** is the only legal reserved word.

Example
```
for i in *            # for and in are reserved words.
do  if foo; then bar  # do, if and then are reserved
                      # words.
fi done               # fi and done are reserved words.
```

Additionally, **ksh** does not recognize a word as a reserved word:
- When used as a pattern in a **case** command, except for **esac**.
- When used as a pattern within ( ).
- After the = within a variable assignment.
- Within a here-document.
- After [[until the end of the compound command, except for]].
- If you quote zero or more characters of the word.

Example
```
case for in           # for is not a reserved word.
do|done) [[ if -eq 0 ]]
                      # do, done and if are not reserved
                      # words.
      x=case ""do;;   # case and do are not reserved words.
esac <<!
while                 # while is not a reserved word.
!
```

IDENTIFIERS

Use identifiers as the names of functions and variables. An identifier is a sequence of characters consisting of one or more of the following: **a-z A-Z   0-9   _** (underscore). The first character cannot be a digit. There is no limit on how many characters an identifier may consist of.

Uppercase and lowercase characters are distinct. For instance, **ksh**
processes **A** and **a** as different identifiers.
Examples
```
PWD   X   x   _x   Foo   A_very_long_identifier
```

ALIAS NAMES

The first character of an alias name can be any printable character except
one of the special characters shown on page 124. The rest of the
characters must be letters, numbers, or underscore. ***Caution***: Since alias
substitution (see page 145) is performed after reserved words are
processed, an alias with the same name as a reserved word is usually
ignored.

Aliases whose names are of the form _ *letter* define macros for the **emacs**
and **vi** built-in editors.

VARIABLE ASSIGNMENTS

The format for a variable assignment is
identifier=value
or
identifier[*expression*]*=value*

identifier must be in the format of an identifier. *expression* is in the format
of an arithmetic expression (see page 129). *value* can be any word.

No unquoted Spaces or Tabs are allowed before or after the =.

PATTERNS

ksh patterns are composed of the pattern characters specified on page 124
and described on the next page, and/or any other characters, called regular
characters. Each regular character matches only itself. The pattern
characters may appear anywhere in a word; at the beginning, middle, or
end. Also, they can appear more than once in a word.

Quote any of the special characters to remove their special meaning and to
cause them to behave like regular characters within a pattern.

ksh patterns are used in pathname expansion, **case** pattern matching,
pattern matching within [[...]], and substring expansion.

ksh patterns differ from the regular expressions that are used in the **ed**,
grep, and other UNIX system commands.

Pattern Characters

[...]
  (Brackets) Delimit a set of characters, any one of which will match the
  character position identified by the brackets. The following characters
  are handled specially within the brackets:
  – (minus) Indicates a range of characters. For instance, **a–z** specifies
    that **ksh** is to match any one character from **a** through **z**. For ranges
    of ASCII characters, see *Character Set*. If you specify characters
    in a reverse order from that shown in the *Character Set* (for
    instance, **z-a**), or if the characters are from two different character
    sets (for instance, ASCII and Kanji), then **ksh** matches only the
    first and last characters. The specification **[a–x–z]** is equivalent to
    [a–xx–z]. *Implementation-dependent*: The ranges of
    characters in the same non-ASCII character set may differ on
    different implementations.
  – Stands for itself when it is the first character after the opening [, the
    character immediately after a **!** following the opening [, or the last
    character before the closing].
  ! Immediately after the opening [, reverses the match. That is, it
    matches any character(s) except those specified.
  ] Stands for itself when it is the first character after the opening [, or
    the character immediately after a **!** following the opening [.
  \ Removes the special meaning of –,], **!**, and \.
  Examples
```
chap[259]
# Matches chap2, chap5, chap9.
para[!1-3]
# Matches para4, para5, parax, etc.
chap[12][01]
# Matches chap10, chap11, chap20, chap21.
para[1-3]
# Matches para1, para2, para3.
```

?

  Matches any single character. In multibyte character sets (e.g.,
  Kanji), matches a complete multibyte character, not just a single byte.
  Example
```
para?
# Matches all 5-character strings, beginning with
# para and ending with any single character.
```

*

Matches zero or more occurrences of any and all characters.
Examples
```
para*
# Matches all character strings that begin
# with para.
x*y
# Matches all strings beginning in x and
# ending in y.
```

Version: The following can be used to form patterns only on versions of **ksh** newer than the 06/03/86 version.

?(*pattern*[|*pattern*]...)

Matches zero or one occurrence of any *pattern*.
Example
```
para?([345]|99)1
# Matches the string para1, para31, para41,
# para51, or para991.
```

*(*pattern*[|*pattern*]...)

Matches zero or more occurrences of any *pattern*.
Example
```
para*([0-9])
# Matches the string para, and para followed by
# any number of digits.
```

+(*pattern*[|*pattern*]...)

Matches one or more occurrences of any *pattern*.
Example
```
para+([0-9])
# Matches para followed by one or more digits.
```

@(*pattern*[|*pattern*]...)

Matches exactly one occurrence of any *pattern*.
Example
```
para@(chute|graph)
# Matches the string parachute or paragraph.
```

!(*pattern*[|*pattern*]...)

Matches all strings except those matched by any of *pattern*.
Example
```
para!(*.[0-9])
# Matches any string beginning with para, and not
# ending in a . followed by a digit.
```

ARITHMETIC EXPRESSIONS

Use an arithmetic expression:
- As an array subscript.
- For each argument in **let**.
- Inside double parentheses. ((...)) is the same as **let** "..."
- As the shift count in **shift**.
- As operands to the arithmetic comparison operators of **test**, [, or [[...]].
- As resource limits in **ulimit**.
- As the right-hand side of a variable assignment to an integer variable.

ksh performs all calculations using the longest integer arithmetic type on your system. **ksh** does not check for overflow.

Caution: Since many of the operators have special meaning to **ksh**, you must quote them.

A constant has the form [*base*#] *number* where:

base   A decimal integer between 2 and 36 that defines the arithmetic base. The default is base 10.

number   Any non-negative number. A number in a base greater than 10 uses uppercase or lowercase letters of the alphabet to represent a digit whose value is 10 or greater. For example, **16#b** or **16#B** represents 11 in base 16. Anything after a decimal point is truncated.

A variable is denoted by an *identifier*. If a variable in an arithmetic expression has the integer attribute (see attributes on page 166), then **ksh** uses the value of the variable. Otherwise, **ksh** assumes that the value of the variable is an arithmetic expression, and tries to evaluate it. A variable whose value is Null, evaluates to **0**. For example, if variable **x** has value **y+1**, variable **y** has value **z+2**, and **z** has value **3**, then the expression **2∗x** evaluates to **12**. **ksh** can evaluate variables 9 levels deep.

Expressions:
- Value: The value of an expression with a comparison operator or a logical operator is **1** if non-zero, or **0** otherwise.
- Precedence: Items are listed below in order of precedence, with the highest ones first. Items of the same precedence are listed under the same bullet.
- Associativity: **ksh** evaluates all items of the same precedence left-to-right, except for = and other assignment operators, which it evaluates right-to-left.

An *expression* is a constant, a variable, or is constructed with the following operator(s) (listed here from highest to lowest precedence):
- (*expression*) Overrides precedence rules.
- −*expression* Unary minus.

- **!***expression* Logical negation. The value is **0** for any *expression* whose value is not **0**.
  ~*expression* Bitwise negation.
- *expression* ***** *expression* Multiplication.
  expression **/** *expression* Division.
  expression **%** *expression* Remainder of 1st expression after dividing by the 2nd expression.
- *expression* **+** *expression* Addition.
  expression **−** *expression* Subtraction.
- *expression* **<<** *expression* Left shift first expression by the number of bits given by the second expression.
  expression **>>** *expression* Right shift first expression by the number of bits given by the second expression.
- *expression* **<=** *expression* Less than or equal to.
  expression **>=** *expression* Greater than or equal to.
  expression **<** *expression* Less than.
  expression **>** *expression* Greater than.
- *expression* **==** *expression* Equal to.
  expression **!=** *expression* Not equal to.
- *expression* **&** *expression* Bitwise and. Value contains a **1** in each bit where there is a **1** in both expressions, and a **0** in every other bit position. Both expressions are always evaluated.
- *expression* **^** *expression* Bitwise exclusive or. Value contains a **1** in each bit where there is a **1** in exactly one of the expressions and a **0** in every other bit position.
- *expression* **|** *expression* Bitwise or. Value contains a **1** in each bit where there is a **1** in either expression, and a **0** in every other bit position. Both expressions are always evaluated.
- *expression* **&&** *expression* Logical and. If the first expression is zero, then the second expression is not evaluated.
- *expression* **||** *expression* Logical or. If the first expression is non-zero, then the second expression is not evaluated.
- *identifier* **=** *expression* Assignment.
  identifier *op***=** *expression* Compound assignment. This is equivalent to *identifier* **=** *identifier* *op* *expression*. *op* must be ***** **/** **%** **+** **−** **<<** **>>** **&** **^** or **|**. **Version**: This feature is available only on versions of **ksh** newer than the 06/03/86 version.

Version: The arithmetic operators **<<**, **>>**, **&&**, **||**, **^**, **&**, **|** and **~** are available only on versions of **ksh** newer than the 06/03/86 version.

CONDITIONAL EXPRESSION PRIMITIVES

Conditional expression primitives are unary and binary expressions that evaluate to True or False. They are used within expressions with the **test** and [simple commands, and within the [[...]] compound command. Spaces or Tabs are required to separate operators from operands.

A primitive can be any of the following unary file expressions:

−r *file*	True if *file* exists and is readable.
−w *file*	True if *file* exists and is writable. True indicates only that the write bit is on. *file* will not be writable on a readonly file system even if this test indicates True.
−x *file*	True if *file* exists and is executable. True indicates only that the execute bit is on. If *file* is a directory, True indicates that *file* can be searched.
−f *file*	True if *file* exists and is a regular file.
−d *file*	True if *file* exists and is a directory.
−c *file*	True if *file* exists and is a character special file.
−b *file*	True if *file* exists and is a block special file.
−p *file*	True if *file* exists and is a named pipe (fifo).
−u *file*	True if *file* exists and its set-user-id bit is set.
−g *file*	True if *file* exists and its set-group-id bit is set.
−k *file*	True if *file* exists and its sticky bit is set.
−s *file*	True if *file* exists and it has a size greater than zero.
−L *file*	True if *file* exists and is a symbolic link.
−O *file*	True if *file* exists and its owner is the effective user id.
−G *file*	True if *file* exists and its group is the effective group id.
−S *file*	True if *file* exists and it is a special file of type socket.

Version: **ksh** checks file descriptor *n* when pathname of *file* is of the form **/dev/fd/***n* on versions of **ksh** newer than the 06/03/86 version.

A primitive can be any of the following unary expressions:

−t [*fildes*]	True if the file whose file descriptor number is *fildes* (default is 1) is open and is associated with a terminal device. *fildes* cannot be omitted when used within [[...]].
−o *option*	True if the *option* is on.
−z *string*	True if length of *string* is zero.
−n *string*	True if length of *string* is non-zero.

Version: **−o** *option*, **−O**, **−G**, and **−S** are available only on versions of **ksh** newer than the 06/03/86 version.

With **test** and [, a primitive can be any of the following binary string expressions:

string1 = *string2*	True if *string1* is equal to *string2*.
string1 != *string2*	True if *string1* is not equal to *string2*.

With [[...]], a primitive can be any of the following binary string expressions:

string = *pattern*	True if *string* matches pattern *pattern*.
string != *pattern*	True if *string* does not match pattern *pattern*.
string1 < *string2*	True if *string1* comes before *string2* based on the ASCII value of their characters.
string1 > *string* 2	True if *string1* comes after *string2* based on the ASCII value of their characters.

A primitive can be any of the following binary file expressions:

file1 **–nt** *file2*	True if file *file1* is newer than file *file2*.
file1 **–ot** *file2*	True if file *file1* is older than file *file2*.
file1 **–ef** *file2*	True if *file1* is another name for file *file2*.

A primitive can be any of the following expressions that compare two arithmetic expressions:

exp1 **–eq** *exp2*	True if the value of *exp1* and *exp2* are equal.
exp1 **–ne** *exp2*	True if the value of *exp1* and *exp2* are not equal.
exp1 **–gt** *exp2*	True if the value of *exp1* is greater than the value of *exp2*.
exp1 **–ge** *exp2*	True if the value of *exp1* is greater than or equal to the value of *exp2*.
exp1 **–lt** *exp2*	True if the value of *exp1* is less than the value of *exp2*.
exp1 **–le** *exp2*	True if the value of *exp1* is less than or equal to the value of *exp2*.

With **test** and [, a primitive can be a string by itself. In this case the primary is True if the string is not Null.

QUOTING

Quoting is the means for negating the normal processing of the following items. You can apply any of the quoting mechanisms to:
- Use any of the special characters with their literal meaning.
- Prevent reserved words from being recognized as reserved words. Quote zero or more characters of the reserved word, for example **"for"**, **\for**, **""for**, or **for""**.
- Prevent alias names from being recognized as aliases. Quote zero or more characters of the alias name.

- Prevent parameter expansion and command substitution within here-document processing. Quote zero or more characters of the delimiter word of a here-document.

\ *Escape Character*

(backslash) When \ is:
- Within a comment, it has its literal meaning.
- Not quoted, the \ is removed and the single next character, other than Newline, is treated with its literal meaning. A Newline following the \ is also removed.
- Within literal quotes, it has its literal meaning.
- Within grouping (double) quotes, it has its literal meaning except when followed by $, `, \, or ".
- Within old command substitution, it has its literal meaning except when followed by $, `, or \.

Example
```
print -r \#   \\\\
# \\
```

\Newline *Line Continuation*

(backslash, followed by Newline) Joins two lines together. This is a special case of the \, in that the \ removes the usual meaning of the Newline character.

Does not have this effect if the \ is within single quotes, or if it follows a # (comment) symbol.

Examples
```
print this is a line \
continuation
this is line continuation
# The following works but is not recommended.
wh\
ile ((x<3)); do let x=x+1;command; do\
ne
```

'...' *Literal (Single) Quotes*

(pair of single quotes) Removes special meaning of all enclosed characters. A single quote cannot appear within single quotes because a single quote denotes the end of the string. That is, even \' is not legal within single quotes. Use \' or " ' " outside of single quotes to refer to the literal ' character.

Example
```
print -r '!*+\'"'"    # Concatenates ' to a
                      # literal string.

!*+\'
```

"..." *Grouping (Double) Quotes*

(pair of double quotes) Removes special meaning of all enclosed characters, except $, `, ", and \.

Inside double quotes, backslash followed by one of the above four characters causes the \ to be removed and that character to be interpreted with its literal meaning. When not preceded by a backslash, the four characters are interpreted as:

$ Parameter expansion.

$(...)   New command substitution. All of the tokens between
            (and) form the command.

`   Old command substitution.

"   End of this string.

\   As stated above, if followed by one of these four characters,
            \ escapes the meaning of the next characters. Otherwise, it
            is interpreted as a literal \.

Examples
```
print -r   "$PWD   \"   \$PWD   \\$PWD   \\\$PWD"
/usr/dgk   "  $PWD   \/usr/dgk   \$PWD
```

`...` *Old Command Substitution*

(pair of backquotes, also known as grave accents) ***Bourne shell***: This is the syntax from the Bourne shell, and is accepted by **ksh**. However, its quoting rules rules are complex, so **ksh** offers a simpler syntax that does the same thing (see new command substitution, below).

ksh constructs the command to be executed from the characters that are left after **ksh** makes the following deletions. A \ that is followed by a $, `, or \, is removed. The following example illustrates the complexity of quoting with ``.

Example
```
print -r "`print -r \$PWD "\$PWD" ')a\`\$\\'`"
/home/dgk /home/dgk )a`$\
```

You can include backquotes, `...`, within grouping (double) quotes. If you do that, and you also want to include one or more double quotes within the backquotes, then you must precede each included double quote by a backslash. **ksh** removes the backslash when it constructs the command.

$(...) *New Command Substitution*

All of the tokens (not characters, as for the old command substitution, above), between the (and the matching), form the command. Thus you do not have to change a command to put it within $(...) as you often do with `...`.

Nesting is legal. That is, you can include $(...) within grouping (double) quotes.

You can use unbalanced parentheses within the command, providing that you quote them. However, you must put a (in front of each pattern list of any **case** commands contained within $(...), to keep the parentheses balanced. *Version*: The optional (in front of the pattern list in **case** commands is available only on versions of **ksh** after 06/03/86.

Example

```
print -r "$(print -r \$PWD "\$PWD" ')a\`\$\\')"
$PWD $PWD )a\`\$\\
```

${...} *Parameter Expansion*

Parameter expansion is described starting on page 170. The characters between the braces are processed as part of the same token. *Version*: This feature is available only on versions of **ksh** after 06/03/86. You had to quote special characters within ${...} on the 06/03/86 and earlier versions of **ksh**.

Example

```
foo=${foo:-<This is the default>}
```

((...)) *Arithmetic Evaluation*

Arithmetic expressions. The characters between the parentheses are processed as if they are contained within double quotes, since this is equivalent to **let** "..." .

Example

```
while (( (X=X+1) )); do print $X; done
```

identifier[...]= *Array Variable Assignment*

Subscript for array variable assignment. The characters within the brackets follow the rules for grouping (double) quotes.

Example

```
X[2*(i+1)]=6
```

I/O REDIRECTION

To redirect the input and/or output of a command, use the notation in this section anywhere in a simple command, or following a compound command.

Example
```
while read -r line
do    print -r "$line"
done <fromfile >tofile
```

You can also use this notation with **exec** to open and close files in the current environment.

Example
```
exec 3< $infile 4>&-
```

See the table on page 147 for how *word*s are expanded. In particular, note that pathname expansion occurs only if a unique pathname would result.

Any of the operators below may be preceded by a single digit, with no intervening Space or Tab allowed. In this case the digit specifies the file descriptor number, instead of the default 0 or 1.

The order in which you specify redirection is significant. **ksh** evaluates each redirection from left-to-right in terms of the file descriptor association at the time of evaluation.

Example
```
cat 1>fname 2>&1
# First associates file descriptor 1 with
# file fname.  It then associates file
# descriptor 2 with the file associated with file
# descriptor 1 (that is, fname).  If the order of
# redirections were reversed, file descriptor 2
# would be associated with the terminal (assuming
# that file descriptor 1 had been specified), and
# then file descriptor 1 would be associated with
# file fname.
```

Note: In the following formats, one or more Spaces or Tabs are optional between the operator and *word*, and no Space or Tab is allowed between the digit and the I/O operator.

< word   *n< word*   **Reading**

> Opens the file with the name that results from the expansion of *word*, for reading as standard input (or file descriptor *n*). When used with a command, redirects the input (or file descriptor *n*) of the command, from the file expanded from *word*.

Example
```
mail abc < F2
# Sends message in file F2 to user whose login
# is abc.
```

<< *word*   *n*<< *word*   **Here-Document**

Creates a here-document file, and opens it as the standard input (or file descriptor *n*).

Any input on the same line after the delimiter *word*, is read normally. You can even have another command on the same line. Common practice is to put *word* at the end of the command it refers to. The here-document begins just after the next Newline even when the Newline is part of a compound command. It continues up to a line that matches *word* character for character (there must be just the one *word* on the line for a match), or to the end of the file. If you specify more than one here-document on a command line, then **ksh** reads them in reverse order.

ksh does not do any parameter expansion, command substitution, or pathname expansion on *word*. If you quote zero or more characters of *word* with a \, single quote, or double quote, then **ksh** does not do any expansions on the characters of the here-document. Otherwise, **ksh** reads and processes the here-document just as it does a double quoted string, except that **ksh** does not process double quotes specially.

Examples
```
cat <<!* | tr '[a-z]' '[A-Z]'
this is a here-document
$HOME is my home directory
!*
THIS IS A HERE-DOCUMENT
/USR/DGK IS MY HOME DIRECTORY
cat << ""EOF
this is a here-document
$HOME is my home directory
EOF
this is a here-document
$HOME is my home directory
```

<<- *word*   *n*<<- *word*   **Here-Document**

Same as above, except that **ksh** strips leading Tabs from the here-document and the line containing the matching delimiter word.

Example
```
cat <<-\!@
    this is a here-document
    $HOME is my home directory
    !@
this is a here-document
$HOME is my home directory
```

<& word   *n<& word*   ## Duplicating Input

word must expand to:
- A digit, in which case **ksh** duplicates standard input (or file descriptor *n*) from the file descriptor whose number is given by digit.
- – (minus), in which case **ksh** closes standard input (or file descriptor *n*).
- **p**, in which case **ksh** connects the output of the co-process (see page 156) to standard input (or file descriptor *n*). This makes it possible to create another co-process and/or to pass the output from the co-process to another command. *Version*: This feature is available only on versions of **ksh** newer than the 06/03/86 version.

Examples
```
exec 3<&4    # Opens file descriptor 3 as a copy of 4.
exec 4<&-    # Closes file descriptor 4.
```

<> word   *n<> word*   ## Reading/Writing

Opens the file with the name that results from the expansion of *word*, for reading and writing as standard input (or file descriptor *n*).
When used with a command, redirects the input (or file descriptor *n*) of the command, from the file expanded from *word*. *Version*: This feature is available only on versions of **ksh** newer than the 06/03/86 version.

Example
```
exec 3<> /dev/tty
# Opens /dev/tty on file descriptor 3 for reading
# and writing.
```

> word   *n> word*   ## Writing
>| word   *n>| word*   ## Writing

ksh opens the file that results from the expansion of *word*, for writing as standard output (or as file descriptor *n*). When used with a command, **ksh** redirects the output (or file descriptor *n*) of the command, to the file expanded from *word*.

If the file does not exist, **ksh** creates it. If the file exists and the **noclobber** option is:

• Set, **ksh** displays an error message. The syntax >| *word* (or *n*>| *word*) causes **ksh** to truncate the file to zero length even if you set the **noclobber** option. *Version*: This feature is available only on versions of **ksh** newer than the 06/03/86 version.

• Not set, **ksh** truncates the file to zero length.

Examples

```
exec 3> foobar    # Opens file foobar for writing.
cat F1 F2 > F3    # Concatenates files F1 and F2, and
                  # places result in F3.
cat F1 F2 >| F3   # Same as above except also works if
                  # F3 exists and noclobber is on.
```

>> *word*   *n*>> *word*   **Appending**

ksh opens the file that results from the expansion of *word* for appending as standard output (or as file descriptor *n*). When used with a command, **ksh** redirects standard output (or file descriptor *n*) of the command, and appends it to the end of the file expanded from *word*.

If the file does not exist, **ksh** creates it.

Example

```
cat F1 >> F2
# Appends file F1 to F2.
# Creates F2 if it doesn't already exist.
```

>& *word*   *n*>& *word*   **Duplicating Output**

word must evaluate to a:

• Digit, in which case **ksh** duplicates standard output (or file descriptor *n*) from file descriptor *word*.

• – (minus), in which case **ksh** closes standard output (or file descriptor *n*).

• **p**, in which case **ksh** connects the input of the co-process (see page 156) to standard output (or file descriptor *n*). This makes it possible to direct the output from any command to the co-process. *Version*: This feature is available only on versions of **ksh** newer than the 06/03/86 version.

Example
```
foobar |&      # Creates cooperating process foobar.
exec 3>&p      # Moves write end of cooperating
               # process to 3.
date >&3       # Directs the output of date to the
               # cooperating process.
exec 3>&-      # Closes connection to cooperating
               # process.
```

EXERCISES

1. Identify each of the following:
   a. `#foo`
   b. `> foo`
   c. `?*`
   d. `esac`
   e. `foo=bar`
   f. `_abc`
   g. `'ab$x'`
   h. `3b2`
   i. `(`
   j. `{`
   k. `~`
   l. `&&`
   m. `select`
   n. `"abc$x"`
   o. `` `date` ``
   p. `$(date)`
   q. `:foo`
   r. `foo[i]=bar+1`

2. What do each of the following patterns match?
   a. `?`
   b. `foo??`
   c. `foo*`
   d. `foo.*`
   e. `foo*bar`
   f. `foo.[cho]`
   g. `foo*.[!cho]`
   h. `foo[!a-z][!a-z]`
   i. `*foo\**`
   j. `foo[-*]`
   k. `*/`
   l. `???[z-a]`
   m. `[a-z]*([a-z0-9])`
   n. `*([0-9])?(.)+([0-9])`
   o. `[0-9]!(*([0-9]))`
   p. `@(foo|bar|bam)?(.c|.o)`

3. In each of the following character strings, identify which characters are special and which characters retain their literal meaning.
   a. `abc\d\$e`
   b. `'abc\d\$e'`
   c. `"abc\d\$e"`
   d. `" "'abc\d\$e'`
   e. `" `abc\d\$e` "`
   f. `' `abc\d\$e` '`

4. What do each of the following I/O redirections do?
   a. `> foobar`
   b. `>> foobar`
   c. `3< foobar`
   d. `4>& -`
   e. `5<> foobar`
   f. `3<< foobar`
   g. `5<<- 'foobar'`
   h. `4<& p`
   i. `5<& 0`
   j. `2>| foobar`

5. Rewrite the **isnum** function from page 70 using patterns not available in the 06/03/86 version of **ksh**.

11 COMMAND PROCESSING

This chapter presents the logical order that **ksh** follows to read and process a command. This is not necessarily the actual order within the code of any given **ksh** implementation.

Commands are processed in two stages. In the first stage, **ksh** reads each command and splits it into tokens. **ksh** determines whether the command is a simple command or a compound command to determine how much to read.

In the second stage, **ksh** expands and executes a command each time that it is used. A compound command such as a **while-do-done** loop is expanded and executed each time that the loop is iterated. A function is expanded and executed each time that it is referenced.

This chapter describes how **ksh** reads its input and how **ksh** expands and executes simple commands. Refer to *Compound Commands* to see how **ksh** processes them.

See *Quick Reference* in the appendix for a more concise description of the grammar for the KornShell language.

READING COMMANDS

ksh first reads commands, and then executes them. This section describes how much **ksh** reads at a time, and how **ksh** splits the input into commands.

Splitting Input into Commands

It is important for you to understand how aliases and **set –k** interact with **ksh** in the reading of commands. You can avoid problems caused by the order in which commands are read and processed by **ksh**, if you:
• Use **alias** and **unalias** with no other commands on the same line.
• Do not use **alias** and **unalias** in compound commands.

- Do not use **set −k** at all. *Bourne shell*: **set −k** is a feature of **ksh** only for compatibility with the Bourne shell.

Caution (Version): For the 06/03/86 and earlier versions of **ksh**, the above comments about aliases also apply to tilde expansion with **~+** and **~−**.

ksh reads at least one line at a time. Therefore new aliases and **set −k** do not affect subsequent commands on the same line, but affect only subsequent lines. This means that if you have two or more simple or compound commands on a single line, **ksh** reads all of the commands on the line before executing them.

Example
```
alias foo=bar; foo
# In this case, foo will not become bar.  If foo were on
# a line following the alias, then foo would become bar.
```

ksh reads entire commands at a time. Therefore, if you use aliases or **set −k** within a compound command, they do not affect the commands within the compound command. They affect only the reading of commands that are read after the execution of the compound command. *Note*: A function definition (see page 162) is a compound command. Therefore, alias definitions within them do not affect how it is read. In addition, a function may be referenced and thus executed many lines after the code for the function definition command, or never at all. Thus an **alias** or **unalias** command in a **function** command may take affect only many lines after the function definition, or never at all.

Example
```
for  i in 0 1
do   if   ((i==0))
     then alias print=date
     fi
     print +%H:%M:%S
done
print +%H:%M:%S
+%H:%M:%S
+%H:%M:%S
11:02:28
```

ksh reads and splits into tokens a complete dot script before it executes any of the commands in the file. The dot script is the file specified as the first argument to the **.** (dot) command. Therefore, if you use aliases or **set −k** in a dot script, they do not affect the commands in the dot script. They affect only the reading of subsequent commands.

ksh reads the smallest number of complete lines that constitute a complete command when it reads its input from your terminal, a shell script other than a dot script, profile files, or your environment file.

When you type an incomplete **ksh** command from a terminal, and then press RETURN, **ksh** displays its secondary prompt, **PS2** (default is >), to indicate that it expects you to continue entering more of the command.
Example

```
for i in One two three
> do print $i
> done
One
two
three
```

Splitting Input into Tokens

The process of splitting your **ksh** input commands into tokens is called lexical analysis. A token is one of the following:
- I/O redirection operator.
- Control operator.
- Newline.
- Reserved word.
- Identifier.
- Word.
- Here-document.

When you type an incomplete token from a terminal, and then press RETURN, **ksh** displays its secondary prompt, **PS2** (default is >), to indicate that it expects you to continue entering more of the token.
Example

```
print "One two three
> four five six
> seven"
One two three
four five six
seven
```

ksh performs alias substitutions (see page 145) as it splits input into tokens.

Determining the Type of a Command

If the first token of the command is one of the following reserved words, then **ksh** reads it as a compound command: **{ case for function if until select time while [[**. *Note*: **ksh** processes these as reserved words only if there are no quotes of any type, or any backslash, in or around them, and they are the first token in the command.

If the first token of the command is one of the following operators:
(**ksh** reads it as a compound command, until the matching closing).
((**ksh** reads it as an arithmetic expression until the matching closing)). **ksh** processes this as though it were a double quoted argument to **let**.

If the first token of the command is one of the following, then **ksh** displays a syntax error and, when not interactive, exits:
- Reserved words:
  do   done   elif   else   esac   fi   in   then   }   ]]
- Operators: | || **&**   **&&**   ;   ;; |**&**

ksh reads any other token at the beginning of a command, including I/O redirection operators, as the first token of a simple command.

Reading Simple Commands

ksh reads all of the tokens until the following as a simple command:
; | **&** || **&&** |**&**   Newline

ksh organizes the tokens in simple commands into three classes:
- I/O redirections (the I/O redirection operator, plus the word following the operator; e.g., >x). **ksh** reads and processes I/O redirections left-to-right. You can mix I/O redirections and command words in any order, although it is not considered good practice to do so. However, this "mixing" ability makes it possible to specify I/O redirections as part of an alias definition, which is sometimes useful.
- Variable assignment words. If the **keyword** option (**set –k**) is on, **ksh** recognizes any word of the syntax of a variable assignment (see page 126) as a variable assignment word. If the **keyword** option is off, **ksh** recognizes any word of the syntax of a variable assignment as a variable assignment word, only until it encounters a token which is not of this format and is not an I/O redirection word. If **ksh** encounters the variable assignment syntax later on, it reads and processes the word as a command word.
- Command words. The remaining words are called command words. **ksh** constructs the command name and the command arguments by expanding command words. **ksh** checks the first command word when it reads it, to see if there is an alias of that name to expand (see next page). *Version*: On versions of **ksh** newer than the 06/03/86 version, if the command name is **alias**, **readonly**, **typeset**, or **export**, **ksh** processes each argument of the format of a variable assignment specially, regardless of whether **keyword** is on or off. These arguments are read and expanded with the same rules as variable assignments, except that they are expanded and evaluated when command arguments are processed.

Alias Substitution

ksh checks the command name word of each simple command to see if it is a legal alias name. If it is not quoted in any way, and it is a legal alias name, and there is a non-tracked alias of that name defined, then **ksh** checks to see if it is currently processing an alias with the same name. If it is, **ksh** does not replace the alias name. If it is not currently processing an alias with the same name, **ksh** replaces the alias name by the value of the alias. *Version*: In the 06/03/86 and earlier versions of **ksh**, **ksh** did not replace the alias name if it was currently processing any alias at all.

ksh performs alias substitution as part of the process of splitting a command into tokens. When **ksh** performs alias substitution, the token containing the alias is replaced by the tokens defined by the value of the alias.

You create, display, and export aliases with **alias**, and remove aliases with **unalias**.

If the value of an alias ends with a Space or a Tab, **ksh** checks the next command word for alias substitution. For example, the preset alias **nohup**, defined below, ends in Space. Thus the word after **nohup** will be processed for alias substitution.
Examples
```
alias foo='print '
alias bar='hello world'
foo bar
hello world
alias od=done
for i in foo bar
do     print $i
od
foo
bar
```

Alias definitions are not inherited across invocations of **ksh**. However, if you specify **alias –x**, the alias remains in effect for scripts invoked by name that do not invoke a separate **ksh**. To export an alias definition, you must specify the **alias –x** and the alias definition in your environment file. See *Invocation and Environment*.

Preset Aliases

Preset aliases are aliases that are predefined by **ksh**. You can unset or change them if you wish to do so. However, we recommend that you do not change them, as this may later confuse you and/or others who expect the alias to work as predefined by **ksh**.

```
autoload='typeset  -fu'
false='let  0'
functions='typeset  -f'
hash='alias  -t'
history='fc  -l'
integer='typeset  -i'
nohup='nohup  '
r='fc  -e  -'
true=:
type='whence  -v'
```

Tilde Expansion

After **ksh** does alias substitution, it checks each word to see if it begins with an unquoted **~**. If it does, then **ksh** checks the word up to a **/** to see if it matches:

~ by itself. It is replaced by the value of the **HOME** variable.

~ followed by **+**. It is replaced by the string **$PWD**. **ksh** expands **$PWD** when the command is executed. *Version*: In the 06/03/86 and earlier versions of **ksh**, **~+** was replaced by the value of **PWD** at the time it was read.

~ followed by **−** (minus). It is replaced by the string **$OLDPWD**. **ksh** expands **$OLDPWD** when the command is executed. *Version*: In the 06/03/86 and earlier versions of **ksh**, **~−** was replaced by the value of **OLDPWD** at the time it was read.

~ followed by user login name. It is replaced by the home (login) directory of the matched user.

~ followed by anything else. The original word is left unchanged.

Also, **ksh** checks the value of each variable assignment to see if a **~** appears after the **=**. If it does, **ksh** attempts tilde expansion. *Version*: In the 06/03/86 and earlier versions of **ksh**, tilde substitution was attempted after each **:** within the value of a variable assignment.

EXPANDING A SIMPLE COMMAND

Prior to execution, **ksh** processes the word tokens of each simple command to generate the command name and/or command arguments as described in this section.

ksh performs command substitution and parameter expansion on a word from left to right first. This is followed by word splitting, and then by pathname expansion. Quote removal is always done last.

As stated above, simple commands are composed of three types of tokens: variable assignment words, command words, and I/O redirections. Command words are expanded first from left to right. The following table summarizes what processing **ksh** does to each type.

	Variable Assignment	Command Word	I/O Redirection
Reading commands			
Alias substitution	No	Note 1	No
Tilde expansion	Note 2	Yes	Yes
Executing commands			
Command substitution	Yes	Yes	Yes,Note 3
Parameter expansion	Yes	Yes	Yes,Note 3
Word splitting	No	Note 4	No
Pathname expansion	No	Yes,Note 5	Note 6
Quote removal	Yes	Yes	Yes

Yes — This is done.
No — This is not done.
Note 1 — Always applies to first word. If the **alias** value ends with a Space or a Tab , then alias substitution also applies to the next word and so on.
Note 2 — Done after the = and after each **:**.
Note 3 — Except after << and <<– operators.
Note 4 — Done only on words generated from command substitution and parameter expansion.
Note 5 — Done, unless **set –f** (**set –o noglob**) is on.
Note 6 — Done only if expansion yields a unique pathname.

Command Substitution

ksh checks each word to see if it contains a command enclosed in **$(...)** (new command substitution), or in a pair of backquotes `` `...` `` (old command substitution). If it does, then **ksh** does the following:
- If you use the old command substitution form, **ksh** processes the string between the backquotes using the quoting rules on page 133 to construct the actual command.
- If you use the new command substitution form, **ksh** executes the command represented by the ellipsis (...).
- **$(...)** or `` `...` `` is replaced by the output of the command represented by the ..., with the trailing Newlines (if any) removed. **ksh** does not process this output for parameter expansion and command substitution.
- If the command substitution appears within grouping (double) quotes, then **ksh** does not process the output from the command for word splitting or for pathname expansion.

$(<*file***)** is equivalent to **$(cat** *file***)**, but executes faster because **ksh** does not create a separate process.

Command substitution is carried out in a subshell environment. No side effects occur in the current **ksh** environment as a result of executing the command substitution. For instance, **$(cd)** does not change the working directory in the current environment.

Examples

```
x=$(date)   # x is assigned the output from date.
```

Parameter Expansion

ksh checks all words that contain an unquoted $ to see if the $ specifies parameter expansion. If it does, then **ksh** replaces the parameter portion of the word.

If the parameter is not set and you specified the **nounset** option (**set −u**), **ksh** displays an error message on standard error. If the error occurs within a script, the program terminates with a False return value.

Example

```
unset foobar
rm $foobar
ksh: foobar: parameter not set
```

If you include a parameter expansion within grouping (double) quotes, then **ksh** does not process the result of the parameter expansion for word splitting and pathname expansion.

Word Splitting

ksh scans the results of command substitution and parameter expansion of command words for the field separator characters (found in the value of the **IFS** variable). **ksh** splits the results of command substitution and parameter expansion into distinct fields where such characters are found.

Example

```
IFS=: foobar="foo:bar"
set foo:bar $foobar "$foobar"
for i
do  print "$i"
done
foo:bar
foo
bar
foo:bar
```

Pathname Expansion

Following word splitting, **ksh** checks each field for the characters *, ?, and [, unless you use the **noglob** option (**set –f**).

If one of these characters does not appear, the field is left unchanged. Otherwise, **ksh** processes the field as a pattern. **ksh** replaces the pattern with all pathnames that match, sorted alphabetically, with the additional rules (that is, in addition to the pattern matching rules):
- * and ? in a pattern do not match /. The pathname must explicitly match each / in the pattern.
- The pathname must explicitly match . (dot) when . is the first character of the pathname, and when the . immediately follows a /.

If there are no matches, **ksh** leaves the word unchanged.

Quote Removal

The special characters \, ", and ' are removed by **ksh** unless they are themselves quoted. **ksh** does not remove quotes that result from expansions.

Null arguments that are:
- Explicit (within single or double quotes, for instance "$*name*" where *name* has no value), are retained.
- Implicit (for instance, $*name* where *name* has a Null value or no value), are removed.

Examples
```
x='"'    y=""
print   "'hello'"   ${x}there${x}
'hello' "there"
set  "$y" $y
print  $#
1
```

EXECUTING A SIMPLE COMMAND

This section describes how **ksh** executes a simple command. A simple command can be a variable assignment command, I/O redirections, a built-in command, a function, or a program.

No Command Name or Arguments

ksh does each of the I/O redirections in a subshell environment. Therefore, the only redirection operators that are useful in this context are > and >|, which you can use to create files.

ksh performs variable assignments from left-to-right in the current environment. *Version*: For the 06/03/86 and earlier versions of **ksh**, the assignments were performed from right-to-left. This change was made to conform to the IEEE POSIX 1003.2 standard.

Return value if:
- Successful: True.
- Otherwise: False (1). If redirection fails within a script or a function, the script or function terminates.

Built-in Commands

ksh executes built-in commands in the current environment. Many of these commands have side effects. They are listed under each command in the *Built-in Commands* chapter.

Except for **exec**, I/O redirection applies only to the built-in command itself. It does not affect the current environment. However, I/O redirection applied to **exec** with no arguments affects open files in the current environment.

ksh processes the following built-ins specially in the ways noted below:
. (dot)   : (colon)   **alias   break   continue   eval   exec   exit export   newgrp   readonly   return   shift   times   trap typeset   wait**.
- **ksh** evaluates variable assignment lists specified with the command before I/O redirection. These assignments remain in effect when the command completes.
- Errors in the built-ins listed above cause the script that contains them to terminate.

Return value: Noted under each command in the *Built-in Commands* chapter.

Functions

If the command is not a built-in, **ksh** checks to see if it is a function.

I/O redirections specified with the function reference apply only to the function itself. They do not affect the current environment. I/O redirections specified within the function with **exec** do affect the current environment.

ksh executes a function in the environment from which the function is invoked. The following are shared by the function and the invoking script, so that they can produce side effects:
- Variable values and attributes, unless you use **typeset** within the function body to declare a local variable.
- Working directory.

- Aliases, function definitions, and attributes.
- Traps other than **EXIT** and **ERR**. *Version*: This applies only to the 06/03/86 and earlier versions of **ksh**.
- Special parameter **$**. *Caution*: Take care that functions do not create a temporary file with the same name as a temporary file created by the invoking script.
- Open files.

The following are not shared between the function and the invoking script and thus cannot cause side effects:
- Positional parameters.
- Special parameter #.
- Variables in a variable assignment list when the function is invoked.
- Variables declared using **typeset** within the function.
- Options.
- Traps. However, signals ignored by the invoking script, will also be ignored by the function. *Version*: On the 06/03/86 and earlier versions of **ksh**, traps other than **EXIT** and **ERR** were shared by the function and the invoking script.

ksh executes a trap on **EXIT** set within a function right after the function completes, but in the environment of the invoking script.

The return value of a function is the return value of the last command executed within the function.

Tracked Aliases

In order to reduce the time that it takes **ksh** to do a pathname search for a command, **ksh** automatically generates some aliases of its own. These are called tracked aliases. They can be displayed with **alias –t**. **ksh** processes these aliases differently from other aliases.

ksh defines a tracked alias for a command name when the command is first encountered if the command name has the syntax of an alias name, the **trackall** option (**set –h**) is set, and the tracked alias is not already an alias.

ksh assigns to a tracked alias a value (which is the pathname corresponding to the given alias name), if the command name is already defined as a tracked alias, and its value is undefined. *Note*: Under these conditions, **ksh** may both define the tracked alias and assign it a value at the same time.

Preset tracked aliases are defined when **ksh** is installed on the system. Since they should be transparent to the user and since they may vary depending on the system, they are not listed in this book.

The value of a tracked alias becomes undefined each time the **PATH** variable is reset, but the alias itself remains defined as a tracked alias. The next subsequent reference to the tracked alias causes its value to be redefined.

When **ksh** encounters a pathname for which there is a tracked alias defined, **ksh** eliminates searching directories defined in the **PATH** variable that begin with a **/**, or that follow the directory defined by the value of the tracked alias.

Programs

ksh executes programs in a separate environment. Therefore the programs cannot have side effects on the current environment.

I/O redirections and variable assignments apply only to the program itself.

If the program terminates with a return value False (non-zero) and if a trap on **ERR** is specified, **ksh** executes the action associated with it. If the **errexit** option (**set −e**) is set, **ksh** exits with a return value of the command that terminated with the False value. Otherwise, **ksh** executes the next command.

If the program terminates with a return value True, **ksh** processes the next command.

EXERCISES

1. Which of the following are simple commands?

   a. `foo  bar`   b. `for  bar`
   c. `>  bar`   d. `for=bar`
   e. `foo`   f. `for>bar`
   g. `foo|bar`   h. `for  ~bar`
   i. `#foo  bar`   j. `fi  bar`

2. Split each of the following commands into parameter assignments, command arguments, and I/O redirections.

   a. `foo  bar  >  file`
   b. `foo=$bar  bar=abc  print  $foo  $bar  >  file`
   c. `foo=$bar  bar=abc  print  >  file  $foo  $bar`
   d. `foo=$bar  bar=abc  print  >  $foo  file  $bar`
   e. `$foo  foo=bar  >  file`
   f. `>  file  foo  bar`
   g. `>  file  foo  <  bar  $bar`

12 COMPOUND COMMANDS

This chapter defines the format and meaning of **ksh** compound commands. A compound command is a pipeline or a list, or it begins with a reserved word or the control operator (.

I/O redirection after any compound command, except a pipeline, the **time** command, or a list, applies to the complete command. I/O redirection applied to a pipeline, the **time** command, or a list applies to only the last command. Use the grouping command beginning with the reserved word { around any command if you need to specify I/O redirection for the complete sequence of commands. I/O redirection does not affect the environment in which **ksh** executes the command.

You cannot specify variable assignments with a compound command.

See the *Quick Reference* chapter for a more concise description of the grammar for the KornShell language.

PIPELINE COMMAND

command [| [*newline...*] *command*]...

A pipeline is a sequence of one or more simple or compound commands, each separated by |. As the above format and definition specify, a pipeline can consist of a single simple or compound command with no pipeline operator |. In practice we would not refer to this as a pipeline (since there is no pipeline operator |). We define it this way so that we do not have to single out this case for commands that allow pipelines within them.

Standard output of each command except the last one, is connected to the standard input of the next command.

ksh runs each command except possibly the last as a separate process. If the **monitor** option is off, **ksh** waits for the last command to terminate. Otherwise, **ksh** runs each pipeline as a separate job. For instance, **date|wc** would be run as a job. **ksh** waits for all processes in a pipeline to complete.

Return value: Return value of last specified *command*.

Example
```
grep foo bar | sort | uniq
food menu
```

TIME COMMAND

time *pipeline*

ksh executes *pipeline*, and displays on standard error the elapsed time, user time, and system time.

Return value: Return value of *pipeline*.

Example
```
time grep foo bar | sort | uniq
food menu

real    0m2.03s
user    0m0.85s
sys     0m0.49s
```

LIST COMMANDS

list

A *list* can be a *pipeline*, or any combination of the following formats. That is, wherever *list* appears in a format below, you can substitute *pipeline* or a complete format recursively, to whatever depth you want.

The list operators have lower precedence than the pipeline operator |. If you specify two or more operators in the same *list*, **ksh** evaluates them left to right, and uses the following precedence:
- Highest: **&&** **||**
- Lowest: **;** **&** **|&**

list [**&&** [*newline...*] *pipeline*]... **And List**

> **ksh** runs the first *pipeline*. If its return value is:
> - True: **ksh** runs the second *pipeline*, and so on to the following *pipeline*(s), as long as the return values of the preceding *pipeline*(s) are True.
> - False (non-zero): **ksh** does not run the remaining *pipeline*(s).
>
> *Return value*: Return value of the last *pipeline* run by **ksh**.
>
> *Example*
> ```
> cd foobar && print -r $PWD
> ```

list [**||** [*newline...*] *pipeline*]... **Or List**

> **ksh** runs the first *pipeline*. If its return value is:
> - True: **ksh** does not run the remaining *pipeline*(s).
> - False (non-zero): **ksh** runs the second *pipeline*, and so on to the following *pipeline*(s), as long as the return values of the preceding *pipeline*(s) are False.
>
> *Return value*: Return value of the last *pipeline* run by **ksh**.
>
> *Example*
> ```
> read -r line || error_exit 'Unexpected end-of file'
> ```

list [**;** *pipeline*]... **Sequential List**

> **ksh** runs each of the *pipeline*(s) in sequence.
>
> *Return value*: Return value of the last *pipeline* run by **ksh**.
>
> *Example*
> ```
> who|wc ; date
> ```

list **&** [*pipeline* **&**]... **Background Processes**

> **ksh** runs each of the *pipeline*(s) without waiting for any of them to complete. If the **monitor** option is on, **ksh** runs each *pipeline* as a separate job.
>
> *Return value*: True.
>
> *Example*
> ```
> nohup find / -name foobar -print &
> ```

list |&   *Co-Processes*

ksh runs **list** as a separate job with its standard input and standard output connected to **ksh**.

To write onto the standard input of this process, use **print –p**. To read the standard output from this process, use **read –p**.

Return value: True.

Example
```
ed - foobar |&
```

[*newline...*] *list* [*newline...*]   *Compound List*

When a list appears within any of the compound commands listed below, it can optionally be preceded and followed by one or more Newlines. We designate this by *compound-list*.

You can use one or more Newlines instead of **;** to specify a sequential list within a compound list.

CONDITIONAL COMMANDS

[[*test-expression* [*newline...*] **]]**
Note: You must type the brackets shown in boldface.

test-expression must be one of the conditional expression primitives defined on page 131, or some combination of these conditional primitives formed by combining one or more of them with one of the following. The following are listed in order of precedence, from highest to lowest:

- **(** *test-expression* **)**. Evaluates to value of *test-expression*. The **( )** are used to override normal precedence rules.
- **!** *test-expression*. Logical negation of *test-expression*.
- *test-expression* **&&** *test-expression*. Evaluates to True if both *test-expression*s are True. The second *test-expression* is expanded and evaluated only if the first *test-expression* is True.
- *test-expression* **||** *test-expression*. Evaluates to True if either of the *test-expression*s is True. The second *test-expression* is expanded and evaluated only if the first *test-expression* is False.

ksh expands the operand(s) for each conditional expression primitive for command substitution, parameter expansion, and quote removal as required to evaluate the command. **ksh** tests the primitive expression to determine whether it is True or False.

Return value: Value of *test-expression*.

Example
```
[[ foo > bar  &&  $PWD -ef . ]]  &&  print foobar
foobar
```

if	*compound-list*
then	*compound-list*
[**elif**	*compound-list*
then	*compound-list*]
...	
[**else**	*compound-list*]
fi	

ksh runs the **if** *compound-list*. If the return value is:
- True: **ksh** runs the **then** *compound-list*.
- False: **ksh** runs each **elif** *compound-list*(s) (if any) in turn, until one has a return value of True. If there are no **elif** *compound-list*(s), or if none have a return value of True, **ksh** runs the **else** *compound-list*, if any.

Return value:
- Return value of the last **then**, **elif**, or **else** *compound-list* that was executed.
- True if no **then** *compound-list* or **else** *compound-list* was executed.

Example
```
if    ((score < 65))
then  grade=F
elif  ((score < 80))
then  grade=C
elif  ((score < 90))
then  grade=B
else  grade=A
fi
```

case *word* **in**
   [[(] *pattern* [| *pattern*] ...) *compound-list* ;;]
...
esac

ksh runs the first command *compound-list* for which *word* matches *pattern*.

ksh expands *word* for command substitution, parameter expansion, and quote removal.

ksh expands each |-separated list of *pattern*s, in turn, for command substitution, parameter expansion, and quote removal. The order of evaluation for patterns within the same list is not defined. If the expanded value of *word* matches the pattern resulting from the expanded value of *pattern*, the corresponding *compound-list* is executed.

Once **ksh** matches a *pattern*, it does not expand any more *pattern*(s).

The parenthesis before each list of *pattern*(s) is optional, except when **case** appears within **$(...)** command substitution. *Version*: With the 06/03/86 and earlier versions of **ksh**, **ksh** did not allow (before the *pattern*(s). Thus you could not use **case** within **$(...)** command substitution.

Return value:
- If *word* matches any *pattern*, return value of the *compound-list* that **ksh** executed.
- If *word* does not match any *pattern*, True.

Example
```
case $x in
-d*)    dflag=1;;
-e*)    eflag=1;;
"")     print -r -u2 - "x must have a value";;
*)      if   test ! -r "$x"
        then print -r - "$x: no read permission"
        fi;;
esac
```

ITERATION COMMANDS

for   *identifier* [**in** *word*...]
do   *compound-list*
done

select   *identifier* [**in** *word*...]
do   *compound-list*
done

ksh does command substitution, parameter expansion, word splitting, pathname expansion, and quote removal for each *word* to generate a list of items, before it processes the **do** *compound-list* command. If you do not specify **in** *word*, **ksh** uses the positional parameters starting at **1** as the list of items as if you had specified **in "$@"**.

In a **for** command, **ksh** sets *identifier* to each item in turn, and runs *compound-list*. Execution ends when there are no more items.

Example
```
for  i  in  fo*
do    print  "$i"
done
food
fool
foot
for
foxy
```

In a **select** command:
- **ksh** displays the items in one or more columns on standard error, each preceded by a number, and then displays the **PS3** prompt. The number of columns is determined by the value of the **LINES** variable and the value of the **COLUMNS** variable.
- **ksh** then reads a selection line from standard input. If the line is the number of one of the displayed items, **ksh** sets the value of the variable *identifier* to the item corresponding to this number. If the line is empty, **ksh** again displays the list of items and the **PS3** prompt; **ksh** does not run *compound-list*. Otherwise, **ksh** sets the variable *identifier* to Null.
- **ksh** saves the contents of the selection line read from standard input, in the variable **REPLY**.
- **ksh** runs *compound-list* for each selection until **ksh** encounters a **break**, **return**, or **exit** command in *compound-list*. The **select** command also terminates when it encounters an *End-of-file*.

Example
```
PS3='Please enter a number '
select i in fo*
do   case $i in
     food|fool|foot)
             print good choice
             break;;
     for|foxy)
             print poor choice;;
     *)      print 'Invalid number';;
     esac
done
1) food
2) fool
3) foot
4) for
5) foxy
Please enter a number
```

Return value:
- Return value of last *compound-list* executed.
- True if no *compound-list* was executed.

while   *compound-list*
do   *compound-list*
done

The **while** command repeatedly runs the **while** *compound-list*. Each time, if the return value of *compound-list* is:
- True: Runs **do** *compound-list*.
- False (non-zero): Loop terminates.

A **break** command within the **do** *compound-list* causes the **while** command to terminate with a return value of True. A **continue** command causes the **do** *compound-list* to terminate and the **while** *compound-list* to be run again.

Return value:
- Return value of last **do** *compound-list* executed.
- True if no **do** *compound-list* was executed.

Example
```
# Reads lines and prints them until an end-of file.
while read -r line
do    print -r - "$line"
done
```

until   *compound-list*
do   *compound-list*
done

The **until** command repeatedly runs the **until** *compound-list*. Each time, if the return value of *compound-list* is:
- False (non-zero): Runs **do** *compound-list*.
- True: Loop terminates.

A **break** command within the **do** *compound-list* causes the **until** command to terminate with a return value of True. A **continue** command causes the **until** *compound-list* to terminate and the **until** *compound-list* to be run again.

Return value:
- Return value of last **do** *compound-list* executed.
- True if no **do** *compound-list* was executed.

Example
```
until cc -c foo.c
do      ed foo.c
done
```

COMMAND GROUPING

(*compound-list*) Subshell Grouping

ksh runs *compound-list* in a subshell environment. Therefore, there will not be side effects in the current environment.

Caution: If you need to nest this command, you must insert Spaces, Tabs, or Newlines between the two open parentheses to avoid arithmetic evaluation.

Return value: Return value of *compound-list*.

Example
```
( find . -print | wc ) >foobar 2>&1 &
```

Brace Grouping

```
{

     compound-list

}
```

ksh runs *compound-list* in the current environment.

Caution: { and } are reserved words here. See page 125 for rules governing reserved words.

Return value: Return value of *compound-list*.

Example
```
{ time foobar ;} 2> savetimes
```

FUNCTION DEFINITION

function *identifier*
{
      compound-list
}

identifier ()
{
      compound-list
}

This defines a function which is referenced by *identifier*. The body of the function is the *compound-list* of commands between { and }. See page 150 for a description of function execution.

Bourne shell: The second format provides compatibility with recent versions of the Bourne shell, except that the braces are required even when *compound-list* consists of a simple command.

Caution: { and } are reserved words here. See page 125 for rules governing reserved words.

Return value: True.

Example
```
function affirmative # question
{
    typeset -l reply
    while true
    do    read -r "reply?$1? " || return 1
          case $reply in
          y|yes)  return 0;;
          n|no)   return 1;;
          *)      print 'Please answer y or n';;
          esac
    done
}
# The following references this function
while affirmative 'Do you want to continue? '
do    foobar
done
```

EXERCISES

1. Write a compound command to do each of the following:
   a. Run a given command once an hour.
   b. Execute a given command only if the variable named **x_flag** is set.
   c. Display the files in your directory in the same format as a **select** list.
   d. Time how long a **while** loop takes to execute.
   e. Display the arguments of a command that do not begin with –.

2. In what ways do the following two commands differ?
   a.
   ```
   for i in *
   do cmd >> output
   done
   ```
   b.
   ```
   for i in *
   do cmd
   done > output
   ```

13 PARAMETERS

ksh entities that store values are called parameters. Some parameters have names predefined by **ksh**, and values set by **ksh**. Other parameters also have names predefined by **ksh**, but values are set by you. And other parameters (called user variables) have names chosen by you, and values set and used by you.

Named parameters, that is, parameters denoted by an identifier, have attributes that you can set. You can use attributes to format data, and for other purposes.

There are several modifiers that you can use to alter the value of a parameter when it is referenced. An important example is substring operations.

All of these operations are discussed in this chapter.

PARAMETER CLASSES

Named Parameters (Variables)

Named parameters are called variables and are denoted by an identifier. You:
• Assign the values of variables with a variable assignment list.
• Assign/unassign attributes with **typeset**.
• Unassign the values and attributes of variables with **unset**.

Caution: By convention, **ksh** uses identifier names that are three or more uppercase characters (for instance, **CDPATH**) for its own use.
Therefore, we suggest that you do not use all uppercase identifier names of three or more characters for user variables. If you do, you run the risk of a future release of **ksh** using that same name for its own use.

Many variables are inherited through the environment of the parent process.

Variables can also be arrays (see page 170).

Positional Parameters

Positional parameters are parameters that are denoted by one or more digits. They are initially assigned values when you invoke **ksh,** or any shell script or function, as follows:
- Parameter **0** is the name of the shell, script, or function.
- Parameter **1, 2,** ... are the values of each of the arguments to the shell, script, or function as it was invoked.

Reassign or unset all of the positional parameters from **1** up with **set.** You cannot reset the value of an individual positional parameter.

Shift positional parameters (except **0**) to the left only (for instance, you can move **3, 4, 5,** ... to **1, 2, 3,** ...), with **shift.**

Special Parameters

Special parameters are parameters denoted by the characters
* **@** # ? – \$!.
ksh automatically sets the values for each of these parameters.

See page 175 for a description of each of these special parameters.

ATTRIBUTES

You can assign each variable one or more of the following attributes. When you change an attribute of a variable, the value that the variable expands to may change to conform to the new attribute. Use **typeset** to turn on/off, or to list the attributes.

–u *Uppercase*

Whenever **ksh** expands the variable, **ksh** changes lowercase characters to uppercase.

ksh turns off the lowercase attribute.

Example
```
typeset -u x=abc
print  $x
ABC
```

–l *Lowercase*

Whenever **ksh** expands the variable, **ksh** changes uppercase characters to lowercase.

ksh turns off the uppercase attribute.

Example
```
typeset -l x=ABC
print   $x
abc
```

–i or –i*base* *Integer*

If, after the **–i**, you:
- Do not specify *base*, the default is base 10 (decimal).
- Do specify *base*, **ksh** expands the value in that arithmetic base. You cannot specify a base above 36.

Whenever you assign a value to the variable, the value is evaluated as an arithmetic expression.

You do not have to specify the integer attribute to use variables within arithmetic expressions. However, performance may be better if you do specify this attribute.

If the base is other than 10, **ksh** prepends the base number followed by a # sign, to the value of the variable when it is expanded.

You can use the preset alias **integer** to declare integer variables.

Example
```
integer x=6
typeset -i8 y=x+x
print $y
8#14
```

–L or –L*width* *Left-justified*

width is any number. If you don't specify *width*, then **ksh** uses the number of characters of the first assignment to the variable.

Whenever **ksh** expands the variable, it left justifies the characters to fit *width*, and puts trailing Spaces at the right, if needed, to fill *width*.

If you assign a value to the variable that is too big to fit *width*, **ksh** truncates excess characters on the right.

ksh turns off the right-justified attribute.

Implementation-dependent: In multibyte versions of **ksh**, *width* refers to the number of columns (rather than to the number of characters). During expansion, if there isn't enough room in *width* for the last complete character, **ksh** does not include that character in the expansion, and uses Spaces to fill up *width*.

Example
```
typeset -L3 x=abcd y
y=3
print "$y-$x"
3  -abc
```

–LZ or –LZ*width* **Strip Leading Zeros**

This is similar to the left-justified attribute (above), except that whenever **ksh** expands the variable, it strips leading zeros at the left.

ksh turns off the right-justified attribute.

Example
```
typeset -LZ3 x=abcd y
y=03
print "$y-$x"
3  -abc
```

–R or –R*width* **Right-justified**

width is any number. If you don't specify *width*, then **ksh** uses the number of characters of the first assignment to the variable.

Whenever **ksh** expands the variable, it right justifies the characters to fit *width*, and puts leading Spaces at the left, if needed, to fill *width*.

If you assign a value to the variable that is too big to fit the *width*, **ksh** truncates excess characters on the left.

ksh turns off the left-justified attribute.

Implementation-dependent: In multibyte versions of **ksh**, *width* refers to the number of columns rather than to the number of characters. During expansion, if there isn't enough room in *width* for the first complete character, **ksh** does not include that character in the expansion and uses Spaces to fill up *width*.

Example
```
typeset -R3 x=abcd y
y=3
print "$y-$x"
  3-bcd
```

–Z or –Z*width* *Zero-filled*

–RZ or –RZ*width* *Zero-filled*

This is similar to the right-justified attribute. However, whenever **ksh** expands the variable it prepends leading zeros at the left. **ksh** does this only if needed, and only if the first character (other than Space or Tab) is a digit, to fill *width*. If the first character is not a digit, then **ksh** fills with leading Spaces.

ksh turns off the left-justified attribute.

Example
```
typeset -Z3 x=abcd y
y=3
print "$y-$x"
003-bcd
```

–r *Read-only*

Once you set this attribute, you will get an error message if you attempt to change the value of this variable, turn off its readonly attribute, or unset it. However, **ksh** can still change the value if it is a variable that **ksh** automatically changes, such as **PWD**.

You can use **readonly** or **typeset** **–r** to set this attribute. Within a function, **typeset** creates a local variable while **readonly** does not.

Example
```
readonly foo=bar
foo=nobar
ksh: foo: is read only
unset foo
ksh: foo: is read only
```

–x *Exported*

ksh automatically sets this attribute for all variables inherited from the parent environment. Therefore, if you change the value of any variable that is inherited from the environment, then **ksh** automatically exports the new value to the environment of each child process.
Bourne shell: This is different from the Bourne shell, where you must explicitly export the variable to export the new value to the environment of any child process.

ksh also passes the attributes of exported variables to the environment of each child process. *Version*: On the 06/03/86 and earlier versions of **ksh**, attributes were passed down only to scripts that did not require a separate invocation of **ksh**. Only the export attribute was passed to new invocations of **ksh**. See *Invocation and Environment* to see when **ksh** requires a new invocation of **ksh** to execute a shell procedure.

Use **export** or **typeset** **−x** to set this attribute. Within a function, **typeset** creates a local variable while **export** does not.

Example
```
export foo=bar PATH
```

−H *Host Operating System Pathname Mapping*

Applicable only to non-UNIX systems. **ksh** ignores this if you specify it on UNIX systems.

Whenever **ksh** expands the variable, **ksh** changes the format of the value from a UNIX system pathname to a host operating system pathname.

Example
In this example, it is assumed that uppercase characters are mapped into the corresponding lowercase characters, each preceded by a **:**.
```
typeset -H file=ABC
print $file
:a:b:c
```

−t *Tagged*

ksh does not use this attribute. It is intended for you to use as you wish.

Example
```
typeset -t PWD foo=bar
typeset +t     # Display names of all variables with the
               # tagged attribute.
PWD
foo
```

ARRAYS

You can use any variable as a one-dimensional array, with the format *identifier*[*subscript*]. Use the syntax on page 126 to assign values to array elements.

The *subscript* must be an arithmetic expression that evaluates to a number in the range **0–511**. *Implementation-dependent*: Some implementations of **ksh** may have a larger limit.

You do not have to declare arrays. However, if you know the size of the array, and/or you want to specify an attribute for the array, use **typeset** to declare the size and or attributes, for instance, **typeset –u x[100]**. When you reference any variable with a valid subscript, an array will be created if you did not declare it. Each attribute applies to all elements of the array.

If you reference an array without a subscript, you will get element zero.

To reference all of the elements of an array, use, as *subscript*, ∗ or **@**. The subscripts ∗ and **@** differ only when the expansion is contained within double quotes. It this case they differ in the same way that the expansion of special parameters ∗ and **@** differ (see page 175).

Caution: Current implementations of **ksh** do not allow you to export array variables to separate invocations of **ksh**.

PARAMETER EXPANSION — INTRODUCTION

$ evokes parameter expansion. Read $ as "value of."

When we say that a parameter is not set, we mean that the parameter has never been given a value or that the parameter has been unset; for example, using **unset** or **shift**.

ksh expands parameters even inside grouping (double) quotes. *Note*: If you put double quotes around the parameter expansion of a command word, or a word in the list of words for the **for** compound command or the **select** compound command, **ksh** does not do word splitting and then pathname expansion on the result of the expansion.

ksh expands parameters inside here-documents if you do not quote the delimiter word.

PARAMETER EXPANSION — BASIC

${*parameter*}

> **ksh** expands this format to the value of the *parameter*.
>
> If the **nounset** option is on and *parameter* is not set, then **ksh** displays an error message. If this occurs within a script, **ksh** terminates execution of this script with a False return value. If **nounset** is off, then **ksh** treats unset parameters as if their value was Null.
>
> *Note*: If *parameter* value is Null, and if you:
> - Put grouping (double) quotes around *parameter*, then when **ksh** does quote removal, it retains the expansion of *parameter*, and counts it as a Null argument. *Exception*: When there are no positional parameters (or array elements), **"$@"** (or **"${*identifier*[@]}"**) does not count as a Null argument.
> - Do not put double quotes around ${*parameter*}, then when **ksh** does quote removal, it throws away the expansion of *parameter* and does not count it as an argument.
>
> { } Braces are optional, except for a:
> - *parameter* followed by a letter, digit, or underscore that is not to be interpreted as part of its name.
> - Variable that is subscripted.
> - Positional parameter of more than one digit.
>
> If *parameter* is one or more digits, then it is a positional parameter.
> *Example*
> ```
> print $PWD ${11} $$
> /usr/dgk arg11 1234
> ```
>
> **ksh** evaluates the subscript before it expands an array variable. You should be alert to this, in case the subscript evaluation causes side effects.
> *Example*
> In the expansion **${x[y=1]}**, **ksh** first evaluates the assignment **y=1,** and then it expands **x[1]**.

PARAMETER EXPANSION — MODIFIERS

${*parameter*:–*word*} *Using default values*
Note: The **:** is optional.

If *parameter* is:
- Unset, **ksh** expands the above format to the expanded value of *word*.
- Null, and you specified **:**, same as above.
- Otherwise, **ksh** expands the above format to the value of *parameter*. **ksh** does not expand *word*.

Example
In this example, **ksh** executes **date** only if **d** is Null or is unset.
```
print ${d:-$(date)}
```

${*parameter*:=*word*} *Assigning default values*
Note: The **:** is optional.

If *parameter* is:
- Unset, **ksh** assigns the expanded value of *word* to *parameter*, and then expands the above format to the value of *parameter*.
- Null, and you specified **:**, same as above.
- Otherwise, **ksh** expands the above format to the value of *parameter*. **ksh** does not expand *word*.

Only variables may be assigned to in this way.

Example
```
unset X
typeset -u X
print ${X=abc}
ABC
```

${*parameter*:?*word*} *Displaying error if Null or unset*
Note: The **:** is optional.

If *parameter* is:
- Unset, **ksh** expands and displays *word* on standard error, and causes your shell script, if any, to terminate with return value False (1). If you omit *word*, then **ksh** displays a message on standard error.
- Null, and you specified **:**, same as above.
- Otherwise, **ksh** expands the above format to the value of *parameter*. **ksh** does not expand *word*.

Example
```
print ${foo?}
```
`ksh: foo: parameter null or not set`

${*parameter*:+*word*} *Using alternate value*
Note: The **:** is optional.

If *parameter* is:
- Unset, **ksh** expands the above format to Null. **ksh** does not expand *word*.
- Null, and you specified **:**, same as above.
- Otherwise, **ksh** expands the above format to the expanded value of *word*.

Example
```
set a b c
print ${3+foobar}
```
`foobar`

PARAMETER EXPANSION — SUBSTRINGS

Note: *pattern* represents any pattern.

${*parameter*#*pattern*} *Remove small left pattern*
The value of this expansion is the value of the *parameter*, with the smallest portion matched on the left by *pattern* deleted.

Example
```
cd $HOME/src/cmd
print ${PWD#$HOME/}
```
`src/cmd`

${*parameter*##*pattern*} *Remove large left pattern*
The value of this expansion is the value of the *parameter*, with the largest portion matched on the left by *pattern* deleted.

Example
```
x=/one/two/three
print ${x##*/}
```
`three`

${*parameter*%*pattern*} *Remove small right pattern*
The value of this expansion is the value of the *parameter*, with the smallest portion matched on the right by *pattern* deleted.

Example
```
x=file.c
print ${x%.c}.o
file.o
```

${*parameter*% %*pattern*} **Remove large right pattern**

The value of this expansion is the value of the *parameter*, with the
largest portion matched on the right by *pattern* deleted.

Example
```
x=foo/fun/bar
print ${x%%/*}
foo
```

PARAMETER EXPANSION — OTHER

${#*parameter*} **String length**

If *parameter* is * or **@**, **ksh** substitutes the number of positional
parameters. Otherwise, **ksh** substitutes the length of the value of
parameter.

Example
```
HOME=/usr/dgk
print ${#HOME}
8
```

${#*identifier*[*]} **Number of elements of an array**
${#*identifier*[@]}

ksh expands the above format to the number of elements in the array
identifier that are set.

Example
```
unset x
x[1]=5 x[3]=8 x[6]=abc x[12]=
print ${#x[*]}
4
```

SPECIAL PARAMETERS SET BY ksh

Note: You cannot initialize or assign values to these parameters.

@ *Positional Parameters*

ksh expands the positional parameters, starting with **$1**, separating them with Space characters.

If you include this parameter expansion in grouping (double) quotes, then **ksh** includes the value of each positional parameter as a separate double quoted string. This is in contrast with the way that * is handled, where **ksh** includes the entire value in one double quoted string (the usual way that parameters are expanded). Therefore, **"$@"** is equivalent to **"$1" "$2"** up to **"$n"** where *n* is the value of **$#**. When there are no positional parameters, **ksh** expands **"$@"** to an unquoted Null string.

Example
```
set "hello there" world
IFS=,$IFS
for i in $@
do print "$i"
done
hello
there
world
for i in "$@"
do print "$i"
done
hello there
world
```

* *Positional Parameters*

ksh expands the positional parameters, starting with **$1**, separating them with the first character of the value of the **IFS** variable.

If you include this parameter expansion in grouping (double) quotes, then **ksh** includes, in double quotes, the values of all of the positional parameters, separated by *d*, where *d* is the first character of the **IFS** variable. Therefore, **"$*"** is equivalent to **"$1***d***$2***d***..."**.

Example
```
set "hello there" world
IFS=,$IFS
for i in $*
do print "$i"
done
hello
there
world
for i in "$*"
do print "$i"
done
hello there,world
```

Number of Positional Parameters

This is initially the number of arguments to **ksh**. Its value can be changed by the **set**, **shift**, and **.** commands.

Example
```
set a b c
print $#
3
```

– Option Flags

(minus) These are the options supplied to **ksh** at invocation or via **set**. **ksh** also automatically sets some options. Each option corresponds to a letter in the value of this parameter.

Example
```
case $- in
*i*) print interactive ;;
*)   print not interactive ;;
esac
interactive
```

? Return Value

The value is that returned by the last executed command, function, or program. If value is:
- Zero, indicates successful completion.
- Non-zero, indicates error or unusual condition. A command terminated by a signal has a return value of 128 plus the signal number.

Example
```
let 0
print $?
1
```

$ *Process Id of this Shell*

The process id is a unique integer guaranteed to be different in every
process active at the same time. It is normally obtained from the
operating system. This parameter expands to the process id.

Suppose you are writing a shell script that may be used by two or
more users at the same time, and that the script creates a temporary file
for its use. You can use this parameter as part of the pathname, to
cause each use of the script to generate a distinct name for the
temporary file.

The value of **$** does not change when **ksh** creates a subshell, even on
systems that create a separate process for a subshell.

Example
```
exec 3> /tmp/foo$$
print /tmp/foo$$
( print /tmp/foo$$ )
/tmp/foo1234
/tmp/foo1234
```

!   *Background Process Id*

The process id number of the last background command or co-process
invoked.

Example
```
sleep 30 &
print $!
784
```

VARIABLES SET BY ksh

If you assign values to most of these variables, you will remove their usual
meanings. For instance, if you change **PWD**, it will not change your
working directory. That is, if you then say **print $PWD**, **ksh** would not
print your working directory. However, the next time **ksh** executes **cd**, it
will set **PWD** to the pathname of your working directory.

_ *Temporary Variable*

(underscore) This variable has several functions:

- Last argument of the previous simple command run in the current environment.
- Holds name of matching **MAIL** file when checking for mail.
- Value is set to the pathname of each program that **ksh** invokes. This value is passed in the environment. *Version*: On versions of **ksh** newer than 06/03/86 version, the value of _ in a script is initialized to the pathname of the script.

Caution: If you unset _, **ksh** removes its special meaning even if you subsequently set it.

Example
```
print hello world
hello world
print $_
world
```

ERRNO *System Error Number*

ERRNO has the integer attribute. Its value is the error number of the most recently failed system call. Its primary use is in debugging. *Implementation-dependent*: The meaning of the error number values is dependent on your system and therefore its use is not portable. *Version*: The **ERRNO** variable is available only on versions of **ksh** newer than the 06/03/86 version.

ksh sets **ERRNO** only for errors that occur in the current process environment. To clear **ERRNO**, assign it a value of zero.

Caution: If you unset **ERRNO**, **ksh** removes its special meaning even if you subsequently set it.

Example
```
> /bin/date
ksh: /bin/date: cannot create
print $ERRNO
13
```

LINENO *Current Line Number*

ksh sets **LINENO** to the current line number within a script or function before it executes each command.

When you assign a value to **LINENO**, it only affects the line number for commands that **ksh** has not yet read.

Version: The **LINENO** variable is available only on versions of **ksh** newer than the 06/03/86 version.

Caution: If you unset **LINENO**, **ksh** removes its special meaning even if you subsequently set it.

Example
```
function foobar
{
    print $0 line $LINENO
}
foobar
foobar line 2
```

OLDPWD *Last Working Directory*

Previous working directory set by **cd**.

Example
```
print $PWD $OLDPWD
/usr/dgk /usr/src
cd -
/usr/src
print $OLDPWD
/usr/dgk
```

OPTARG *Option Argument*

ksh sets the value of the **OPTARG** variable when **getopts** encounters an option that requires an argument. *Version*: The **OPTARG** variable is available only on versions of **ksh** newer than the 06/03/86 version.

Caution: If you unset **OPTARG**, **ksh** removes its special meaning even if you subsequently set it.

OPTIND *Option Index*

getopts sets the value of the **OPTIND** variable to the index of the argument to search for the next option. *Version*: The **OPTIND** variable is available only on versions of **ksh** newer than the 06/03/86 version.

OPTIND is initialized to **1** whenever **ksh**, a script, or a function is invoked. You can assign a **1** to **OPTIND** to reinitialize **getopts** to process another argument list.

Caution: If you unset **OPTIND**, **ksh** removes its special meaning even if you subsequently set it.

Example
```
OPTIND=1
while getopts u:xy:z foo -y bar -zx -unew foobar
do    print OPTIND=$OPTIND OPTARG=$OPTARG foo=$foo
done
OPTIND=3 OPTARG=bar foo=y
OPTIND=3 OPTARG=bar foo=z
OPTIND=4 OPTARG=bar foo=x
OPTIND=5 OPTARG=new foo=u
```

PPID *Parent Process Id*

Process id of the process that invoked this shell. *Caution*: If you unset **PPID**, **ksh** removes its special meaning even if you subsequently set it.

Example
```
print $PPID
777
```

PWD *Working Directory*

Working directory set by **cd**.

Example
```
cd /usr/src
print $PWD
/usr/src
```

RANDOM *Random Number Generator*

RANDOM has the integer attribute. **ksh** assigns **RANDOM** a uniformly distributed random integer from **0** to **32767** each time it is referenced.

You can initialize the sequence of random numbers, by assigning a numeric value to **RANDOM**.

Caution: If you unset **RANDOM**, **ksh** removes its special meaning even if you subsequently set it.

Example
```
RANDOM=$$    # Initialize the random number generator.
print $RANDOM $RANDOM
7269 32261
```

REPLY *Reply Variable*

When you use the **select** compound command, the characters that you type are stored in this variable.

When you use the **read** built-in command, and you do not specify any arguments, the characters that are read are stored in this variable.

Example
```
read; print "$REPLY"
hello    world
hello    world
```

SECONDS *Elapsed Time and Seconds*

SECONDS has the integer attribute. Its value is the number of seconds since you invoked **ksh**. If you assign a value to **SECONDS**, then the value of **SECONDS** is the value that you assigned, plus the number of seconds since the assignment. See *Customizing Your Prompt*.

Caution: If you unset **SECONDS**, ksh removes its special meaning even if you subsequently set it.

Example
```
SECONDS=35
print $SECONDS; sleep 10; print $SECONDS
35
45
```

VARIABLES USED BY ksh

This section describes variables you can set to affect the behavior of **ksh**. Many people assign values to these variables in their profiles, so that they do not have to do it each time they log in.

System administrators often assign values to some of these variables in the **/etc/profile** file. You can use **cat** to display the contents of **/etc/profile**. However, normally only system administrators can make changes to this file.

Defaults: You can assign values to these variables. If you do not, **ksh** does one of the following:
• Assigns an explicit default value. In this case, you could print the value of the variable.
• Uses an implicit default value. In this case, you could not print the value of the variable.

- Has no default. In this case, **ksh** does neither of the above, and does not use that variable at all. For instance, if you do not assign a value to **CDPATH**, then if you specified **cd**, it would not do a search.

CDPATH *Search Path for* **cd** *Built-in*

: (colon)-separated list of directories used by the **cd** command as described below. The working directory is specified by a **.** or a Null directory name, which can appear before the first **:**, after the last **:**, or between **:** delimiters.

If the directory that you specify for **cd** does not begin with a **/**, then **ksh** searches each of the directories in the **CDPATH** in order for the specified directory, and tries to **cd** to that directory.

No Default

Example
```
CDPATH=$HOME:/usr/src
cd cmd
/usr/src/cmd
```

COLUMNS *Number of Columns on Terminal*

If you set **COLUMNS**, **ksh** uses the value to define the width of the edit window for the **ksh** edit modes, and for printing **select** lists.

Besides **ksh**, several other programs also use this variable.

Implicit Default: 80

EDITOR *Pathname for Your Editor*

If you set the value of **EDITOR** to a pathname that ends in **emacs**, **gmacs**, or **vi**, and if the **VISUAL** variable is not set, then **ksh** turns on the corresponding option.

Implicit Default: /bin/ed

ENV *User Environment File*

Each time that you invoke **ksh**, it expands this variable to generate the pathname of the shell script, if any, that will be executed when **ksh** is invoked. Typical uses are for **alias** and **function** definitions, and for setting options with **set**.

When the **privileged** option is set, **ksh** does not expand this variable, and does not execute the resulting script.

No Default

Example
```
ENV=$HOME/envfile
```

FCEDIT   *Editor for* fc *Built-in*

You assign a value to **FCEDIT** if you want to change the editor that **fc** will use, when you do not specify an editor on the **fc** command line.

Implicit Default: /bin/ed

FPATH   *Search Path for Auto-load Functions*

: (colon)-separated list of directories that **ksh** searches in order for a function definition file. The format of the **FPATH** variable is the same as the **PATH** variable. *Version*: The **FPATH** variable is available only on versions of **ksh** newer than the 06/03/86 version.

No Default

Example
```
FPATH=$HOME/fundir  # Look for function definitions here.
autoload foobar     # Specify that foobar is a function.
foobar              # Load $HOME/fundir/foobar to define
                    # function, and then execute it.
```

HISTFILE   *History Pathname*

If **HISTFILE** is set when **ksh** first accesses the history file, then **ksh** uses this value as the name of the history file. **ksh** first accesses the history file when it encounters the first function definition which does not have the **nolog** option set, or after it completes processing the environment file, whichever occurs first.

If the history file does not exist and **ksh** cannot create it, or if it does exist and **ksh** does not have permission to append to it, then **ksh** uses a temporary file as the history file.

Implicit Default: $HOME/.sh_history

Example
This example shows how to create a separate history file for each "window" on systems that have windows (sometimes termed "layers"), and that also have a program named **tty** that returns a separate pathname for each window.
```
ttyname=$(tty)
HISTFILE=$HOME/${ttyname##*/}
```

HISTSIZE *Number of History Commands*

If **HISTSIZE** is set when **ksh** first accesses the history file, then the maximum number of previously entered commands that you can access via **ksh** will be equal to this number.

Caution: Setting this number to an outrageously large value, such as 10000, may result in a slow startup for a new invocation of **ksh**.

Implicit Default: 128

HOME *Your Home Directory*

The value of the **HOME** variable is the default argument used by **cd**.

Default: The value of **HOME** is automatically set when you log in, as assigned by your system administrator.

IFS *Internal Field Separator*

ksh uses each of the characters in the value of the **IFS** variable to split into fields:
- The result from command substitution or parameter expansion of command words.
- The result from command substitution or parameter expansion of words after **in** with **for** and **select**.
- The characters that **ksh** reads with **read**.

ksh uses the first character of the value of **IFS** to separate arguments when **ksh** expands the * parameter, and when **ksh** expands ${*identifier*[*]}.

Version: On versions of **ksh** newer than 06/03/86 version, the value of **IFS** is reset to the default value after executing the environment file and before the execution of a script begins. Therefore, you cannot influence the behavior of a script by exporting **IFS**.

Default: Space-Tab-Newline characters, in that order.

Example
```
IFS=:
read name passwd  uid gid rest
root::0:0:superuser:
print "User $name has userid $uid and groupid $gid"
User root has user id 0 and group id 0
```

LINES *Number of Lines on Terminal*

If you set **LINES**, **ksh** uses the value for printing **select** lists (**select** compound command). **select** lists will display vertically until about two-thirds of **LINES** lines are filled.

Besides **ksh**, several programs also use this variable.

Implicit Default: 24

MAIL *Name of Your Mail File*

If **MAIL** is set to the name of a file that has grown, and **MAILPATH** is not set, then **ksh** informs you when there is a change in the modification time of the file whose name is the same as that of the value of **MAIL**. **ksh** does this periodically as determined by **MAILCHECK** (see below).

Default: Set by system administrator.

MAILCHECK *Frequency of Mail Check*

MAILCHECK has the integer attribute. You can set the value of **MAILCHECK** to specify how often (in seconds) **ksh** will check for changes in the modification time of any of the files specified by the value of **MAIL** (see just above) or **MAILPATH** (see just below). When the time has elapsed, **ksh** will check before issuing the next prompt.

If **MAILCHECK** is not set or is zero, then **ksh** checks the file before each prompt.

Caution: If you unset **MAILCHECK**, **ksh** removes its special meaning even if you subsequently set it.

Default: 600 seconds.

MAILPATH *List of Mail Files*

: (colon)-separated list of pathnames. You can follow each pathname with a **?** and a message for **ksh** to display. Default message is `You have mail in $_.`

Before **ksh** displays a message, **ksh** sets the variable _ (underscore) to the name of the file that changed and performs parameter expansion on the message.

No Default

Example
```
MAILPATH=~uucp/dgk:/usr/spool/mail/dgk
```

PATH *Path Search Directories*

: (colon)-separated list of directories. The working directory is specified by a **.** or a Null directory name, which can appear before the first **:**, after the last **:**, or between **:** delimiters.

Use the **PATH** variable to specify where **ksh** should search for the command that you want it to execute. Searches apply only to programs that do not contain a **/** in their names. **ksh** searches for the program in each of the directories in the **PATH** in the order specified, until it finds the program to execute.

Whenever you assign a value to the **PATH** variable, **ksh** unsets the values of all tracked aliases.

You may not change **PATH** if the **restricted** option is on.

Default: **/bin:/usr/bin:**

The path in the following example causes **ksh** first to look in your own bin directory, then in **/bin**, then in **/usr/bin**, and finally in the working directory.

Example
```
PATH=$HOME/bin:/bin:/usr/bin:
```

PS1 *Primary Prompt String*

If the **interactive** option is on, **ksh** does parameter expansion on the value of **PS1** and displays it via standard error when **ksh** is ready to read a command.

ksh replaces the character **!** in **PS1** by the command number. If you want to include an **!** in your prompt, use **!!**.

For more information and examples, such as how to customize your prompt, see **Customizing Your Prompt**.

Default: **$** (# for superuser)

PS2 *Secondary Prompt String*

ksh displays **PS2** via standard error after you have pressed RETURN and thus started a new line, without your having entered a complete command.

Default: **>**

Example
```
print Tod\
> ay is Tuesday
Today is Tuesday
```

PS3 *Select Command Prompt*

ksh displays **PS3** via standard error to prompt you to select one of the choices that you specified with the **select** compound command.

Default: #?

Example
```
PS3='Please enter a number: '
select i in foo bar1 bar2 bar3
do    command
done
1) foo
2) bar1
3) bar2
4) bar3
Please enter a number:
```

PS4 *Debug Prompt String*

ksh does parameter expansion on the value of **PS4**, and displays it via standard error when **ksh** is ready to display a command during execution trace.

Version: This feature is available only on versions of **ksh** newer than the 06/03/86 version.

Default: +

Example
```
PS4='[$LINENO]+ '
set -x
print $HOME
[3]+ print /usr/dgk
/usr/dgk
```

SHELL *Pathname of the Shell*

If the value of **SHELL** contains an **r** in the last component of the pathname when **ksh** is invoked, then **ksh** sets the **restricted** option. Several UNIX system commands use the **SHELL** variable to invoke a new shell.

Default: May be set to the pathname for **ksh** during login.

TERM *Terminal Type*

The **TERM** variable specifies what terminal you are using. It is not used by **ksh**. However, it is used in some examples in this book and several other programs use this variable.

No Default

TMOUT *Timeout Variable*

TMOUT has the integer attribute.

If you set **TMOUT** to a value greater than zero, **ksh** terminates if you do not enter a command within the prescribed number of seconds after **ksh** issues the **PS1** prompt (plus an additional 60 second grace period).

Implementation-dependent: **ksh** may have been compiled on your system with a maximum bound for this value that you cannot exceed.

Caution: If you unset **TMOUT**, **ksh** removes its special meaning even if you subsequently set it. However, the value of **TMOUT** at the time that it is unset continues to be the timeout value for terminating **ksh**.

Default: Zero, which means unlimited. Or set by system administrator.

Example
```
# In this example, it is assumed that 5 minutes have
# elapsed after the $ prompt.
TMOUT=300
$
shell timeout in 60 seconds
```

VISUAL *Visual Editor*

If you set the value of **VISUAL** to a pathname that ends in **emacs**, **gmacs**, or **vi**, then **ksh** turns on the corresponding option no matter what the value of **EDITOR**.

No Default

14   BUILT-IN COMMANDS

INTRODUCTION

Built-in Commands

Built-in commands (we refer to them as "built-ins") are processed by **ksh** itself. On most systems **ksh** causes a separate process to be created for programs but not for built-ins. Most built-ins behave the same as do programs. However, some built-ins differ in the way that I/O redirection and variable assignment lists work. These differences are defined on page 191. These special built-ins are denoted by a dagger (†) next to the formats for the command.

Reasons for having built-ins:
• You can change the current environment with them, either directly or via side effects.
• **ksh** executes them much faster than other commands doing the same thing.
• They always behave as documented in this chapter. The behavior of programs may differ on different systems.

Return Values

The normal return value is specified under each built-in. The return value is False (1) for all built-ins for which you have specified:
• An invalid option.
• An incorrect number of arguments.
• An incorrect argument (for instance, an argument that should be numeric, is not numeric).
• An invalid I/O redirection.
• An invalid variable assignment, such as an invalid identifier or a non-numeric assignment to an integer variable.
• An invalid alias name.
• An expansion for a parameter that has not been set and the **nounset** option is on.

Output

Unless otherwise specified, **ksh** writes output for a built-in on standard output, file descriptor 1. Thus you can use built-ins in pipelines.

ksh writes error messages on standard error.

Example
```
set | wc
29   43   310
```

Caution about Side Effects:
- The current implementation of **ksh** executes each element of a pipeline, except the last, in a subshell environment. Therefore, any side effects of built-ins, except in the last element of a pipeline, do not affect the current environment as built-ins normally do.
- This behavior may be changed in a future implementation of **ksh**. Therefore, we strongly recommend that you enclose the command in parentheses if you need to guarantee that the built-in will execute in a subshell environment, as illustrated in the second example, below.
- *Version*: The 06/03/86 and earlier versions of **ksh** execute the last element of a pipeline in a subshell environment.
- *Example*
```
word=murrayhill
print foobar | read word
print $word
foobar
# Above example displays murrayhill with 06/03/86 version.
```
- *Example*
```
word=murrayhill
print foobar | (read word)
print $word
murrayhill
```

Notation

Each built-in command described below uses the notation defined on page 12. Whenever a command is specified as allowing options of the form ±*letters*, you can specify each of the options separately, each preceded by a + or a −. You can specify −− to cause the next argument to be processed as an argument rather than an option. This is required whenever the first argument to a command begins with a + or a −. *Version*: The 06/03/86 and earlier versions of **ksh** did not allow separate arguments for all commands and did not recognize −− for some commands.

† A dagger designates built-ins that are treated differently as follows:
- **ksh** processes variable assignment lists specified with the command before I/O redirection. These assignments remain in effect when the command completes.
- Errors in these built-ins cause the script that contains them to terminate.

DECLARATIONS

Version: On versions of **ksh** newer than the 06/03/86 version, **ksh** expands command arguments to declaration commands that are in the format of a variable assignment specially. **ksh** performs tilde expansion after the equal sign and does not perform word splitting or pathname expansion on these arguments.
- *Example*
```
export foo=~morris
print $foo
/usr/morris
# This example displays ~morris with 06/03/86 version.
```

† **alias** [**-tx**] [*name* [=*value*] ...]

Use **alias** to define and display aliases.

Do not specify any *name* arguments if you want to display aliases. **ksh** displays the list of aliases, one per line, on standard output, in the form *name=value*. If you specify **-t** and/or **-x**, then **ksh** displays only those aliases with the corresponding attribute(s).

Use **-t** to set and list tracked aliases. The value of a tracked alias is the full pathname corresponding to the program of given *name*. It becomes undefined when the value of the **PATH** variable is reset, but the alias remains tracked.

Use **-x** to set or display exported aliases. An exported alias remains defined across scripts invoked by name that do not cause a separate invocation of **ksh**. *Note*: Exported aliases are not defined across separate invocations of **ksh**. You must put alias definitions in your environment file to have aliases defined for separate **ksh** invocations.

If *name* is specified, it must be a valid alias name, or **alias** displays an error message. In a valid alias name, the first character is a printing character other than one of the special characters listed on page 124, and the other characters are alphanumeric.

ksh defines an alias for each *name* whose *value* you specify. Previous definitions for each *name* are removed.

If you specify *name* only, then:
- Without **−t** and **−x**, **ksh** displays the name and value of the alias *name*.
- With **−x**, **ksh** sets the export attribute on the alias *name*.
- With **−t**, **ksh** sets the tracked attribute, and sets the value of the alias *name* to the pathname obtained by doing a path search.

value can contain any valid shell text. If the last character of *value* is a Space or a Tab, **ksh** also checks the word following the alias to see if it should do alias substitution. Use a trailing Space or a Tab when the next argument is supposed to be a command name.

Enclose *value* in single quotes if you want *value* expanded only when **ksh** executes a reference to the alias. Otherwise, **ksh** also expands *value* when it processes **alias**.

Example
```
x=1
alias foo='print $x' bar="print $x"
x=2
foo
2
bar
1
```

Caution: Setting the export attribute to change the meanings of commands, as in the example below, may cause scripts to run incorrectly.

Return value:
- If all *name*(s) are aliases or if you specify attributes: True.
- Otherwise: False. Value is the number of *name*(s) that are not aliases.

Examples
```
alias ls='ls -C'     # Setting export would be
                     # dangerous here.
alias nohup='nohup '
```

† **export** [*name* [*=value*]] ...

name(s) are marked for automatic export to the environment of subsequently executed commands.

export is the same as **typeset −x**, except that if you use **export** within a function, **ksh** does not create a local variable.

If you do not supply any arguments to **export**, then **ksh** displays a list of variables that have the export attribute, and their values. Each *name* starts on a separate line.

Return value: True.

Examples
```
export PWD HOME    # Exports PWD and HOME variables.
export PATH=/local/bin:$PATH
                   # Sets and exports PATH variable.
export             # Lists all exported variables.
```

✝ **readonly** [*name* [=*value*]] ...

name(s)
- You cannot change *name* by subsequent variable assignment in this **ksh** environment.
- **ksh** itself can still assign a new value to a readonly variable. For instance, if **PWD** is set to **readonly**, you cannot assign it a new value. But **ksh** will assign it a new value whenever you change your working directory (see **cd**).

readonly is the same as **typeset −r**, except that if you use **readonly** within a function, **ksh** does not create a local variable.

If you do not specify any *name*(s), **ksh** displays a list of your variables that have the readonly attribute, and their values. You cannot unset readonly variables.

Version: The 06/03/86 and earlier versions of **ksh** did not pass down the readonly attribute to separate invocations of **ksh**.

Return value: True.

Example
```
readonly HOME PWD
```

✝ **typeset ±f**[**tux**] [*name...*]

Use this form of **typeset** to display function names and values, and to set and unset function attributes.

Use the flags:
t To specify the **xtrace** option for the function(s) specified via *name*.
u To specify that *name* refers to a function that has not yet been defined. *Version*: This feature is available only on versions of **ksh** newer than the 06/03/86 version.

─────────

✝ See page 191

x To specify function definitions to remain in effect across shell
scripts that are not a separate invocation of **ksh**.

To set attributes, specify **−f** and one or more of the above flags and the
*name*s to which they apply.

To unset attributes, specify **+f** and one or more of the above flags and
the *name*s to which they apply.

Use **typeset** to display function names and definitions on standard
output. Use **−f** to display both function names and definitions. Use
+f to display function names only. Because **ksh** stores function
definitions in your history file, even if you specify a **−f, ksh** will not
display a function definition if you do not have a history file, or if the
nolog option was on when the function was read. To display:
- Specific functions, specify *name* and none of the above flags.
- All functions with a given attribute, specify a flag and no *name*.
- All functions, specify neither *name* nor flags.

Return value:
- If all *name*(s) are functions or you specify **−u**: True.
- Otherwise: False. Value is the number of *name*(s) that are not
  functions.

Examples
```
typeset -f   # Displays all functions, and their values
             # if known.
typeset -fx  # Displays all functions with x attribute,
             # and their values if known.
typeset -fu foobar
             # Specifies foobar to be an undefined
             # function.  Only with new version.
```

† **typeset** [±**HLRZilrtux** [*n*]] [*name* [=*value*]] ...

Use this command on variables to:
- Set attributes. Specify a **−** and the *name*(s).
- Unset attributes. Specify a **+** and the *name*(s).
- Set *value*(s). Specify *name*(s) and *value*(s). You can also specify
  − to set attribute(s) after setting *value*(s), and **+** to unset attribute(s)
  after setting *value*(s).
- Display on standard output, variables and/or their attributes. Do not
  specify any *name*(s), and specify:
  - To display names and values of all variables that have the
    attribute(s) that you specify.

---

† See page 191

+ To display only the names.
Nothing (neither – nor +) to display names and attributes of all
variables.

If you specify **typeset** inside a function, **ksh** creates new instances of
name(s). That is, **ksh** creates local variable(s), and restores the
value(s) and attribute(s) of these variables when the function
completes.

You can specify the following attributes:

–u   Uppercase.
–l   Lowercase.
–i   Integer. *n* specifies arithmetic base.
–L   Left-justifies. *n* specifies field width.
–LZ Left-justifies and strips leading zeros. *n* specifies field width.
–R   Right-justifies. *n* specifies field width.
–RZ Right-justifies. *n* specifies field width and fills with leading
         zeros.
–Z   Zero-filled. *n* specifies field width. Equivalent to **–RZ**.
–r   Readonly.
–x   Export.
–H   UNIX system to host operating system pathname mapping.
–t   User defined tag.

Return value: True.

Examples
```
typeset             # Displays names and attributes
                    # of all variables.
typeset -xi         # Displays names and values of all
                    # variables with both the
                    # export and integer attributes.
typeset +xi         # As above, but displays names only.
typeset a b c       # Defines variables a, b, and c
                    # without any special attributes.
                    # If executed inside a function,
                    # this creates local variables.
typeset -i8 x       # x will be an integer variable
                    # and will print in octal (base 8).
typeset -u x        # Whenever x is given a value,
                    # all lowercase characters are
                    # converted to uppercase.
typeset -r x=abc
                    # First gives x the value abc,
                    # and then makes it readonly.
typeset -L4 z       # Whenever z is given a value, it
                    # is truncated to four places and
                    # filled with trailing spaces as needed.
```

```
typeset -LZ4 z     # Same as above, except that
                   # leading zeros are stripped.
typeset -R4 z      # Whenever z is given a value,
                   # it is truncated on the left to
                   # four characters.  It is filled in
                   # with leading spaces if the value is
                   # fewer than four characters.
typeset -RZ4 z     # Same as above, except leading zeros
                   # are prepended instead of spaces.
typeset -H file    # On non-UNIX systems, this takes a UNIX
                   # system pathname and converts it to the
                   # host system name.  On UNIX systems,
                   # the -H has no affect.
```

unalias *name...*

unalias removes the *name*(s) from the alias list.

Return value :
- If all *name*(s) are aliases: True.
- Otherwise: False. Value is the number of *name*(s) that are not aliases.

Example
```
unalias ls nohup   # Remove ls and nohup
                   # alias definitions.
```

unset [**−f**] *name...*

If you do not specify **−f**, then *name* refers to a variable. In this case, for each of the *name*(s):
- **ksh** unsets value(s) and attribute(s).
- An unsubscripted array name refers to all elements of the array.
- You cannot unset readonly variables.

If you specify **−f**, then *name* refers to a function. In this case **ksh** unsets the function definition(s) and removes *name*.

Caution: If you specify **unset** with the following predefined variables, **ksh** removes their special meaning even if you subsequently set them:
_ (Temporary) **ERRNO   LINENO   MAILCHECK
OPTARG   OPTIND   RANDOM   SECONDS   TMOUT**

Return value :
- If all *name*(s) are functions or variables: True.
- Otherwise: False. Value is the number of *name*(s) that are not functions or variables.

Examples
```
unset VISUAL         # Unsets VISUAL variable.
unset -f foo bar     # Unsets functions foo and bar.
```

POSITIONAL PARAMETERS AND OPTIONS

set [±**aefhkmnopstuvx–**] [±**o** *option*]... [±**A** *name*] [*arg...*]
Note: You can repeat the [±**o** *option*] argument.

You can specify options on your **ksh** invocation line (see page 235), as well as with **set**.

Use **set** to:
- Set options. Specify – (minus) and option letter, or –**o** *option*.
- Unset options. Specify + and option letter, or +**o** *option*.
- Set positional parameters. Specify *arg*(s).
- Assign values to an array variable. Specify ±**A** *name* and *arg*(s).
- Sort positional parameters or *arg*. Specify –**s**.
- Unset positional parameters. Specify –– and do not specify *arg*.

Do not specify *arg* for the following:
- Display option setting(s) on standard output. Specify –**o** and do not specify *option*. *Note*: The – parameter contains the letter of each option that has a letter and that is set.
- Display names and values of all variables. Specify **set** by itself, with nothing else.

Option names are shown below, together with option letters in parentheses.

allexport (a)

        While **allexport** is set, **ksh** sets the export attribute for each variable to which you assign a value.

bgnice   **ksh** runs all background jobs at a lower priority.

emacs   Puts you in the **emacs** built-in editor.

errexit (e)

        If a command has False return value, **ksh** executes the **ERR** trap if set, and immediately exits. **ksh** disables **errexit** while reading profiles and environment files.

(f)   See **noglob**, below.

gmacs   Puts you in the **gmacs** built-in editor.

(h)   See **trackall**, below.

ignoreeof

        When the **interactive** option is also set, **ksh** does not exit on *End-of-file* (default CONTROL d). Type **exit** to terminate **ksh**.

keyword (k)

When **ksh** reads a command, **ksh** places each word that has the syntax of a variable assignment in the variable assignment list. Ordinarily, variable assignments must precede the command name word, and words that look like variable assignments but appear after the command name word are treated as command argument words.

Caution (*Bourne shell*): **keyword** is provided for compatibility with the Bourne shell. We recommend that you not use it. It is not essential. It may be omitted from future versions of **ksh**.

markdirs

ksh appends a trailing **/** to all directory names resulting from pathname expansion.

monitor (m)

ksh runs background jobs in a separate process group, and displays a line upon completion. **ksh** reports the return value of background jobs in a completion message. **ksh** automatically turns on **monitor** for interactive shells on systems with job control.

noclobber

ksh will not overwrite an existing file with the **>** redirection operator. You must specify **>|** to overwrite an existing file. *Version*: This option is available only on versions of **ksh** newer than the 06/03/86 version.

noexec (n)

ksh reads commands but does not execute them. You can use this option to have **ksh** check your shell script for syntax errors. **ksh** ignores **noexec** for interactive shells.

noglob(f)

ksh disables pathname expansion.

nolog

ksh does not store function definitions in the history file. *Version*: This option is available only on versions of **ksh** newer than the 06/03/86 version.

nounset (u)

ksh displays an error message when it tries to expand a variable that is unset.

privileged (p)

>*Version*: This option is available only on versions of **ksh** newer than the 06/03/86 version. Turning **privileged** off sets the effective user id to the real user id, and the effective group id to the real group id. Turning **privileged** on, restores the effective user id and effective group id to their values when **ksh** was invoked (see page 233). The **privileged** option is on whenever the effective user id is not equal to the real user id, or the effective group id is not equal to the real group id. When **privileged** is on, **ksh**:
>- Disables processing of the **$HOME/.profile** file.
>- Uses the file **/etc/suid_profile** instead of the file you specify with the **ENV** variable. The system administrator can use this file to change **PATH** or insert commands.

protected (p)

>*Version*: This option is available only on the 06/03/86 version of **ksh**. **ksh** automatically turns on **protected** whenever the effective user id is not equal to the real user id, or the effective group id is not equal to the real group id. When **protected** is on, **ksh**:
>- Disables processing of the **$HOME/.profile** file.
>- Resets **PATH** variable to its default value.
>- Uses the file **/etc/suid_profile** instead of the file you specify with the **ENV** variable. The system administrator can use this file to change **PATH** or insert commands.

(t)   **ksh** reads and executes one command, and then exits.

trackall (h)

>**ksh** causes each command whose name has the syntax of an alias name to become a tracked alias when it is first encountered. **ksh** automatically turns on **trackall** for non-interactive shells.

(u)   See **nounset**, above.

verbose (v)

>**ksh** displays its input on standard error as it is read.

vi   Puts you in **vi** built-in editor.

viraw   Specifies **vi** character-at-a-time input.

xtrace (x)

>After expanding each simple command, **ksh** expands **PS4** and displays it on standard error followed by the command and its expanded arguments. The **set +x** command that turns off this option will not be displayed. *Version*: The **PS4** variable is available only on versions of **ksh** newer than the 06/03/86 version. Earlier versions preceded each command execution trace with a +.

–s sorts positional parameters. This option has a different meaning when used on the **ksh** invocation line.

Use ±**A** *name* to assign values *arg* to array *name* starting sequentially from zero. When **–s** is also specified, *arg* is sorted before the assignment. Use **–A** to cause **ksh** to unset *name* prior to the assignment. *Version*: Array assignment with **set** is available only on versions of **ksh** newer than the 06/03/86 version.

Options are terminated by an argument not beginning with a + or –, a –, or a – –. **ksh** interprets any argument(s) that follow the – or – –, even if the argument(s) begin with a –, as an *arg*, not as an option. Thus you must use – or – – to set positional parameter **1** to a value beginning with a –. Use:

– Turns off **–x** and **–v** options. *Caution (Bourne shell)*: This is included only for compatibility with the Bourne shell. Use **+xv** to turn off the **–x** and **–v** options instead.

– – Does not change any of the options. If you do not specify any arguments following the – –, then **ksh** unsets the positional parameters.

Return value: True.

Examples

```
set              # List all variables and their values.
set +            # List all variables without the values.
set -o           # Lists all option settings.
set c a b        # Sets $1 $2 and $3.
set -s           # Sorts $1 $2 and $3.
set -o vi -o viraw
                 # Turns on vi and viraw options.
set -xv          # Turns on verbose and xtrace options.
set --           # Unsets all positional parameters.
set -- "$x"      # Sets $1 to value of x, even if x
                 # begins with -.
set -- $x        # Splits x by IFS variable, then does
                 # pathname expansion on each item.
                 # Then sets positional parameters to
                 # the items that result, even if x
                 # begins with -.
set -A foo c a b # Assigns foo[0]=c foo[1]=a foo[2]=b.
set +A foo d x   # Assigns foo[0]=d foo[1]=x, leaves
                 # foo[2] alone.
```

† **shift** [*n*]

ksh shifts positional parameter(s) to the left by *n*. **ksh** discards the first *n* positional parameter(s).

n is an arithmetic expression that must evaluate to zero, or a positive number less than or equal to the value of special parameter **#**. Default is 1.

Return value: True.

Example
```
set a b c d e
shift 2
print $*
c d e
```

CONTROL FLOW

† **.** *file* [*arg...*]   **Dot Command**

ksh reads the complete *file* (called a dot script), and then executes commands from it in the current environment. *Note*: **ksh** reads the complete dot script before executing commands in it. Thus, if you set or unset aliases or use **set –k** within a dot script, they will not affect the commands within that dot script.

ksh uses the search path specified by the **PATH** variable to find the file. If you specify *arg*s, they replace the positional parameters. Otherwise, positional parameters are unchanged.

Return value: Return value of last command.

Example
```
cat foobar
foo=hello bar=world
print $foo $bar
. foobar
hello world
```

† **break** [*n*]

break exits from the smallest enclosing **for, while, until,** or **select** loop, or from the *n*th enclosing loop if you specify *n*. Execution continues with the command immediately following the loop(s).

---

† See page 191

n is an integer equal to or greater than 1.

Return value: True.

Example
```
for i in *
do    for j in foo bar bam
      do    if    test "$j" = "$i"
            then  break 2  # Break out of both for loops.
            fi
      done
done
```

† **continue** [*n*]

continue is the opposite of **break**. Goes to top of smallest enclosing **for**, **while**, **until**, or **select** loop, or to top of *n*th enclosing loop if specified, and causes it to repeat execution.

n is an integer equal to or greater than 1.

Return value: True.

Example
```
for i in *
do    if    test -d "$i"
      then  continue   # Continue with next for value.
      fi
      print -r - "$i is not a directory"
done
```

† **eval** [*arg...*]

eval constructs a command by concatenating *arg* together, separating each with a Space. **ksh** then reads and executes this command in the current environment. Note that command words are expanded twice; once to construct *arg* and again when **ksh** executes the constructed command.

Return value: Value of the command determined by *arg*(s).

Examples
```
foo=10 x=foo
y='$'$x
print $y
$foo
eval y='$'$x
```

---

† See page 191

```
print $y
10
if      eval [ -d \${$#} ]
then    print $0: Last argument must be a directory.
        exit 1
fi
```

[†] **exec** [*command*] [*arg...*]   (See page 205)

[†] **exit** [*n*]

Causes **ksh** to exit. If this is the login shell, **ksh** logs you out. Otherwise, **ksh** returns to the program that invoked **ksh**. A trap on **EXIT** is executed before **ksh** terminates.

End-of-file also causes **ksh** to exit, unless the **ignoreeof** option is on.

Return value
- *n*, if you specify it.
- Otherwise, value of preceding command.

Examples
```
exit 0      # Exits True.
exit 1      # Exits False.
```

[†] **return** [*n*]

Causes a **ksh** function to return to the invoking shell script. **return** outside a function is equivalent to **exit**.

A trap on **EXIT** is executed in the environment of the calling program after the function returns.

Return value
- *n*, if you specify it.
- Otherwise, value of preceding command.

Example
```
function foo # filename
{
    if      test ! -d "$1"
    then    print "$PWD/$1: No such directory"
            return 1
    fi
    cd "$1"
    foo "$1"
    cd ..
}
```

[†] See page 191

† **trap** [*action*] [*condition...*]

Use **trap** to:
- Specify the action for **ksh** to take when the *condition*(s) arise. If *action* is:
  - Null, then when any specified *condition* arises, **ksh** ignores it.
  - –, or omitted, then **ksh** resets *condition*(s) to their original value(s).
  - A command, then **ksh** executes the command each time that any of the *condition*(s) arise.
- Display a list of *action*(s) and *condition*(s) for all of your trap settings. To do this, specify **trap** with no *action* and no *condition*(s).

ksh expands *action* once when it executes **trap**, and again whenever one of the *condition*(s) arise.

A *condition* is one of:
- Name or number of a signal.
  Implementation-dependent: The specific signal numbers and names differ on different systems. Use **kill –l** to list signal names and numbers on your system. For portability, we recommend that you specify names rather than numbers, because names are more likely to be the same on different systems.
- **ERR**. **ksh** executes *action* whenever a command has a non-zero return value. This trap is not inherited by functions.
- **0** or **EXIT**. If **trap** is executed inside the body of a function, *action* is executed after the function completes, in the environment that called the function. If outside the body of a function, *action* is executed upon exit from **ksh**.
- **DEBUG**. **ksh** executes *action* after each simple command. This trap is not inherited by functions.

If more than one condition arises at about the same time, **ksh** executes:
- First, **DEBUG**, if specified.
- Second, **ERR** , if applicable.
- Then, any other applicable trap command(s) in order of signal number.
- Last, **EXIT**.

When **ksh** is invoked, it ignores traps that were ignored by its parent process. Even if you specify an action for a signal that the parent ignored, the signal will never reach **ksh**.

---

† See page 191

Version: The **DEBUG** trap is available only on versions of **ksh** newer than the 06/03/86 version.

Return value: True.

Examples
```
trap      # Displays all traps and actions.
trap '$HOME/.logout' EXIT
          # Sets a trap so that logout in your HOME
          # directory will execute when shell terminates.
trap '$HOME/.logout' 0
          # Same.
trap - INT QUIT TERM EXIT
          # Unsets traps on INT QUIT TERM EXIT.
```

INPUT/OUTPUT

echo [*arg...*]

Echos each *arg* on standard output, separating each by a Space.

Implementation-dependent: The behavior of **echo** depends on your system:
- On UNIX System V compatible systems, **echo** is equivalent to **print –**.
- On other systems that have a command named **/bin/echo**, and for which **/bin/echo –n** means not to print a trailing Newline, **echo** depends on the **PATH** variable. If a path search for **echo** would yield **/bin/echo**, **echo** is equivalent to **print –R**. Otherwise, **echo** is equivalent to **print –**.
- On all other systems, **echo** is equivalent to **print –**.

Return value: True.

Example
```
echo - foobar
- foobar
```

† **exec** [*command*] [*arg...*]

Use **exec** to:
- Replace **ksh** with *command*, without creating a new process. You must specify *command* . If you specify *arg*(s), they are arguments to *command*. I/O redirection affects the current process environment.

---

† See page 191

- Open, close, and/or copy file descriptors as specified by I/O redirection. Do not specify *command* or *arg*. **ksh** sets to close-on-exec file descriptor numbers greater than **2** that are opened in this way, so that they will be closed when **ksh** invokes another program.

Return value:
- If you specify *command*, **exec** does not return to **ksh**.
- Otherwise, True.

Examples

```
exec 3< readfile   # Opens readfile as file descriptor 3
                   # for reading.
exec 4> writefile  # Opens writefile as unit 4 for
                   # writing.
exec 5<&0          # Makes unit 5 a copy of unit 0.
exec 3<&-          # Closes file unit 3.
exec prog          # Overlays ksh with prog.
```

print [−**Rnprsu** [*n*]] [*arg...*]

Use **print** to display output on standard output, or wherever you specify. **print** displays each *arg*, separating each by a Space, and normally adding a Newline after all the *arg*(s).

Unless you specify **−r** or **−R** , **print** formats using the following escape conventions:

\a	Bell character. *Version*: This feature is available only on versions of **ksh** newer than the 06/03/86 version.
\b	Backspace.
\c	Print line without adding Newline. The remaining *arg*s are ignored.
\f	Formfeed.
\n	Newline.
\r	Return.
\t	Tab.
\v	Vertical Tab.
\\	Backslash.
\0*x*	The 8-bit character whose ASCII code is the 1-, 2-, or 3-digit octal number *x*.

Caution: \ is a quote character. **ksh** removes it when it expands the command, unless the \ is quoted.

You can specify the following with **print**:

–   **ksh** processes anything following the – as an *arg*, even if it begins with a –.

–R **ksh** does not use the \ conventions listed above. **ksh** processes anything following the **–R**, other than **–n**, as an *arg*, even if it begins with a –.

–n **ksh** does not add a trailing Newline to the output.

–p **ksh** redirects *arg*(s) onto the co-process.

–r **ksh** does not use the \ conventions listed above.

–s **ksh** redirects *arg*(s) to the history file.

–u **ksh** redirects *arg*(s) to file descriptor *n*, or to default 1. *n* must be 1, 2, or a file descriptor that you opened with **exec**. The **–u** option has the same effect as redirecting the standard output of **print** but does not cause the file to be opened and closed, or the file descriptor to be duplicated, each time.

Return value: True.

Examples
```
print -r 'hi\\\\there'
hi\\\\there
print 'hi\\\\there'
hi\\there
print -r hi\\\\there
hi\\there
print hi\\\\there
hi\there
```

read [**–prsu** [*n*]] [*name*?*prompt*] [*name*...]

Use **read** to read a line and split it into fields, using the characters in the **IFS** variable as separators. Ordinarily, a trailing \ at the end of a line causes the line to be continued onto the next line; **ksh** removes both the \ and the Newline.

Each *name* must be a valid identifier. The first field is assigned to the first *name*, the second field to the second *name*, etc., with leftover fields assigned to the last *name*. The default *name* is **REPLY**.

If you specify *name*?*prompt*, then, when **ksh** is interactive, it displays *prompt* on standard error.

You can also specify:

–p **ksh** reads the input line from the co-process. An *End-of-file* causes **ksh** to disconnect the co-process so that you can create another co-process.

–r A \ at the end of a line does not signify line continuation.

−s   **ksh** saves a copy of the input line as a command in the history file.

−u   **ksh** reads from file descriptor *n*; default is 0. Before you specify **read** with a file descriptor other than 0 or 2, you must open a file on the descriptor with **exec**.

Return value: True, unless an *End-of-file* is encountered.

Example
```
while read -r
do    print -r "$REPLY"
done <<!
My Home directory is $HOME.
!
My Home directory is /usr/dgk
```

OPERATING SYSTEM — ENVIRONMENT

cd [*directory*]

Use **cd** to change the working directory.

If *directory* is:
- − (minus). **ksh** changes the working directory to the previous directory, and displays the new working directory name.
- */string*. **ksh** changes the working directory to */string*. The **CDPATH** variable is not used.
- Specified, but it does not begin with a **/**.
  - If **CDPATH** is set, and *directory* does not begin with a **./**, or **../**, **ksh** prepends, in turn, each directory in the **CDPATH** variable to *directory* to construct a directory name. **ksh** changes the working directory to the first constructed name, if any, that corresponds to a directory that you have permission to change to. **ksh** displays the directory name.
  - If **CDPATH** is not set, **ksh** changes the working directory to *directory*.
- Not specified. **ksh** changes the working directory to the value of the **HOME** variable.
- Non-existent, or you don't have appropriate permission. **ksh** displays an error message.

Caution: **ksh** interprets the filename **..** as meaning move up one level towards **/**, even if the operating system doesn't. Thus, **cd ./foo** followed by **cd ..** changes the working directory to **foo** and then restores the working directory.

ksh sets the **PWD** variable to the working directory, and the **OLDPWD** variable to the previous working directory.

cd cannot be executed while the **restricted** option is set.

Return value:
- If the change of working directory was successful, True.
- Otherwise, False (1).

Example
pwd
```
/usr/src/cmd
```
cd;pwd
```
/usr/dgk
```
cd -
```
/usr/src/cmd
```

cd *oldstring newstring*

ksh substitutes *newstring* for *oldstring* in the working directory name, **PWD**, and tries to change to this new directory. **ksh** displays the new working directory name.

Return value:
- If the change of working directory was successful, True.
- Otherwise, False (1).

Example
cd /usr/foo/src/cmd
cd foo bar
```
/usr/bar/src/cmd
```

pwd

Use **pwd** to display the working directory. **pwd** is equivalent to **print –r – $PWD** if you have not changed **PWD**.

Return value: True.

Example
cd /usr/src/cmd
pwd
```
/usr/src/cmd
```

† **times**

Use **times** to display how much time your current **ksh** has consumed, and the time consumed by child processes invoked by **ksh**.

---

† See page 191

ksh displays two lines on standard output, showing accumulated user time and system time in hundredths of a second for:
- 1st line, **ksh**.
- 2nd line, child processes invoked from **ksh**.

Implementation-dependent: Both the division between user time and system time, and the accuracy of the time, may vary on different systems.

Return value: True.

Example
```
times
0m1.26s  0m2.98s
2m7.91s  0m27.46s
```

ulimit [−acdfmpst] [*n*]

Use **ulimit** to set or display system resource limits. These limits apply to the current process and to each child process created after the resource limit has been specified. If you:
- Specify *n*. **ksh** sets the specified resource limit to *n*. *n* can be any arithmetic expression or **unlimited**.
- Do not specify *n*. **ksh** displays the specified resource limit.

Different systems allow you to specify different resource limits. Some systems restrict how much you can raise the limit of a resource. Other systems do not allow you to raise limits for some or all of these resources at all. If your system has the capability, you can specify the following for **ksh** to set or display (−a displays only):

−a   All current resource limits.
−c   Size limit of *n* blocks on the size of core dumps. Each block is 512 bytes.
−d   Size limit of *n* kilobytes on the size of the data area.
−f   Size limit of *n* blocks on files written by child processes (files of any size may be read). Each block is 512 bytes.
−m   Limit of *n* kilobytes on the size of physical memory that this process or any of its children can use.
−s   Size limit of *n* kilobytes on the size of the stack area.
−t   Time limit of *n* seconds to be used by each process.

If you do not specify a resource, the default is the file size limit, **−f**.

Return value: True.

Example
```
ulimit -f 1000
ulimit -f
1000
```

umask [*mask*]

Use **umask** to set or display the file creation mask. If you:
- Specify *mask*, **ksh** sets the file creation mask to *mask*.
- Do not specify *mask*, **ksh** displays the file creation mask on standard output.

mask is a 3 digit octal number called the file creation mask. It specifies what permissions the system should remove whenever **ksh** or any of its child processes create a file. See page 17 for an explanation of file permissions.

Return value: True.

Example
```
umask 002  # Removes write permission for others.
umask
002
```

OPERATING SYSTEM — JOB CONTROL

Note: When a command in this section takes an argument called *job*, *job* can be a process id. When the **interactive** option is on, *job* can also be specified as one of the following:

%number	To refer to the job by *number*.
%string	The job whose name begins with *string*.
%?string	The job whose name contains *string*. **Version**: This is available only on versions of **ksh** newer than the 06/03/86 version.
%+ or *%%*	Current job.
%−	Previous job.

bg [*job...*]
fg [*job...*]

Implementation-dependent: **bg** and **fg** are built-ins only on systems that support job control.

Use **bg** to resume stopped jobs and run them in the background. Use **bg** without arguments to refer to the current job (the job that you most recently stopped). Use **bg** *job*s to refer to specific jobs.

Use **fg** to move background jobs into the foreground one at a time. Use **fg** without arguments to refer to the current job (the job that you most recently stopped or started). Use **fg** *job*s to refer to specific jobs.

Return value: If **monitor** option is:
- On, True.
- Off, False (1).

Examples
```
alias %=_fg
function _fg
{
      fg %${1-%}
}
bg
bg %2
fg
% 10
bg %cc
```

jobs [−lp] [*job...*]

Use **jobs** to display information about specified *job*s (or all active jobs when job is omitted) that the current **ksh** invoked. **ksh** displays:
- Job number, in [ ], with + in front of current job number, and − in front of previous job number.
- Status. **Running**, **Stopped**, **Done**, **Terminated**, etc.
- A number in ( ) after **Done** is the return value of that job. If there is no ( ) after **Done**, the return value is True.
- Command line. **ksh** obtains the command line from the history file. If **ksh** cannot access the history file, then it does not display the command line.

If you specify −l, **ksh** displays process id's after the job number, in addition to the usual information.

If you specify −p, **ksh** displays only the process id's.

Return value: True.

Example
```
jobs -l
+[4] 139  Running        cc -c foo.c&
-[3] 465  Stopped        mail morris
 [2] 687  Done(1)        foo.bar&
jobs -p %m
465
```

kill [−*signal*] *job...*

Use **kill** to send a signal to the specified *job*s. This normally terminates processes that do not catch or ignore the signal.

signal
- Specify either number(s) or name(s). See **kill −l** (just below), to display the list of possible signal names and numbers.
- If you do not specify *signal*, then **ksh** sends the **TERM** signal.

If the signal being sent is **TERM** (terminate) or **HUP** (hangup), then **ksh** first sends *job* a **CONT** (continue) signal if *job* is stopped.

Return value: Number of processes that **kill** was not able to send signal to.

Example
```
kill -HUP %cc
```

kill −l

Use **kill −l** to display signal numbers and names.

Implementation-dependent: The signal numbers vary on different systems.

Return value: True.

Example
```
kill -l        # Lists signals.
```

† **wait** [*job*...]

Use **wait** to have **ksh** wait for the specified *job*s to terminate.

ksh waits for the given process if you specify *job* as a number. Otherwise, **ksh** waits for all its child processes of the specified *job* to terminate. *Version*: *job* had to be a number with the 06/03/86 and earlier versions of **ksh**.

ksh waits for all currently active child processes to complete if you omit *job*.

Return value: Termination status of last process waited for.

Examples
```
wait       # Waits for all background commands
           # to complete.
wait %2    # Waits for job 2 to complete.  New
           # version only.
wait 346   # Waits for process 346 to complete.
wait $!    # Waits for last background process
           # to complete.
```

---

† See page 191

MISCELLANEOUS

† : [*arg...*]   ***Null Command***

Use **:** where you must have a command, as in the **then** condition of an **if** command, but you do not want the command to do anything.

The arguments to **:** are expanded. *Caution:* Parameter expansions can have side effects in the current environment.

Caution (Bourne shell): Some early versions of the Bourne shell did not have the comment syntax (**#**). Users therefore used this command to include a comment. However, unlike the real comment syntax, **ksh** splits the arguments of the **:** command into tokens, and expands them. Thus you should use the comment syntax for comments.

Return value: True.

Examples
```
:  ${X=abc}
if    false
then  :
else  print $X
fi
abc
```

fc [**−e** *editor*] [**−nlr**] [*first* [*last*]]

fc (fix command) provides access to your history file. Use **fc** to:
- Display commands from your history file; specify **−l**. An alternative is to use the preset alias **history** instead of **fc −l**.
- Edit and reexecute previous commands. Do not specify **−l**. **ksh** creates a file containing the commands that you specify, and invokes an editor on this file. **ksh** uses the editor (as specified by the following sources, in the order listed):
  - *editor*
  - **FCEDIT** variable
  - **/bin/ed**

When you finish editing the commands, **ksh** reads, displays, and executes them.

---

† See page 191

first and *last* define the range of commands to which **fc** applies. **ksh** limits the number of previous commands that you can specify, to the value of the **HISTSIZE** variable. You can specify *first* and/or *last* as:

- Positive number, denotes command numbers.
- Negative number, is subtracted from current command number.
- String, denotes most recent command starting with specified string.
- *last* not specified. **ksh** defaults it to *first*.
- *first* and *last* not specified. **ksh** defaults as follows:
  first   **−16** if you specified **−l**. Otherwise, to **−1**.
  last   **−1** (the previous command).

You can also specify:

−n   Suppresses command numbers when the commands are displayed.
−r   Reverses order of the commands.

Return value:
- Invalid arguments, False (1).
- Otherwise, if **−l** argument is specified, True. If not specified, value of last command is reexecuted.

Examples
```
fc     # Invokes editor defined by FCEDIT variable
       # (default /bin/ed) on the most recent command.
       # The command is executed when you finish editing.
fc -l  # Lists the last 16 commands.
```

fc −e − [*old=new*] [*command*]

Use this command to reexecute a previously entered command. **ksh** displays the command before reexecuting it.

Instead of this command, you can use the preset alias **r**, with or without *old=new* and *command*.

If you specify *old=new*, **ksh** replaces the string *old* with the string *new* before reexecuting it.

command specifies the command to be reexecuted. **ksh** limits the number of previous commands that you can specify, to the value of the **HISTSIZE** variable. You can specify *command* as:

- Positive number. Denotes command numbers.
- Negative number. Is subtracted from current command number.
- String. Denotes most recent command starting with specified string.
- Nothing. **ksh** defaults to the previous command.

Return value: Value of the reexecuted command.

Examples
```
fc -e ${VISUAL-vi}
          # Same as above, except uses the editor defined
          # by VISUAL variable, or defaults to vi.
r         # Displays and reexecutes most recent command.
r cc      # Displays and reexecutes the most recent
          # command starting with cc.
r foo=bar cc
          # Finds the most recent command that starts with
          # cc, changes foo to bar, and displays and
          # executes the command.
```

getopts *optstring name* [*arg...*]

> **getopts** checks the argument list *arg* for legal options. If *arg* is omitted, **getopts** uses the positional parameters instead.
>
> An option-argument begins with a + or a –. An *arg* not beginning with a + or a – delimits the end of options, as does the argument ––.
>
> *optstring* contains the option letters that **getopts** recognizes. If a letter is followed by a :, that option is expected to have an argument. The option can be separated from the argument by Spaces and/or Tabs.
>
> Each time you invoke **getopts**, it places the next option letter it finds in the variable *name*. A + is prepended to *name* if the option is found in an *arg* beginning with +. **ksh** stores the index of the next *arg* to be processed in the **OPTIND** variable. Whenever **ksh** or a script is invoked, **OPTIND** is initialized to 1. When an option requires an option-argument, **getopts** places it in the **OPTARG** variable.
>
> A leading : in *optstring* affects the behavior of **getopts** when **getopts** encounters an option letter not in *optstring*. If *optstring* begins with :, **getopts** puts the letter in **OPTARG** and sets *name* to **?** for an unknown option, and sets *name* to **:** when a required option argument is omitted. Otherwise, **getopts** displays an error message and sets *name* to **?**.
>
> *Version*: **getopts** is available only on versions of **ksh** newer than the 06/03/86 version.
>
> *Return value*: True until **getopts** encounters the end of options.
>
> *Example*
> ```
> while getopts :abo: c
> do   case $c in
>      a)   aflag=1;;
>      +a)  aflag=;;
>      b)   bflag=1;;
>      +b)  bflag=;;
> ```

```
     o)   oflag=$OPTARG;;
     :)   print -u2 "$0: $OPTARG requires a value:
          exit 2;;
    \?)   print -u2 "$0: unknown option $OPTARG"
          print -u2 "USAGE: $0 [ -a -b -o value] file ..."
          exit 2;;
       esac
done
shift OPTIND-1
```

let *arg...*

Use **let** to evaluate one or more arithmetic expressions.

ksh evaluates each *arg* as a separate arithmetic expression. Therefore, if you specify Spaces or Tabs within an arithmetic expression, you must quote them. Since many of the operators have special meaning to **ksh**, you must quote them.

You can use the command ((*expression*)) instead of **let** if you want to evaluate only a single expression. When you use ((*expression*)) you do not have to quote the Spaces, Tabs, or any other special characters in *expression*. **ksh** processes them as if they were in grouping (double) quotes.

Return value:
• If value of last expression is non-zero, True.
• Otherwise, False (1).

Examples
```
let x=x+1 y=x%4+2
# The following script displays the first n lines
# of the standard input, where you can specify n
# as an optional argument whose default is 20.
typeset -i n=${1-20}                      # Set n.
while (((n=n-1)>=0)) && read -r line # At most n lines.
do    print -r - "$line"
done
```

† newgrp [*group*] [*arg...*]

newgrp is equivalent to **exec /bin/newgrp** *arg...*

Implementation-dependent: **newgrp** is only on systems that have a command **/bin/newgrp**. The command **/bin/newgrp** changes the group id of the process to the *group* that you specify.

---

† See page 191.

Return value: This command does not return.

Example
```
newgrp system        # Changes your group to system.
```

test [*expression*]

[[*expression*] **]**   *Left Bracket Command*
Note: You must type the brackets shown in boldface.

> Use **test** or [...] to check the type of a file, whether two pathnames are the same file, or permissions on files. Also use **test** or [...] to compare two files to see which is older or newer, to compare two strings, or to compare two arithmetic expressions.

> *Cautions*:
> - *expression* indicates all the arguments that together make up the *expression*. Each of the operators is a separate argument to **test** and [...].
> - **ksh** expands all of the words in the command before evaluating *expression*. Therefore you should use grouping quotes around words that are expanded. This will avoid errors due to words that expand to Null, due to words with embedded Spaces or Tabs, and due to words with embedded pathname expansion characters.

> Use any of the conditional expression primitives defined on page 131 to form *expression*. In addition, specify the following operators to combine these primitives within an *expression*:
>
> **!**   Unary **negation** operator.
> **–a** Binary **and** operator.
> **–o** Binary **or** operator (**–a** has higher precedence than **–o**).
> (*expression*)
>   Parentheses for grouping. *Note*: Parentheses are **ksh** tokens. Therefore, you must quote them to use them as arguments to **test** or [...].

> *Version*: Versions of **ksh** newer than the 06/03/86 version have the [[...]] compound command which makes **test** and [obsolescent.

> *Return value*:
> **test** evaluates *expression*. If the value is:
> - True, returns True.
> - Otherwise, returns False (1). **test** also returns False if you do not specify *expression*.

Examples
```
test -r "$x"     # Tests if value of x names a file
                 # that you can read.
```

```
if    [ -x "$file" -a ! -d "$file" ]
then  print "$file is an executable program"
fi
test x+1 -gt y  # True if x+1 is greater than y.
test X"$y" = X  # True if value of y is not set or is
                # Null.  The reason for the X is that
                # the value of y might start with a -.
```

whence [−v] *name...*

Use **whence** without −v to find the absolute pathname, if any, corresponding to each *name*. You can also use **whence** to find out what type of item each *name* is; specify −v (or use the preset alias **type**, which is defined as **whence −v**). For each *name* you specify, **ksh** displays a line that indicates if the *name* is:
- Reserved word.
- Alias.
- Exported alias.
- Built-in.
- Undefined function.
- Function.
- Tracked alias.
- Program.
- Not found.

Return value: True if all *name*s are found, otherwise False .

Examples
```
whence vi      # Displays full pathname of vi.
/usr/bin/vi
whence -v vi
vi is a tracked alias for /usr/bin/vi
whence echo
echo
whence -v echo
echo is a shell built-in
type for
for is a reserved word
```

EXERCISES

1. What do each of the following built-in commands do?
   a. **print -r - $PWD**   b. **print "foo\tbar\c"**
   c. **kill -l**   d. **kill -HUP %cc**
   e. **eval print \$$foo**   f. **. foobar**
   g. **exec 3< foobar**   h. **read -r -u3 foobar**
   i. **set -- "${a[@]}"**   j. **set -s**

k. `export   foo`
l. `typeset   -Lu3   x=foobar`
m. `alias   foo`
n. `unalias   foo`
o. `let   x=x+1`
p. `whence   let`
q. `test   -r   foobar`
r. `[   X"$foo"   =   X"$bar"   ]`
s. `cd   -`
t. `cd   foo   bar`
u. `umask`
v. `umask   022`
w. `shift   3`
x. `set   -x`
y. `:   ${foo?bar}`
z. `jobs   -l`

2. Write a built-in command to do each of the following:
   a. Display the current traps.
   b. Declare an integer variable.
   c. Declare a local variable in a function.
   d. Open a file to read on file descriptor 4.
   e. Read a line on file descriptor 4 and split it into three fields using **:** as a field separator.
   f. Cause a message to be displayed on standard error when a program is interrupted.
   g. Tell whether a pathname is a directory that you can write.
   h. Display all aliases.
   i. Unset all variables with the tagged attribute.
   j. Display the absolute pathname of the **date** command.
   k. Wait for the last background command to complete.
   l. Display the last positional parameter.
   m. Close file descriptor 4.
   n. Turn on execution tracing for a function named **foobar**.

3. Write an alias that repeats a range of commands stored in your history file. Hint: Use an "editor" that does nothing.

---

15   OTHER COMMANDS

The programs in this chapter are referred to elsewhere in this book, in the text, and/or in the examples. They exist on all UNIX systems and on many non-UNIX systems. If your system does not have any of them and you want to use them, you can write some of them in **ksh** language, and all of them in the C language.

Note: The descriptions here are not necessarily complete. They do, however, describe the features that are used by the examples in this book.

COMMANDS

cat [*file...*]

Concatenates one or more *file*(s) and writes their contents on standard output.

If you do not specify *file*, or if the argument − is encountered, **cat** reads from standard input.

Caution: Since **ksh** performs I/O redirection before **cat** is invoked, the command **cat** *file1 file2* > *file1* in the example below would not work as expected.

Example
```
cat file1            # Displays contents of file1.
cat file1 file2 > file3
                     # Concatenates file1 and file2,
                     # and places result in file3.
```

chmod *mode file...*

Changes file permissions according to *mode*. Only the owner of a file, or the superuser, may change its permissions.

Specify *mode* in the one of the following two formats:
- An octal number constructed from the bitwise or of the following modes:

4000	Set effective user id on execution.
2000	Set effective group id on execution. The group of the file must correspond to your current group id, in order for you to set the group id.
0400	Read by owner.
0200	Write by owner.
0100	Execute (search in directory) by owner.
0070	Read, write, execute (search) by group.
0007	Read, write, execute (search) by others.

- One or more of [*who*] *op* [*permission*] separated by a comma, where:

who is a combination of the letters:

u	User's permissions.
g	Group permissions.
o	Other permissions.
a	Default if you do not specify *who*. Specifies user's, group, and other permissions.

op is one of the following:

+	Add *permission* to each *file*.
−	Delete *permission* from each *file*.
=	Assign *permission* to each *file*.

permission can be any or all of:

r	Read.
w	Write.
x	Execute.
s	Set owner id and/or group id when used with **u** and/or **g**.

Note: Omitting *permission* is useful only with =, to take away all permissions.

Examples

```
chmod o-w file1   # Denies write permission to others.
chmod +x file1    # Makes a file executable.
chmod 755 file1   # Sets permission on file1 to 755.
```

cp *file... target*

Copies *file*(s) to *target*. *file* and *target* cannot refer to the same file.

If *target* is:
- Directory. *file*(s) are copied to that directory.
- File. Copying a file into *target* does not change the mode, owner, or group of the file. All links remain and the file is changed.

- Nonexistent. A new file is created with the same mode as *file*. The owner and group of *target* are those of the effective user and group.

Example

```
cp *.c newdir    # Copies filenames in the current
                 # directory ending in .c to
                 # directory newdir.
```

date [+*format*]

Displays date and time on standard output.

You can specify a *format* string preceded by a +, to display the date.
- All output fields are of fixed size, zero-padded if needed.
- Each field descriptor is preceded by %, and is replaced in the output by its corresponding value. A single % is encoded by %%. All other characters are copied to the output without change.
- Some field descriptors:
  - H   Hour 00 to 23
  - M   Minute 00 to 59
  - S   Second 00 to 59

Examples

```
date
Tue May 10 10:34:08 1987
date +%H:%M:%S
10:34:09
```

ed [−]   [*name*]

ed is a line-oriented text editor for creating files consisting of any kind of alphanumeric text, adding or deleting text, locating a word or string of characters, moving lines of text around within a document or program, duplicating lines of text, and substituting words or strings of characters for other words or strings of characters.

ed operates on a copy of the file it is editing. Changes made to the copy have no effect on the file until a **w** (write) directive is given. The copy of the text being edited resides in a temporary file called the buffer. There is only one buffer.

name is the name of the file you wish to edit. If you do not specify *name*, **ed** will ask you to specify a pathname when you write the file.

Use − when the standard input is an editor script, to suppress the display of explanatory output.

Example
```
ed - foobar <<\!  # Prepends >> to each line of foobar.
1,$s/^/>> /
w
q
!
```

find *directory... expression*

Generates a list of all pathnames that are in each of the given *directory*(s), and applies *expression* to each of them.

expression indicates all of the arguments that together make up the expression. Each of the operators are separate arguments to **find**.

Some primitive *expression*(s):

–name *pattern*
> True if the last component of pathname matches the given *pattern.*

–perm *mode*
> True if the permission of the file matches *mode.*

–print   Displays the pathname. Always True.

–type *t*   True if the type of the file is *t*, where *t* is **d** for directory, or **f** for file.

–exec *command* [*arg*] ... ;
> True if the executed command has a return value of zero. Replaces *arg* {} with the current pathname.

–size [±] *n*
> True if file is size *n.*

–mtime [±] *n*
> True if file was modified in the last *n* days.

A + in front of a number means greater than. A – in front of a number means less than.

The following operators combine *expressions*:

!   Unary **negation** operator.

–a   Binary **and** operator.

–o   Binary **or** operator (**–a** has higher precedence than **–o**).

(*expression*)
> Parentheses for grouping.

Quote *pattern*, ;, (, and) to prevent **ksh** from interpreting them.

Example
```
find / -type d -print  # Displays all directory names
                       # in the file system.
```

grep [*option...*] *pattern* [*file...*]

Searches the input *file*(s) (default is standard input), for lines matching *pattern*. Normally, each line found is copied to standard output. **grep** patterns are limited regular expressions (regular expressions are beyond the scope of this book).

*option*s:
- **−c** Prints a count of matching lines.
- **−e** *pattern*
  Same as a simple *pattern*, but useful when the *pattern* begins with a −. Not available on all versions of **grep**.
- **−f** *file*
  The *pattern* is taken from *file*.   Not available on all versions of **grep**.
- **−i** Ignores upper/lowercase distinction during comparisons.
- **−l** Displays (once) only the names of files with matching lines, separated by Newlines.
- **−n** Precedes each line by its relative line number in the file.
- **−s** Suppresses error messages produced for nonexistent or unreadable files.
- **−v** Displays all lines but those matching.
- **−x** Displays only lines matched in their entirety. Not available on all versions of **grep**.

In all cases, the pathname is displayed if there is more than one input file. *Caution*: Take care when using characters that may also be meaningful to **ksh**. It is safest to enclose the entire *pattern* in literal (single) quotes.

Return value:
- True If any matches found.
- 1 If no matches found.
- 2 For syntax errors or inaccessible files (even if matches found).

Example
```
grep bar foobar
A foobar is defined as
law without the bar exam, therefore
```

ln *file... target*

Links *file*(s) to *target*. *file* and *target* cannot refer to the same file.

If *target* is a:
- Directory. For each *file* specified, a link, the name of which is the last component of *file*, is placed inside this directory .

- File. The file *target* must not exist and *file* must be a single argument.

  Example
  ```
  ln $olddir/foobar $newdir
          # Creates filename foobar in $newdir that refers
          # to the same file as foobar in $olddir.
  ```

lp [*file...*]
lpr [*file...*]

Prints named *file*(s), or standard input if no file is specified, on a printer queue.

On some systems, this command is named **lp**. On other systems it is named **lpr**.

Example
```
lpr file1   # Prints file named file1.
```

ls [*–altCF*] [*directory...*]

Displays the filenames in one or more *directories*, one filename per line. **ls** displays the contents of the current directory if you do not specify *directory*.

The meaning of the options is as follows:
- **–a**   Also displays filenames beginning with a **.** (dot).
- **–l**   Displays a longer listing that also shows its permission string, number of links, owner, group, size of the file, and the time that it was last modified.
- **–t**   Causes the filenames to be sorted in order of the time that they were last modified, most recent first.
- **–C**   Displays the filenames more than one to a line, using Tabs to separate the names. Some systems do this by default when displaying them to a terminal.
- **–F**   Displays directory names with a trailing **/**, and executable files with a trailing ∗.

Example
```
ls -l bin     # Displays a long listing for
              # files in bin.
```

mail [*–b*] [*user...*]

Sends or displays mail messages to and from users on your system or on other systems.

If you specify **–b**, the messages are displayed in a first-in, first-out order. ***Implementation-dependent***: Some systems use **–r** instead of **–b**.

Specify one or more *user*(s) if you want to send a message. The message will consist of all the characters on standard input until the end of file.

Example
```
mail morris <<!
We should get the book finished and to publisher ASAP.
!
```

mkdir *directory*...

Creates specified *directory*(s) with permission 777, less those permissions specified in the file creation mask.

mkdir requires write permission in the parent directory.

Return value:
• True, if all directories were successfully created.
• Otherwise, non-zero, and displays a diagnostic.

Example
```
mkdir foobar  # Creates subdirectory foobar.
```

more [*file*...]

See **pg** on the next page.

mv [**–f**] *file*... *target*

Moves or renames *file*(s) to *target*. *file* and *target* cannot refer to the same file.

file may be a directory. On some systems the directories may be renamed only if the two directories have the same parent, and *file* is renamed *target*.

If *target* is a directory, one or more *file*s are moved to that directory.

If *target* is a file, and if **mv** determines that the mode of *target* forbids writing, it:
• Prints file permissions. See **chmod**.
• Asks for a response.

- Reads standard input for one line. If the line begins with **y**, **mv** occurs if permissible. Otherwise, the command exits with a False return value. **mv** requires write permission in the directory to remove the old file. It does not require write permission to the file.
- Asks questions if standard input is a terminal and the **−f** option is not specified.

Example

```
mv /tmp/foo$$ savefile   # Moves /tmp/foo$$ to filename
                         # savefile in current directory.
```

pg [*file...*]

Displays one or more files, a screenful at a time. If you do not specify *file*, **pg** displays its standard input. It normally pauses after each screenful, printing at the bottom of the screen. If you then press:

SPACE	Another screenful is displayed.
q	**pg** exits.
h	Displays help information.

Some systems use a command named **more** instead.

Example

```
ls -l | pg    # Displays ls -l output a screenful
              # at a time.
```

rm [**−f**] [**−r**] [**−i**] *file...*

Removes filename entries for *file*(s) from a directory. If an entry is the last link to the file, the file is destroyed. Removal of a filename requires write permission in its directory, but neither read nor write permission on the file itself.

If a file has no write permission and the standard input is a terminal, its permissions are displayed and a line is read from standard input. If that line begins with **y**, the file is deleted. Otherwise, the file remains.

Asks questions if standard input is a terminal and the **−f** option is not specified.

file cannot refer to a directory unless you specify **−r**. **rm** recursively deletes the entire contents of the specified directory, and the directory itself.

If you specify **−i**, files are removed interactively. **rm** asks whether to delete each file and, under **−r**, whether to examine each directory.

It is forbidden to remove the filename **..** (two dots) to avoid the consequences of inadvertently doing something like **rm −r .*** .

Example
```
rm *.o   # Removes all files from current directory
         # whose names end with .o.
```

rmdir *directory...*

Removes one or more *directory*(s), which must be empty.

sleep *time*

Suspends execution for *time* seconds.

Example
```
sleep 3600;date      # Runs date in an hour.
```

sort [*option...*] [*file...*]

Sorts lines in one or more file(s). If you do not specify *file*, **sort** uses its standard input.

*option*s:

+n   Skips the first *n* fields.

−b   Ignores leading blanks.

−f   Folds upper and lowercase letters.

−n   Sorts by numeric value.

−o *ofile*
  Puts output in *ofile*.

−t*c*   Uses *c* as the field separator character. Otherwise, fields are separated by Spaces and Tabs.

Example
```
who | sort   # Sorts the output of the who command.
```

stty [**erase** *erase*] [**kill** *kill*] [**eof** *eof*] [**int** *int*] [**quit** *quit*]

If you do not specify options, **stty** displays terminal settings. Otherwise, **stty** sets the characteristics that you specify. Different systems allow different settings to be specified.

Example
```
stty eof ^d   # Sets the end-of-file character to ^d.
              # ^ indicates a control character.
```

tail [±*number*] [**–f**] [*file*]

Displays the last part of a file. Copies *file* to standard output, starting at a designated place. If *file* is not specified, standard input is used. Copying begins at distance +*number* of lines from the start, or –*number* from the end of the input. Specifying **–f** causes **tail** not to exit at the end of the file, but rather to wait and try to read repeatedly in case the file grows.

Example
```
ls -l | tail -3     # Displays last three lines
                    # of ls output.
```

tee [**–a**] *file...*

Reads standard input, and writes to standard output and *file*(s).

– a appends to *file*(s).

Example
```
date | tee file1 file2
# Writes date to standard output, file1, and file2.
```

tr [**–c**] [**–d**] [**–s**] [*string1* [*string2*]]

Transliterates characters in a file. Copies standard input to standard output, substituting or deleting characters based on *string1* and *string2*. Input characters in *string1* are mapped to corresponding characters in *string2*.

You can specify the following options:
- **–c** Complements the set of characters in *string1* with respect to the ASCII character set.
- **–d** Deletes input characters in *string1*.
- **–s** Squeezes multiple occurrences of characters in *string2*.

Example
```
tr "[a-z]" "[A-Z]" < filein > fileout
          # Changes characters in filein to uppercase.
          # Stores output in fileout.
```

uniq [**–c**] [**–d**] [**–u**] [*input* [*output*]]

Copies lines from its input to its output, eliminating any adjacent lines that are duplicates.

You can specify the following options:
- **–c** Causes each line of the output to be preceded by the number of times that line appears. This option supersedes the **–d** and **–u** options.
- **–d** Displays duplicated line(s).
- **–u** Displays only lines that are not repeated.

uniq reads from standard input if you do not specify *input*.

uniq displays its output to standard output if you do not specify *output*.

wc [**–l**] [**–w**] [**–c**] [*file...*]

Word count. Counts lines, words (a maximal string of characters delimited by Spaces, Tabs, or Newlines), and characters. It also keeps a total count for all named *file*(s).

–l, **–w**, **–c** causes only **l**ines, **w**ords, and/or **c**haracters to be reported. Default is that all are reported.

file, if specified, causes pathnames to be printed along with the counts. Otherwise, count is taken from standard input.

Example
```
wc -l foobar  # Displays number of lines in foobar.
```

what *file...*

Looks for character strings in each of the *file*(s) prefixed by **@(#)** and displays them. **ksh** has a character string containing the version in this format.

Example
```
what $(whence ksh)
/bin/ksh:
    Version 06/03/86a
```

who [**am i**]

Displays the list of users who are currently logged onto your system, the filename of each terminal, and the time logged in. Use **am i** to restrict the listing to your own login.

Example
```
who am i
dgk      tty09     May 10 12:07
```

EXERCISES

1. Write a command that does each of the following:
   a. Displays the number of users currently logged onto the system.
   b. Displays all files in your home directory and subdirectories that have not been accessed in more than three days.
   c. Displays the last 10 lines in a file named **foo** that contains the string **bar**.
   d. Removes a file called **?*]**.
   e. Lists files in the working directory in order of increasing size.

2. What would be the effect of each of the following commands run in the order shown?
   a. `mkdir foobar`
   b. `date > foobar/foodate`
   c. `ln foobar/foodate foobar/bardate`
   d. `cat foobar/*date`
   e. `ls -l foobar | tee foobar/out`
   f. `grep foo foo/*`
   g. `rm foobar/foodate`
   h. `chmod 600 foobar/out`
   i. `ls -lt foobar`
   j. `find foobar -type f -exec cat {} \;`
   k. `rm -f foobar`

16 INVOCATION AND ENVIRONMENT

This chapter specifies what **ksh** does when you invoke **ksh**, **ksh** scripts, and **ksh** functions. It also discusses what constitutes an environment for a **ksh** process, and how the **ksh** environment is shared or inherited across different types of invocations.

ENVIRONMENT

The environment of a **ksh** script or function is defined by:
- Open files.
- Access rights to files and processes.
- Working directory.
- Value of the file creation mask.
- Resources that you can set with **ulimit**.
- Current traps.
- Shell variables and attributes.
- Aliases.
- Functions.
- Option settings.

SHELL INVOCATION

ksh creates a new process each time that you invoke **ksh** explicitly, with or without arguments. You can also cause **ksh** to be invoked implicitly.

The items below are in the order that **ksh** sets up the environment.

Inheritance

A **ksh** child process inherits a copy of the environment of its parent process which includes:
- All the open files not set close-on-exec.

- Access rights to files and processes. **ksh** sets the effective user id of the process to the real user id of the process, and the effective group id of the process to the real group id of the process unless you invoke it with the **privileged** option (**–p**). *Version*: Resetting of the effective user and group id and the **privileged** option apply only on versions of **ksh** newer than the 06/03/86 version.
- The working directory.
- Value of the file creation mask.
- Values of resource limits.
- Signals that are ignored by the parent. **ksh** does not allow you to set traps for these signals.
- Signals not ignored by the parent process. **ksh** sets default actions for these but they can be changed.
- Shell variables, with the exception of **IFS**, with the export attribute in the parent process, are inherited by the new **ksh** process. Other shell variables are not inherited. The attributes of the variables are also inherited. *Version*: Only the export attribute is inherited on the 06/03/86 and earlier versions of **ksh**. Also, **IFS** can be inherited with the 06/03/86 and earlier versions.
- Alias definitions and function definitions are not inherited. Even exported aliases and functions are not inherited. You must put these definitions in the environment file to cause child processes to have access to them.
- Option settings are not directly inherited. However, option settings can be specified on the command line and some option settings can be inherited indirectly through the value of exported variables.

Positional Parameters

ksh sets the positional parameters to the values of non-option arguments that you provide.

If you do not specify any non-option arguments to **ksh**, **ksh** sets parameter **0** to the name of **ksh**.

Otherwise, **ksh** sets parameter **0** to the first non-option argument, and the rest of the arguments become parameter **1**, **2**, **3**, etc.

Example
```
ksh -x -v prog abc
# Runs ksh with the x and v options.
# $0 is set to prog.
# $1 is set to abc.
```

Invocation Line Options

You can specify all of the options to the **set** command. You can also specify the following options at invocation:

–c *string*
> **ksh** reads commands from *string*.

–i **ksh** runs as an interactive shell. In this case the **TERM** signal is ignored, and the **INT** signal is caught and causes the current command to be terminated and a new prompt to be issued.

–r **ksh** runs as a restricted shell.

–s **ksh** reads commands from standard input. **ksh** automatically turns on the **–s** option if you do not specify **–c** option, or any arguments to **ksh** other than options. **ksh** ignores the **–s** option if you specify **–c**.

ksh initially turns off all options that you do not specify, except that:

- **ksh** turns on the **interactive** option if you do not specify any non-option arguments to **ksh**, and standard input is directed from a terminal, and standard output is directed to a terminal.
- **ksh** turns on the **trackall** option, when **ksh** is not interactive.
- **ksh** turns on the **monitor** option if the **interactive** option is on, and if **ksh** can determine that the system can handle job control.
- **ksh** sets **emacs**, **gmacs**, and/or **vi** options based on your settings of the **EDITOR** and **VISUAL** variables.
- **ksh** turns on the **bgnice** option. *Version*: This is the default behavior for versions of **ksh** newer than the 06/03/86 version.
- **ksh** sets the **restricted** option if the **SHELL** variable or the filename of the shell contains an **r**.
- **ksh** turns on the **protected** option if the effective user id of the process is not equal to the real user id of the process, or the effective group id of the process is not equal to the real group id of the process. *Version*: The **protected** option is available only on the 06/03/86 version of **ksh.**

Environment File

If the **privileged** (**–p**) option is:

- Off. **ksh** expands the value of the **ENV** variable for parameter expansion. If the expansion yields the name of a file that you have permission to read, then **ksh** reads and executes each of the commands in this file in the current environment.
- On. If the file named **/etc/suid_profile** exists and **ksh** has permission to read this file, then **ksh** reads and executes each of the commands in this file in the current environment.

To cause function definitions and/or alias definitions to remain in effect for subsequent invocations of **ksh**, you must:
- Put alias and/or function definitions into a file.
- Export aliases and/or functions that you want to be inherited by shell scripts that are invoked by the new **ksh** process.
- Set the value of the **ENV** variable to the name of this file.
- Export **ENV**.

Alias and function definitions within the environment file without the **–x** attribute are removed for non-interactive shells.

History File

For interactive shells, **ksh** opens or creates the history file at the earlier of:
- The first function definition it reads while the **nolog** option is off.
- After the environment file has been read and executed.

For non-interactive shells, **ksh** opens or creates the history file when it is first referenced, for example, with **read –s** or **print –s**.

LOGIN SHELLS

If the name of the **ksh** program starts with a – (minus), then **ksh** is a login shell. A login shell is the same as a regular **ksh** invocation except that:
- You cannot specify any non-option arguments.
- **ksh** reads and executes the file **/etc/profile** if it exists. This file is created by the system administrator.
- If the **privileged** option is off, then **ksh** reads and executes the commands from the file defined by expanding **$HOME/.profile**.

These profile files are read and executed one command at a time so that aliases defined in these files affect subsequent commands in the same file.

RESTRICTED SHELLS

A restricted shell is an execution environment that is more controlled than that of the standard **ksh** shell. With a restricted shell you cannot:
- Change the working directory.
- Set the value of **SHELL**, **ENV**, or **PATH** variables.
- Specify the pathname of a command with a **/** in it.
- Redirect output of a command with > , >|, <>, or >>.

These restrictions do not apply when **ksh** processes the **.profile** file, and the file defined by the **ENV** variable.

If a restricted shell executes a shell script, **ksh** executes it in a non-restricted environment.

SHELL SCRIPTS

A script can be invoked by name or as the first argument to **ksh**. Except as listed in the next paragraph, invoking a script by name does not cause a separate invocation of **ksh** on most systems. Scripts invoked by name take less time to begin. They also inherit the exported functions, exported aliases, and exported arrays from the calling program.

Shell scripts are carried out as a separate invocation of **ksh** when:
- The script has execute permission but does not have read permission.
- The script has the setuid or setgid permission set.
- *System-dependent*: On some systems, shell scripts are carried out as a separate invocation of **ksh** for all scripts whose first line begins with the characters **#!** followed by the pathname for **ksh**. The characters after the **#!** define the interpreter to run to process the script.

When **ksh** executes a script without a separate **ksh** invocation:
- The file defined by the **ENV** variable is not processed.
- The history file is inherited.
- Exported aliases and exported functions are inherited. All other aliases and functions are not inherited.
- Exported arrays are inherited.
- Variable attributes are inherited. *Version*: On versions of **ksh** newer than the 06/03/86 version, variable attributes are also inherited with separate invocations of **ksh**.

A script runs until it:
- Has no more commands left to run.
- Runs the **exit** command.
- Runs the **return** command when outside a function.
- Runs the **exec** command with an argument. In this case the script will be replaced by the program defined by the first argument to **exec**.
- Detects one of the errors listed on page 189 while processing a built-in command listed with a dagger.
- Receives a signal that is not being ignored, for which no trap has been set, and that normally causes a process to terminate.
- Exits from a command with a False return value while the **errexit** option is on and no **ERR** trap has been set.

SUBSHELLS

A subshell is a separate environment that is a copy of the parent shell environment. Changes made to the subshell environment do not affect the parent environment.

ksh creates subshells to carry out:
- (...) commands.
- Command substitution.
- Co-processes.
- Background processes.
- Each element of a pipeline except the last. *Version*: On the 06/03/86 and earlier versions of **ksh**, the last element of a pipeline was run in a subshell environment.

SHELL FUNCTIONS

Shell functions share all of the environment with the calling process except:
- Variable assignments that are part of the call.
- Positional parameters.
- Option settings.
- Variables declared within the function with **typeset**.
- Traps. Version: On the 06/03/86 and earlier versions of **ksh**, traps other than **EXIT** were shared with the caller.

DOT SCRIPTS

A dot script is a script that is specified with the **.** command. A dot script is read in its entirety and then expanded and executed in the current process environment. A syntax error in a dot script causes the script that referenced it to terminate.

Arguments specified with the **.** command replace the positional parameters.

BUILT-IN COMMANDS

Each built-in is evaluated in the current process environment.

I/O redirection applied to built-ins does not affect the current environment.

Variable assignments for built-ins denoted by a † in the *Built-in Commands* chapter, affect the current environment. Other assignments affect only the specific built-in.

PART V

APPLICATION
PROGRAMMING

17 SHELL FUNCTIONS AND PROGRAMS

This chapter contains several functions and programs written in the KornShell language. They are included here primarily for illustrative purposes. However, you may find some of these functions and/or programs useful.

SAMPLE LOGIN PROFILE

```
#
# This is a sample KornShell login profile
#

# First set and export the following:

export ENV=$HOME/.envfile \
       PATH=$HOME/bin:${PATH#:}: \
       HISTFILE=$HOME/sh_history \
       HISTSIZE=250 \
       LOGNAME=${LOGNAME:-${HOME##*/}} \
       MAIL=/usr/spool/mail/$LOGNAME \
       MAILPATH=~uucp/$LOGNAME:$MAIL \
       MAILCHECK=60 \
       EDITOR=$(whence vi) \
       PAGER=$(whence pg) \
       CDPATH=":$HOME:/usr" \
       PWD=$HOME \
       OLDPWD=$HOME

# Put first character of hostname into prompt
# Different systems have different ways to get hostname
# Here we try them all
typeset -uxL1 HOSTCHAR=$( {
                       uname -n || hostname ||
                       cat /etc/whoami || print '?'
                  } 2>/dev/null
             )
```

```
# Put the hostname and working directory into the prompt
PS1="$HOSTCHAR"':${PWD#$HOME/}:!$ '

# Initialize some options
set -o ignoreeof -o trackall

# Set the terminal the way I like it
stty intr '^?' erase '^h' kill '^x'

# Find out what terminal I am on
export COLUMNS=80 LINES=24 TERM TERMCAP
case $TERM in
""|dialup|network)
      if    [ "$(whence termid)" ]
      then  TERM=$(termid)
      else  PS3='Please enter number or terminal name: '
            select TERM in 745 hp2621 4014 vt100 \
                   ansi 5620 630 vt52 sun
            do  TERM=${TERM:=$REPLY}
            done
      fi
      ;;
esac

# Special terminal setups

case $TERM in
745|735)
      stty cr1 nl1 -tabs erase \#; tabs
      ;;
2621|hp*)
      stty cr0 nl0 tabs; tabs
      ;;
4014|tek)
      stty cr0 nl0 -tabs ff1
      print "\033;\c"
      ;;
4105) LINES=30
      print '\033%!0\033KY5\033KDH575A;E;C3C0E35\c'
      print '\033KDH675A;E;C3C0E45\033%!1\c'
      ;;
4404) LINES=32
      ;;
630)  LINES=${LINES:-68} COLUMNS=${COLUMNS:-92}
      export DMD=/usr/add-on/630 DMDSGS
      ;;
5620) LINES=${LINES:-34} COLUMNS=${COLUMNS:-88}
      export DMD=/usr/add-on/dmd DMDSGS
```

```
        ;;
sun)    LINES=${LINES:-34}
        ;;
esac

case $DMD in
"")     break;;
*)      DMDSGS=$DMD PATH=$PATH:$DMD/bin;;
esac
umask 022    # Set file creation mask.
```

SAMPLE ENVIRONMENT FILE

```
#
# This is a sample ENV file
#

# set options
set -o trackall
# set up aliases and functions
alias -x sh=${SHELL:-/bin/sh} \
        suspend='kill -STOP $$' \
        nmake=~gsf/bin/nmake

case $- in
*i*)    # interactive
        alias cd='$HOME/funlib/cd;cd' \
              mcd='$HOME/funlib/cd;mcd' \
              cx='chmod +x' \
              h='fc -l' \
              @u='rlogin ulysses'
        if      test "$(whence more)"
        then    alias pg=$(whence more)
        fi
        function l   # list files in columns
        {
            set -o markdirs
            if    [ $# = 1  -a  -d "$1" ]
            then  cd "$1"
                  trap 'cd $OLDPWD' EXIT
                  set --
            fi
            PS3=
            typeset i
            select i in ${@-*}
            do      :
            done < /dev/null
        }
esac
```

pushd, popd, *AND* dirs

These functions show how you can define functions to provide the C shell directory management interface. Compare them to the directory manipulation functions in the next section.

Three **ksh** functions provide the C shell directory stack management interface. The function:

pushd   When you specify:
- A pathname, **pushd** changes the working directory to this pathname and pushes the previous working directory onto the stack.
- No argument, **pushd** exchanges the top two elements of the directory stack and changes back to the previous working directory.
- +*n*, **pushd** rotates the whole stack so that the *n*th argument of the directory stack becomes the top element and changes the working directory to it.

popd   When you specify:
- No argument, **popd** removes the previous working directory from the directory stack and changes the working directory to it.
- +*n*, **popd** deletes the *n*th previous working directory from the stack.

dirs   Displays the current directory stack starting from the working directory.

```
#
# DIRECTORY MANIPULATION FUNCTIONS pushd, popd AND dirs
#
# Uses global variables _push_max _push_top _push_stack
integer _push_max=100 _push_top=100
```

dirs

```
# Changes home directory to ~
# Shares variable dir with caller
function to_tilde
{
    case $dir in
    $HOME)
        dir=\~ ;;
    /*) ;;
    *)  dir=\~/$dir;;
    esac
```

```
}

# Display directory stack -- $HOME displayed as ~
function dirs
{
    typeset dir=${PWD#$HOME/}
    to_tilde
    print -r - "$dir ${_push_stack[@]}"
}
```

pushd [*directory*]
pushd +*n*

```
# Change directory and put directory on front of stack
function pushd
{
    typeset dir= type=0
    integer i
    case $1 in
    "") # pushd
        if    ((_push_top >= _push_max))
        then  print pushd: No other directory.
              return 1
        fi
        type=1 dir=${_push_stack[_push_top]}
        ;;
    +[1-9]|+[1-9][0-9]) # pushd +n
        integer i=_push_top$1-1  # Note, $1 contains +
        if    ((i >= _push_max))
        then  print pushd: Directory stack not that deep.
              return 1
        fi
        type=2 dir=${_push_stack[i]}
        ;;
    *)  if    ((_push_top <= 0))
        then  print pushd: Directory stack overflow.
              return 1
        fi;;
    esac
    case $dir in
    ~*)   dir=$HOME${dir#~};;
    esac
    cd "${dir:-$1}" || return 1
    dir=${OLDPWD#$HOME/}
    to_tilde
    esac
    case $type in
```

```
    0)  # pushd name
        _push_stack[_push_top=_push_top-1]=$dir
        ;;
    1)  # pushd
        _push_stack[_push_top]=$dir
        ;;
    2)   # push +n
        type=${1#+} i=_push_top-1
        set -- "${_push_stack[@]}" "$dir" "${_push_stack[@]}"
        shift $type
        for dir
        do   (((i=i+1) < _push_max)) || break
             _push_stack[i]=$dir
        done;;
    esac
    dirs
}
```

popd [+*n*]

```
# Pops the top directory
function popd
{
    typeset dir
    if      ((_push_top >= _push_max))
    then  print popd: Nothing to pop.
          return 1
    fi
    case $1 in
    "")
        dir=${_push_stack[_push_top]}
        case $dir in
        ~*)    dir=$HOME${dir#~}
        esac
        cd "$dir" || return 1
        ;;
    +[1-9]|+[1-9][0-9])
        integer i=_push_top$1-1
        if      ((i >= _push_max))
        then  print pushd: Directory stack not that deep.
              return 1
        fi
        while ((i > _push_top))
        do _push_stack[i]=${_push_stack[i-1]}
              i=i-1
        done
```

```
        ;;
  *)  print pushd: Bad directory.
      return 1;;
  esac
  unset _push_stack[_push_top]
  _push_top=_push_top+1
  dirs
}
```

AN ENHANCED cd INTERFACE

These functions provide an alternative to the C shell directory stack interface routines. We use an alias to replace the **cd** command with an upward compatible function. Thus, you can continue to use **cd** and still benefit from the directory stack.

This directory stack management interface consists of three functions and an alias. The function:

_cd   When you specify:
- *−n*. **_cd** changes back to the *n*th previous working directory.
- *n*. Changes to the *n*th directory displayed with the **dirs** function.
- Anything else. **_cd** changes the working directory exactly the same as **cd** and saves the previous working directory onto a stack. If there are more directories than specified with the **CDSTACK** variable, the least recently referenced directory is removed from the list.

mcd   Displays a menu of the directories it has saved, each preceded by a number. You can then enter the number of a previous directory, or the name of a new directory to change the directory.

dirs   Displays the current directory stack, starting from the working directory.

The alias **cd** is defined to **_cd**.

```
#
# DIRECTORY MANIPULATION FUNCTIONS, REPLACES CD
#
# Uses global variables _push_max _push_top _push_stack
integer _push_max=${CDSTACK-32} _push_top=${CDSTACK-32}
unalias cd
alias cd=_cd
# Display directory stack -- $HOME displayed as ~
function dirs
{
    typeset dir="${PWD#$HOME/}"
    case $dir in
```

```
    $HOME)
        dir=\~
        ;;
    /*)  ;;
    *)  dir=\~/$dir;;
    esac
    PS3=
    select i in "$dir" "${_push_stack[@]}"
    do  :
    done < /dev/null
}

# Change directory and put directory on front of stack
function _cd
{
    typeset dir=
    integer n=0 type=4
    case $1 in
    -|-1|2)  # cd -
        n=_push_top type=1
        ;;
    -[1-9]|-[1-9][0-9])  # cd -n
        n=_push_top+${1#-}-1 type=2
        ;;
    1)   # keep present directory
        print -r - "$PWD"
        return
        ;;
    [2-9]|[1-9][0-9])  # cd n
        n=_push_top+${1}-2 type=2
        ;;
    *)  if    ((_push_top <= 0))
        then  type=3 n=_push_max
        fi;;
    esac
    if    ((type<3))
    then  if    ((n >= _push_max))
          then  print cd: Directory stack not that deep.
                return 1
          else  dir=${_push_stack[n]}
          fi
    fi
    case $dir in
    ~*)   dir=$HOME${dir#~};;
    esac
    \cd "${dir:-$@}" > /dev/null || return 1
    dir=${OLDPWD#$HOME/}
    case $dir in
    $HOME)
```

```
            dir=\~
            ;;
    /*)  ;;
    *)   dir=\~/$dir;;
    esac
    case $type in
    1)   # swap first two elements
         _push_stack[_push_top]=$dir
         ;;
    2|3)   # put $dir on top and shift down by one until top
         integer i=_push_top
         for dir in "$dir" "${_push_stack[@]}"
         do   ((i > n)) && break
             _push_stack[i]=$dir
             i=i+1
         done
         ;;
    4)   # push name
         _push_stack[_push_top=_push_top-1]=$dir
         ;;
    esac
    print -r - "$PWD"
}

# Menu-driven change directory command
function mcd
{
    typeset dir="${PWD#$HOME/}"
    case $dir in
    $HOME)
         dir=\~
         ;;
    /*)  ;;
    *)   dir=\~/$dir;;
    esac
    PS3='Select by number or enter a name: '
    select dir in "$dir" "${_push_stack[@]}"
    do   if    _cd $REPLY
         then   return
         fi
    done
}
```

SHELL VERSION OF cat *COMMAND*

```
#
#       SHELL VERSION OF cat
#
alias open=exec                     # more descriptive
alias duplicate=exec                # more descriptive
duplicate 3<&0                      # save descriptor 0
for i                               # do for each file
do  if      test x"$i" != x         # open file if needed
    then    if      test x"$i" != x- # - is standard input
            then    open 0< $i
            else    duplicate 0<&3  # use standard input
            fi
    fi
    IFS=
    while read -r line              # read in a line
    do      print -r - "$line"      # print out the line
    done
done
```

SHELL VERSION OF grep *COMMAND*

```
#
#          SHELL VERSION OF grep
#
vflag= xflag= cflag= lflag= nflag= arg=$1
set -f                  # Disable pathname generation
while true              # Look for options
do     case    $arg in
       -v*) vflag=1;;   # Displays lines not matched
       -x*) xflag=1;;   # Must be an exact match
       -c*) cflag=1;;   # Only a count of matches
       -l*) lflag=1;;   # Only pathnames of matched files
       -n*) nflag=1;;   # Precede line with number
       -e*) shift;expr="$1"; arg=;;
       -f*) shift;expr=$(< $1); arg=;;
       -*)  print -u2 -r - $0: 'unknown flag'; exit 1;;
       *)
            if      test "$expr" = ''
            then    expr="$1";shift
            fi
```

```
                    test "$xflag" || expr="*${expr}*"
                    break;;
            esac
            arg=${arg#-?}                # compute next arg
            case $arg in
            "")    shift; arg=$1;;
            *)     arg=-$arg;;
            esac
    done
    noprint=$vflag$cflag$lflag          # don't print if set
    integer n=0 c=0 tc=0 nargs=$#       # initialize counters
    for i in "$@"                       # go thru the files
    do  if    ((nargs<=1))
        then fname=''
        else fname="$i":
        fi
        test "$i"  &&  exec 0< $i       # open file if needed
        while read -r line              # read in a line
        do    let n=n+1
              case "$line" in
              $expr)                    # line matches pattern
                  if   test "$noprint" = ""
                  then print -r "$fname${nflag:+$n:}$line"
                  fi
                  let c=c+1 ;;
              *)                        # not a match
                  if   test "$vflag"
                  then print -r "$fname${nflag:+$n:}$line"
                  fi;;
              esac
        done
        if    test "$lflag" && ((c))
        then  print $i
        fi
        let tc=tc+c n=0 c=0
    done
    if    test "$cflag"
    then  print $tc
    fi
    let tc                              # set the exit value
```

SHELL VERSION OF nohup COMMAND

```
#
#          SHELL VERSION OF nohup
#
trap '' HUP                 # ignore hangup
set -o trackall
command=$(whence "$1")
exec 0< /dev/null           # disconnect input
if    test -t               # redirect output if necessary
then  if     test -w .
      then   echo 'Sending output to nohup.out'
             exec >> nohup.out
      else   echo "Sending output to $HOME/nohup.out"
             exec >> $HOME/nohup.out
      fi
fi
if    test -t 2             # direct unit 2 to a file
then  exec 2>&1
fi
# run the command
case $command in
*/*)  exec "$@"
      ;;
*)    "$@"
      ;;
esac
```

EXERCISES

1. Modify the function **_cd** so that it executes a script named **.ente**r
    when it enters a directory, and a script **.leave** when it leaves it.

2. Modify the new **cd** functions so that it uses a circular stack instead of
    the downward growing stack. What advantages does this have?

3. Write the **wc** command.

4. Suppose that you are on a system that does not have the **cp** command.
    It only has a command named **copy** that takes two arguments; a
    source file that must exist; and a destination file that must not exist.
    Write the **cp** command for this machine.

5. Write a command that generates all the pathnames of files starting
    from a specified directory, and executes a specified action for each
    pathname. The action can be specified as a function.

6. Write the **getopts** built-in command, defined on page 216, as a function. Assume that *arg* is required. How could you define an alias and function for **getopts** that works even when you do not specify *arg*?

7. Use the above function in **grep.sh** to replace the argument parsing.

8. Write a command to compare two files and print out the first line of each where they differ.

9. Write a command that does arithmetic on roman numerals. The answer should also be in roman numerals.

10. Write a command that takes any number of single letters as arguments and displays all word combinations of these letters in alphabetic order, one per line. Do not use any of the commands in the *Other Commands* chapter.

11. Write a command that can quiz you on any number of subjects. Each subject is a file consisting of lines, where each line contains a question, followed by the number of the correct answer, followed by the list of choices, each separated by a **:**. All quizzes should be stored in the same directory. The command should take the subject to be quizzed on as an argument, and should then present each question and the choices to the user. After two tries, the user should be told the correct answer. At the end of the quiz the user should be given a score, both as a raw score and as a percent. The raw score is obtained by giving one point for each correct answer, and one-half point for each question answered correctly on the second try.

12. Write a command to display a list of files where each file begins on a separate page. Each page should have a heading that defaults to the name of the file left-justified on the left top of the page, and the date, right-justified on the right. Each line of each file should be numbered starting at 1. The command should allow option arguments:
–l *pagelength*	To specify the page length, default 60.
–w *pagewidth*	To specify the page width, default 80.
–h *string*	To specify the heading.

18   A COMPLETE APPLICATION

This chapter contains an example of how you can use **ksh** as a high-level programming language to program an application. The example that we use is a slightly modified version of the MH (Message Handling) system. MH was originally written at the Rand Corporation in the C language. It was later modified by the Department of Information and Computer Science at the University of California, Irvine. We have rewritten it in **ksh** for this book.

We chose MH because it is in the public domain and because it illustrates many of the features of **ksh** as a high-level programming language. It is a useful system that you might want to adapt and install on your system for your actual use. Of course, this certainly is not necessary for you to understand and use **ksh**. It is a moderately sized application; the source code for the MH system consists of tens of thousands of lines of C code.

Disclaimer: Although we believe that the MH code in this chapter should work if you correctly adapt and install it on your system, we make no claims for it, do not support it, and do not supply it in machine-readable form.

THE MH MESSAGE HANDLING SYSTEM

With MH you can send messages to other people on your system, and you can read messages that other people send to you. Depending on how things have been set up on your system, it may be possible for you to send messages to people on remote systems. You can also reply to messages that you have received, review them, organize them in folders, and delete them.

MH differs from other mail programs in that it is composed of many small programs instead of just one very large program. Among new users this sometimes causes some confusion along the lines of, What program do I run? With MH, you use **ksh** to invoke one command at a time. This means that when you handle mail, the entire power of **ksh** is at your disposal in addition to the facilities that MH provides.

Summary of Commands

The minimal list of MH commands that you can get by with (the complete list of commands in this book) is:

comp   Composes a new message to send.
folder   Tells you what the current folder is.
folders   Lists all folders.
inc   Incorporates mail (gets new mail).
next   Shows the next message.
prev   Shows the previous message.
refile   Files messages in folders.
repl   Replies to a received message.
rmm   Removes a message.
scan   Scans a folder and displays a summary of what is in it.
show   Shows the current message.

Messages and Folders

A message takes the form of a memorandum, and is composed of two major parts: A header, which contains information such as "To" and "From" addresses, "Subject," "Date," etc.; and the body, which is the actual text of the message. Each component in the header starts with a keyword followed by a : (colon) and additional information. If header lines continue past one line, then each subsequent line begins with one or more leading Spaces or Tabs. For example, in the message

```
Date: 12 Aug 87 11:21:34 EST (Wed)
To: ihnp4!ulysses!dgk
Subject: Software Development Environments
From: cbosgd!pds (Pat Sullivan)

This is the text.
```

there are four header items, and one line of text in the body. Note that a blank line separates the body from the headers.

MH stores a message as an ordinary file in a directory. This directory is called a folder. If you choose to keep and organize your messages, you may create as many folders as you wish. There is no limit to the number of messages in a folder. Typically, messages are numbered from 1 up.

All of your personal folders, along with some other information that MH needs to know, are kept in a special directory that you can specify, whose default is called **Mail** under your home directory. Normally, MH manages these files and directories automatically, so that you need not work with them directly unless you really want to.

Reading New Mail

When you are notified that you have mail (usually when you log in), perhaps with the message
```
You have mail.
```
then you know that messages are waiting in your maildrop. To read these messages, you first have to incorporate the mail into your in-box by typing the command **inc**.

This incorporates the new mail from your mail drop to your in-box, which is a folder named, naturally enough, **+inbox**.

As **inc** incorporates your new mail, it generates a scan listing of the mail.
```
Incorporating new mail into inbox...
2+ 10/10 gsf             nmake <<A new version of nmak
3  10/10 ..!ulysses!dgk ksh <<I found a bug in the la
4  10/11 root            space << Please clean up any
```

Each time **inc** is invoked, any new messages are added to the end of your **+inbox** folder.

To read the first message, use the **show** command. This displays the current message. To read each subsequent message, use the **next** command.

If you want to back up, the **prev** command shows the previous message.

Another way to read your messages is to name them all at once with **show all**. This command displays them all, one after the other.

The **all** argument to **show,** above, might also be replaced with **next** or **prev**, as in **show next** or **show prev**, which are respectively equivalent to the **next** and **prev** commands.

If you have had occasion to type **inc** more than once, then you will find that **show all** is showing not only the new messages, but also the old messages that you have already seen. Therefore, you might find it better to use **show cur-last** instead. This command displays messages from the current message (**cur**), to the last message (**last**). Each time **inc** is invoked, it makes the first new message the current message.

It should be noted here that the name **all** given in a previous example, is equivalent to the message range **first–last**, where **first** is the name of the first message in **+inbox**. Also, **show** by itself is equivalent to **show cur**.

As mentioned earlier, with **ksh** as your interface to MH, it becomes easy to list a message on a line printer or to another file. For example, **show all | lpr** (or **show all | lp** on some systems) sends all the messages in the current folder to the line printer.

To summarize, the preceding has introduced these important concepts:
- Folders (in particular, the **+inbox** folder).
- Messages.
- Message names (e.g., **prev**, **next**, **cur**, **first**, **last**).
- Message ranges (e.g., **cur–last**, **all**).
- More will be said about folders and messages in following sections.

Originating Messages

To create a message draft from scratch, use the **comp** command. You will be placed in whatever editor you specify, with a default header template that you must fill in. If you make a mistake, you may correct it later with a text editor. The draft will be sent only if you give an explicit request before you exit this command, so you do not have to worry about the draft getting away from you prematurely.

To start, you simply type **comp**. The default draft template contains the following header fields:

To: Type the address of the person to whom you wish the message sent. If this person is on the same system as you, then that person's login id should serve as the address (e.g., **morris** or **dgk**). A discussion of addresses outside your system is beyond the scope of this book.

cc: "Carbon copy" (an archaism) address. It is customary, but not required, to put your own address here so that you get a copy of the message when it is sent. To put more than one address in the **To:** and/or **cc:** components, just use a **,** (comma) between each address on a line.

Subject: A line of any descriptive text will do.

The subject line is followed by a dashed line, and you are then expected to type the body of the message. When you finish, just exit your editor in the customary fashion.

Caution:

- While in the editor, do not delete colons in the headers or change the spelling of **To:**, **cc:**, or **Subject:**, and do not leave blank lines between these lines.
- Feel free to change the addresses that you typed previously, or to add these lines if they are missing.
- Do not delete the dashes that separate the header lines from the text of the message.
- Do not add additional header lines unless you understand precisely what you are doing. This means particularly that you should not type or fill in a **From:** line. When the message is sent, the system automatically adds this line.
- Also, you should not type a **Date:** line in the header. When the message is sent, the system automatically adds the current date and time.

An example of a complete message draft, as it appears on your screen, might be:

```
To: morris
cc: gsf, ekrell
Subject: Korn Shell Programming Language Talk
-------

A presentation on the ksh implementation of the
Rand/UCI Mail Handling System (MH), will be given in
1D-451 on April 1st at 1:30 PM. Refreshments will be
served afterward.

David Korn
```

At this point, you are asked **What now?**. This is known as being at the "What now," level. For now, there are probably only four options that will interest you:

edit   Edit the draft.

list   List the draft on your screen.

quit   Quit, without sending the draft.

send   Send the draft, then quit.

edit   All of these options take various arguments. For example, the **edit** option will let you edit the draft before sending it. When you leave the editor, you will come back to the **What now?** level, where you can reedit the draft, send it, list it, or simply quit without sending the draft at all.

quit   If you **quit** without sending the draft, the draft is saved in a file whose default name is **Mail/draft** under your home directory. You can recall this file later using the **–use** argument to **comp**, **comp –use**. The **What now?** level permits you to do further editing and to send the final draft when you are ready.

send When it is time to send the draft on its way, use the **send** option by itself. If there are any problems with the draft (for example, if one or more of the people whom you specified in the **To:** and **cc:** components do not exist), then you are notified at this time.

Replying to Messages

To reply to a message, use the **repl** command. For example, **repl** creates a reply to the current message. You may also reply to a specific message (other than the current one) by giving a message number (e.g., **1**, **4**), or a message name (e.g., **first**, **last**, **prev**), for example, **repl prev**.

We haven't really introduced message numbers yet. We discuss them in the next section.

The process of replying to a message is very similar to composing a message from scratch (see the previous section), but **repl** conveniently constructs and displays the header of the reply draft for you. You need only type in the text of the reply. The draft is sent only if you give an explicit **send** after you finish editing it, so you do not have to worry about the draft getting away from you prematurely. An example of a complete reply draft, as it appears on your screen, might be:

```
To: dgk
cc: morris
Subject: Re:Korn Shell Programming Language Talk
In-reply-to: Your message of 27 Mar 87 18:15:08 EST.
------
    I'll be there.
gsf
```

At this point, you are asked **What now?**. Refer to the previous section regarding how to edit, display, or send the draft at this point.

As with **comp**, if you **quit** without sending the reply draft, the draft is saved in a file whose default name is **Mail/draft**, under your home directory. You can recall this file later using the **–use** argument to **comp**, **comp –use**. The **What now?** level permits you to do further editing and to send the final draft when you are ready.

Scanning Messages

The scan listing created by **inc** shows the message number, the date on which the message was sent, the sender, and the subject of the message. If there is sufficient space remaining on the line, the beginning of the text of the message is displayed as well, preceded by **<<** (two left angle brackets). An example of a scan listing is:

```
1  10/10 attunix!crume  ksh in Japan << ksh is beginn
2+ 10/10 gsf            nmake <<A new version of nmak
3  10/10 ..!ulysses!dgk ksh <<I found a bug in the la
4  10/11 root           space << Please clean up any
```
Note that all messages have message numbers.

To generate your own scan listing, use the **scan** command. Typing just **scan** will list all the messages in the current folder.

To scan a subset of these messages, you can specify the numbers of the messages that you consider interesting, e.g., **scan 2 3**.

You may display message names in addition to discrete message numbers. The built-in message names recognized by MH are:

all All messages in the folder, **first–last**.

first First message in the folder.

last Last message in the folder.

prev Message immediately before the current message.

cur Current message.

next Message immediately after the current message.

You can specify message ranges in addition to discrete message numbers or names by separating the beginning and final message numbers with a – (minus). For example, **scan 5–10** scans messages 5 through 10 inclusive.

You can also specify a range of messages by separating a beginning message number and a relative number of messages with a **:**. For example:

scan last:3 scans the last three messages in the folder. Similarly, **scan first:3** scans the first three messages in the folder.

scan next:3 scans the next three messages.

scan cur:–3 scans backwards for three messages beginning from the current message.

scan 100:4 scans four messages beginning from message number 100.

To summarize, the important concepts discussed in this section are message ranges, message numbers, and message names. When an MH command is described as taking a *msg* argument, it accepts either a message name or a message number. Most MH commands are described as taking *msgs* arguments, meaning that more than one message or message range is accepted.

Deleting Messages

To delete a message, use the **rmm** command. By default, **rmm** deletes the current message, but you can give **rmm** a list of messages to be removed as well. There is no corresponding **unrmm** command. However, you can specify the command that removes the file and can therefore change the way **rmm** works so that it simply moves messages to another folder (say, **+wastebasket**).

Filing Messages

The possibility of having folders other than **+inbox** has been mentioned previously. The methods for moving messages between folders and manipulating folders are discussed here.

The **refile** command moves messages from a source folder to one or more destination folders.

By default, the current message is moved from the current folder (typically **+inbox**) to another folder specified as an argument to **refile**. For example, **refile +todo** moves the current message from the current folder to the folder **+todo**.

To move messages from a folder other than the current folder, use the **−src +folder** switch, as in **refile −src +todo last +save +notes** which moves the last message in the **+todo** folder to the folders **+save** and **+notes**. Note that this operation is a move, not a copy. It removes the message from the source folder. To keep a copy in the source folder as well, use the **link** switch as in **refile −link −src +todo last +save +notes**.

Whenever you give a folder argument to an MH command, that folder becomes the current folder. To find out which folder is current, use the **folder** command. The **inc** command sets the current folder back to **+inbox** by default.

To find out about all of a user's folders, use the **folders** command. Since folders can contain other folders, the **folders −recurse** command will recursively examine each folder for you.

To set the current folder without doing anything else, use the **folder** command with a folder argument. Hence, **folder +inbox** makes **+inbox** the current folder.

The Profile

The profile in this version of MH differs from the profile in the original MH system both in the names of variables and in the syntax. In our implementation, the profile file is in the format of a shell script.

You can customize the MH environment by creating and editing a profile file named **.Mhprofile** in your home directory. Although there are lots of options, here are the most useful:

MhPath   The pathname of the directory which all the folders are under. The default is **$HOME/Mail**.

MhEditor

Lists the default editor that **comp** and **repl** should use. The default is **${VISUAL:-${EDITOR:-/bin/ed}}**, but you might prefer another editor.

MhMsg_protect

Whenever MH creates a message (for example, with **inc**), this is the octal access permission that the message is created with; the default is **MhMsg_protect=644**. This permission allows all other users on the system to read your messages. Note that changing the mode in the MH profile does not change the permission of messages that have been created already; use **chmod** to change the modes of your existing messages. *Caution*: To maintain privacy, use the access permission 600.

MhFolder_protect

Whenever MH creates a folder (for example, with **refile**), this is the access permission that the folder is created with. The default is **MhFolder_protect=751**. This permission allows other users on the system access to specific messages in your folders. *Caution*: To maintain stricter privacy, use the access permission 700.

MhSignature

When MH posts mail for you, it looks at this variable for your "real world" name. All the escape conventions understood by **print** get expanded. For example, **MhSignature='David Korn\nulysses!dgk'** causes a two-line signature to be appended to each message that you send.

MhAuditfile

A scan listing of each message that is placed in your **+inbox** folder will be appended to this file.

MhRm   The name of the command that removes message files. Default is **rm**.

MhList   The name of the command that displays messages to you. Default is **cat**.

MhStdform

The name of the default template that is used when you compose a message and when you reply to a message. Default is **$MhPath/.std_form**.

Use the alias feature of **ksh** to set your own default switch settings in your environment file. For example, if you want the default editor for **repl** to be **emacs**, the line **alias repl='repl –editor emacs'** is sufficient. Command line arguments tend to override alias settings. Given the environment file setting for **repl** above, if you invoked **repl** with **repl –editor vi**, **repl** would use the **vi** built-in editor instead of **emacs**.

Note that the **.Mhprofile** is a **ksh** script. Be sure that it is properly formatted.

Conventions

Now let's summarize the conventions that MH commands use:
- You can give any MH command that deals with messages a +*folder* argument to say which folder to use. However, you may give only one +*folder* argument per command in most cases.
- If an MH command accepts a *msgs* argument, then you can give any number of messages to the command. The MH command expands all the ranges and processes each message, starting with the lowest numbered message and working its way to the message with the highest number.
- If an MH command accepts a *msg* argument, then you can give at most one message.
- Switches to MH commands start with a –. Unlike the standard UNIX system convention, each switch consists of more than one character, for example, **–header**. To minimize typing, you need type only a unique abbreviation of the switch. Thus, for **–header**, **–hea** is probably sufficient, depending on the other switches accepted by the command.
- All MH commands have a **–help** switch, which you must spell out fully. When an MH command encounters the **–help** switch, it displays the syntax of the command and the switches that it accepts. In the list of switches, parentheses indicate required characters. For example, all **–help** switches will appear as **–(help)**, indicating that no abbreviation is accepted.
- Most MH switches have both on and off forms, such as **–format** and **–noformat**. In these cases, the last occurrence of the switch on the command line determines the setting of the switch.
- Since most switches have both on and off forms, it is easy to customize the default options for each MH command by defining aliases in your environment file, and to override those defaults on the command line.

DESIGN

The above description is not a complete specification. We fill in details as needed. We experimented with the original MH commands to determine their precise behavior. In most cases the format of the output is the same as the original MH system.

We will rely on the **mail** command for the posting and delivery of messages.

Folders and Messages

Folders are represented by directories. Messages are represented by files.

You always have a current folder, and each folder has a current message. We have chosen to use a file named:

.cur in each folder, to keep track of the current message.

.master in the **Mail** directory, to keep track of the current folder.

We experimented with the original MH commands to discover how each command affected the current folder and the current message.

Architecture

We had to decide whether to write each command as a function or as a script. To make this decision you must be aware of the following tradeoffs:

- Scripts take longer to start executing because **ksh** must find the file that contains the shell script.
- Function definitions take time for **ksh** to read and process. They also use memory which causes **ksh** to take a little longer to invoke a process.
- You cannot use the *Suspend* character to stop a function even if your system has job control.

There are tradeoffs for each choice you make. You have to weigh the benefits and drawbacks to each approach. Since it is easy to change a function to and from a script, you can make this decision after you have written most of the code.

We have chosen to write each command as a separate shell script. Each script uses a common set of functions stored in a file named **mh_init**. When each command is invoked, it checks to see if the common set of functions are defined in the environment. If they are not, then each script causes **mh_init** to be read as a **.** (dot) script.

If you read the shell script containing the common function definitions with the **.** (dot) built-in, the MH commands will be executed faster. You would ordinarily put the **.** built-in in your login profile or your environment file.

Performance

Our objective was that the most frequently used commands (**show**, **next**, **refile**, and **scan**) respond without any noticeable delay. With the common functions pre-loaded, the response for **show** and **next** outperformed the C language versions. **scan** and **refile** were only slightly slower. Even without pre-loading the common functions, the performance was adequate.

Shared Functionality

The following functionality is shared by all the commands:
- Processing arguments. Each command must check for invalid switches, display help information, and decode message specifications.
- Keeping track of the current folder and message number.
- Displaying error messages.

The following functionality is shared by two or more of the commands:
- Reading a message header by **repl**, **scan**, and **inc**.
- Disposition of a draft by **comp** and **repl**.
- **What now?** portion of **comp** and **repl**.
- Reading a folder to determine its contents by **folder** and **folders**.
- Displaying a scan message by **inc** and **scan**.

Naming Convention

It is good practice to choose a naming convention for variables so that functions and shell scripts are easier to read, and to minimize the number of name conflicts that can arise.

We use the following conventions:
- Names with all uppercase letters are predefined by **ksh** or by the system.
- All variables shared by any shell script and one or more functions start with the prefix **Mh**.
- Local variables are used within functions whenever possible. Local variables are all lowercase.
- Variables that correspond to field names in the header portion of the header start with an uppercase letter.
- Each switch name is used to hold the switch setting.

IMPLEMENTATION

In this section we show and describe each of the functions and commands that we wrote to implement our modified version of the MH system.

Each of the following headings contains the name of a function or a command. Under the heading is a description of the code, and the code itself.

The code uses the following global variables in addition to the variables that you can specify in your MH profile file:

MhCommand
> The name for the current MH command. Each command sets this value from parameter **0** by stripping off any path prefix.

MhCurfolder
> Name of the current folder.

MhCurmsg
> Number of the current message.

MhFirst Message number corresponding to the first message in a range of messages.

MhFolder
> Name of the folder specified for this command.

MhLast Message number corresponding to the last message in a range of messages.

MhLastmsg
> Number of the last message in the current folder.

MhMany This variable is set to ... for each command that allows you to specify multiple folders.

MhMsg Message that is being processed by this command.

MhMsgs List of messages for this command.

MhSwitches
> List of legal switches for the command. Each switch is a separate argument. The value of **MhSwitches** is as follows:
> - Each switch that can take an argument is specified as *−name=value*.
> - Each switch that can have an optional **no** in front of it is specified as *−name−*.
> - Each switch that can only be turned on is specified as *−name*.

The order of presentation of the **ksh** code is bottom up, with the shared functions first.

Note the use of quoting throughout the code. We try to protect against errors that occur if:
- A parameter is Null or unset.
- A parameter or folder name contains one or more Spaces or Tabs.

- A parameter or folder name contains the pathname expansion characters, [ ], **?**, and/or **∗**.
- A parameter or folder name contains a ****.

err_exit [*message...*]

err_exit displays on standard error the command name, a **:**, and a brief description of the error as provided by *message*.

The command exits with a False (1) return value.

```
function err_exit # message...
{
  print -u2 -r - "$MhCommand: $@"
  exit 1
}
```

check_setup

Each command calls **check_setup** to read your **.Mhprofile** file and to read the **.master** file.

If you do not have a **.master** file then the current folder is set to **inbox**.

```
function check_setup
{
  set -o noglob
  MhPath=$HOME/Mail
  test   -r "$HOME/.Mhprofile"  && . "$HOME/.Mhprofile"
  if     test ! -d "$MhPath"
  then   err_exit "$MhPath: not a directory"
  elif   test -r "$MhPath/.master"
  then   . "$MhPath/.master"
  else   MhCurfolder=inbox MhCurmsg=0 MhLastmsg=1
  fi
}
```

check_args [*arg...*]

check_args checks each *arg* supplied with the command line and reports any syntax errors.

The outer **while** loop shifts through each *arg* and checks whether *arg* is a:
- Folder. It starts with a +. **check_args** sets the **MhFolder** variable, and checks to see if any other folder is specified.
- Message. It starts with a digit, or begins with one of the message names **all**, **cur**, **prev**, **next**, **first**, or **last**. **check_args** checks whether multiple messages are permitted.
- Help request. It is **–help**. **check_args** uses the **MhSwitches** variable to display the help message, and calls **exit**.
- A switch. It starts with a – and is followed by a lowercase letter. **check_args** checks that it matches one of the switches in **MhSwitches** and that the specification is not ambiguous, and it creates a variable whose name is the name of the switch.

```
function check_args # arg ...
{
  # process the arguments
  typeset switch first=first val state
  while test "$1"
  do    case $1 in
        +*)  # folder
             case $first in
             first)
                 MhFolder=${1#+} first=
                 ;;
             "")
                 if   test ! "$MhMany"
                 then err_exit "only one folder at a time!"
                 fi
                 MhFolder="$MhFolder ${1#+}";;
             esac
             ;;
        [0-9]*|all|cur*|prev*|next*|first*|last*)
             if   test "$MhMsg"
             then MhMsgs="$MhMsgs $1"
             else usage_error
             fi
             ;;
        -help)
             print -n "syntax: $MhCommand"
             print -n "[+folder]${MhMany+...} "
             print -r - "${MhMsg+[msgs]} [switches]"
             print '  switches are:'
             for i in ${MhSwitches}
             do    IFS==
                   case $i in
                   *-)
                       i=${i#-}
                       print "   -[no]${i%-}" ;;
```

```
                        *)
                                print "    "$i;;
                        esac
                done
                print -r - '    (-help)'
                exit 1
                ;;
        -[a-z]*[!-]) # switches
            val=$1 state=1
            case $1 in
            -no*) # strip off leading no
                    val=-${1#-no} state=;;
            esac
            case $MhSwitches in
            *$val*)
                switch=${val#-}${MhSwitches#*$val}
                case $val in
                ${switch})
                    err_exit "$1: ambiguous";;
                esac
                switch="${switch%% *}"
                case $switch in
                *=*)
                    shift
                    case $1 in
                    -*|"")
                        err_exit "missing argument to" \
                            "-${switch%=*}"
                        ;;
                    esac
                    eval ${switch#*=}=$1
                    ;;
                *)
                    eval ${switch%-}=$state;;
                esac
                ;;
            *)
                err_exit "usage: [+folder]$MhMany"\
                    "${MhMsg+[msgs]} [switches]"
                ;;
            esac
            ;;
        *)
            err_exit "bad message list $1"
        esac
        shift
    done
}
```

check_folder

check_folder checks to see whether **MhFolder** exists. If it exists, **check_folder** returns True. If it does not exist, **check_folder** creates the folder, sets the protection mode, and returns False (1).

```
function check_folder
{
  typeset dir=$MhPath/$MhFolder\
          mode=${MhFolder_protect:-751}
  if    test ! -d "$dir"
  then  read reply?"Create folder \"$dir\"? "
        case $reply in
        y|yes)
              if    mkdir "$dir"
              then  chmod "$mode" "$dir"
                    MhCurmsg=1 MhLastmsg=1
                    return 1
              else  err_exit "cannot create folder +$MhFolder"
              fi
              ;;
        *)    exit 1;;
        esac
  fi
  return 0
}
```

set_folder

set_folder changes to a new folder if **MhFolder** is not the current folder. It calls **check_folder** if the folder does not already exist. Otherwise it reads the **.cur** file in the new folder. It does not update the **.master** file.

```
function set_folder
{
  typeset dir="$MhPath/$MhFolder"
  if    test "$MhFolder" != "$MhCurfolder"
  then  MhCurfolder=$MhFolder
        if    check_folder && test -r "$dir/.cur"
        then  . "$dir/.cur"
        fi
  fi
}
```

restore_env

restore_env updates the **.cur** file in the current folder and the **.master** file. Several commands specify this routine as a trap on **INT** and **EXIT**.

```
function restore_env
{
  print > $MhPath/.master "MhCurfolder=$MhCurfolder\
        MhCurmsg=$MhCurmsg \
        MhLastmsg=$MhLastmsg"
  print > $MhPath/$MhCurfolder/.cur\
        "MhCurmsg=$MhCurmsg\
        MhLastmsg=$MhLastmsg"
  rm -f /tmp/Mh*
}
```

read_header *mfile*

read_header reads the header portion of the message file *mfile* and gives values to the variables:

From   Second word on the first line beginning with **From** or **From:**.

Subject
        Remainder of the line starting with **Subject:**.

Cc   Remainder of the line starting with **cc:** or **Cc:** plus any continuation lines beginning with a Space or Tab.

Message_id
        Remainder of the line starting with **Message-id:**.

month and **day**
        These are set from the first line that contains a time stamp of the form **HH:MM:SS.**

value   Beginning of the body of the message. **read_header** uses the variable **size** to determine how many bytes of the message body it should read.

```
function read_header # msg_file
{
  typeset field= IFS= from='From[ :]*' \
      date='*[0-2][0-9]:[0-5][0-9]:[0-5][0-9]*'
  test  -r "$1" || err_exit "no current message"
  exec 3< $1
  while read -u3  -r
  do    case $REPLY in
        $from|$date)     IFS='   '; set -- $REPLY
            IFS=
            test "${1%:}" = From && From=${From-2}
            (($# > 7 )) || continue
            shift $#-5
```

```
            month=$2
            case $1 in
            [0-9]|[0-3][0-9])
                  day=$1
                  ;;
            *)
                  day=$3;;
            esac
            date=$from
            ;;
      Subject:*)
            Subject=${REPLY#Subject:}  field=subject
            ;;
      Message-Id:*)
            message_id=${REPLY#Message-Id:}  field=message
            ;;
      [Cc]c:*)
            Cc=${REPLY#[Cc]c:} field=cc
            ;;
      [Tt]o:*)
            To=${REPLY#[Tt]c:} field=to
            ;;
      *:*)     field=${REPLY%%:*}
            ;;
      [\ \     ]*)
            if    test "$field" = cc
            then  Cc="$Cc $REPLY"
            fi
            ;;
      *)  break;;
      esac
   done
   test "$Mh_size" || return
   Mh_size=Mh_size-${#Subject}-3
   while read -u3  -r && ((Mh_size>0))
   do    Mh_size=Mh_size-${#REPLY} \
         Mh_value="$Mh_value $REPLY"
   done
   exec 3<&-
}
```

scan_message *mfile* [*auditfile*]

scan_message formats and displays a one-line summary for the message
file **mfile** that is specified. **scan** and **inc** call this function.

scan_message uses **read_header** to extract the fields from the header
portion of the message.

inc allows you to specify *auditfile*, where a log of these one-line messages is kept for all incoming mail.

```
function scan_msg # msg_file [auditfile]
{
  set -o noglob
  typeset label Mh_value Subject Message_id
  typeset -Z2 day mon
  integer month Mh_size=${COLUMNS:-80}-31 \
      Jan=1 Feb=2 Mar=3 Apr=4 May=5 Jun=6 \
      Jul=7 Aug=8 Sep=9 Oct=10 Nov=11 Dec=12
  typeset -R4 n
  typeset -L1 flag=' '
  typeset -L17 From
  typeset -L$Mh_size message
  n=${1##*/}
  if    test "$MhCurmsg" = "${1##*/}"
  then  flag=+
  fi
  read_header $1
  message="$Subject  <<$Mh_value"
  print -r - "$n$flag ${mon=$month}/$day $From " $message
  if    test "$2"
  then  print -r - "$n  $month/$day $From "$message >> $2
  fi
}
```

back_to_prev [*n*]

back_to_prev is only called by the function **message_range**. It checks to see whether the message whose number is defined by the variable **MhFirst** exists. If it does, the function returns. If it does not, **ksh** keeps decrementing the **MhFirst** variable until a message by this number exists or it reaches the number 1.

back_to_prev assumes that you are in the correct folder when you call it.

```
function back_to_prev # [n]
{
  integer n=${1-1}
  while true
  do    until test -r $MhFirst || ((MhFirst <= 1))
        do    MhFirst=MhFirst-1
        done
        let n=n-1 || return
        MhFirst=MhFirst-1
  done
}
```

skip_to_next [*n*]

skip_to_next is only called by the function **message_range**. It checks to see whether the message whose number is defined by the variable **MhFirst** exists. If it does, the function returns. If it does not, **ksh** keeps incrementing the **MhFirst** variable until a message by this number exists or it reaches the **MhLastmsg** value.

skip_to_next assumes that you are in the correct folder when you call it.

```
function skip_to_next # [n]
{
  integer n=${1-1}
  while true
  do    until test -r $MhFirst || ((MhFirst >= MhLastmsg))
        do    MhFirst=MhFirst+1
        done
        let n=n-1 || return
        MhFirst=MhFirst+1
  done
}
```

set_message

set_message checks to see that only one message was specified and then sets **MhCurmsg** to the numerical value corresponding to this message.

```
function set_message
{
  case $MhMsgs in
  "")   ;;
  \ *\ *)
      err_exit 'only one (current) message at a time!'
  *)
      if    test "$Mhmsgs" != "$MhCurmsg"
      then  message_list '' $MhMsgs
            MhCurmsg=$MhFirst
      fi;;
  esac
}
```

message_list *action message...*

message_list sets the working directory to the current folder and then calls **message_range** for each *message* that is supplied.

action is the command or function to be executed for each message. *message* can be either a single message or a range.

```
function message_list # action messages
{
  typeset action="$1"
  if    \cd "$MhPath/$MhCurfolder"
  then  shift
        for i
        do    message_range "$i" "$action"
        done
  else  err_exit "$MhCurfolder: no such folder"
fi
}
```

message_range *message* [*command*]

message_range converts a message or a range of messages to numbers and sets the variables **MhFirst** and **MhLast**.

If *command* is specified, **message_range** calls *command* for each message from **MhFirst** to **MhLast**. **MhMsg** is set to the current message when *command* is called.

```
function message_range # message command
{
  integer last=0 skip=0
  typeset msg
  MhMsg=$1
  case $1 in # check for : modifier
  *:-[0-9]*)    # check for msg:-number
      msg=${1%:-*} skip=${1##*:}
      ;;
  *:[0-9]*)   # check for msg:number
      msg=${1%:*} skip=${1##*:}
      ;;
  *)
      msg=$1;;
  esac
  case $msg in
  *-*)   # check for a range, no : modifier allowed
      let skip && err_exit "bad message list $1"
      message_range ${msg#*-}
```

```
            last=MhFirst MhLast=MhFirst
            message_range ${msg%-*}
            ;;
all)
            MhFirst=1 MhLast=MhLastmsg last=MhLastmsg
            ;;
last)
        MhFirst=MhLastmsg
        back_to_prev
        if    ((skip>0))
        then  skip=-skip
        fi
        ;;
first)
        MhFirst=1
        skip_to_next
        ;;
next)
        MhFirst=MhCurmsg+1
        skip_to_next
        ;;
prev)
        MhFirst=MhCurmsg-1
        back_to_prev
        ;;
cur)
        MhFirst=MhCurmsg
        ;;
[1-9]*)
        MhFirst=$msg
        ;;
*)   err_exit "bad message list $1"
        ;;
esac
if    ((skip > 0))
then   last=MhFirst
        skip_to_next $skip
        MhFirst=last MhLast=MhFirst
elif  ((skip < 0))
then   last=MhFirst MhLast=MhFirst skip=-skip
        back_to_prev $skip
fi
test "$2" || return
set +o noglob
if    ((last>0)) && ((MhLast!=MhFirst)) # range
then  for i in [1-9] [1-9][0-9] [1-9][0-9][0-9] \
            [1-9][0-9][0-9][0-9]
      do    case $i in
            \[*|*-*)              ;;
```

```
              *)   if     ((i>=MhFirst)) && ((i<=MhLast))
                   then   $2 $i
                          last=$i
                   fi
                   ;;
              esac
        done
        MhLast=last
  else  $2 $MhFirst
        MhLast=MhFirst
  fi
}
```

folder_walk *folder*

folder_walk walks through *folder* and provides some statistics on messages in it. It is called by the **folder** and **folders** commands.

If the **pack** variable is set, then messages are renumbered sequentially from 1 up.

If the **recurse** variable is set, then **folder_walk** calls **folder_walk** for each directory in *folder*.

The working directory must be set to *folder* before this function is called.

folder_walk increments the variable **tfolder** and adds the number of messages in folder to variable **tmsg**.

```
function folder_walk # folder
{
  integer min=0 n=0 cur=0 max=0 newcurrent=0
  typeset -R4 nmsg first current last
  typeset -R22 folder=$1
  typeset other=
  typeset -L1 curf=' '
  if    test -r .cur
  then  . .cur
        cur=MhCurmsg
  fi
  if    test "$1" = "$MhCurfolder"
  then    curf=+
  fi
  set +o noglob
  for i in ? ?? ??? ???? ?????*
  do  case $i in
      [1-9]|[1-9][0-9]|[1-9][0-9][0-9]|[1-9][0-9][0-9][0-9])
            n=n+1
            if    test "$pack" && ((i!=n))
```

```
          then   if      ((i==cur))
                  then   newcur=n
                  fi
                  mv $i $n
          else   let min  || min=i
                  max=i
          fi
          ;;
     \*)  err_exit "$1 has no messages"
          ;;
     ,*|'?'|'??'|'???'|'????'|'?????*')
          ;;
     *)   if     test "$recurse" -a -d "$i"
          then   \cd "$i"
                  folder_walk "$1/$i"
                  \cd  ..
          fi
          other=';'
          ;;
    esac
done
if     test "$pack"
then   max=n min=1 cur=newcur
fi
((cur<=max))  || cur=0
print > .cur "MhCurmsg=$cur\tMhLastmsg=$max"
if     test "$curf" = +
then   print > $MhPath/.master "MhCurfolder=$1\
        MhCurmsg=$cur\tMhLastmsg=$max"
fi
print -rn - "$folder$curf has "
if     ((min))
then   nmsg=$n last=$max first=$min curf=s
        ((n==1)) && curf=' '
        print -rn - "$nmsg message$curf ($first-$last)"
else   print -rn "  no messages${other:+            }"
fi
if     test "$other" || let cur
then   if     ((cur))
        then   current=$cur
                print -rn - "; cur=$current$other"
        else     print -rn "$other            "
        fi
        test "$other" && print -rn - ' (others)'
fi
print .
tmsg=tmsg+n tfolder=tfolder+1
}
```

dispose_draft [*draft*]

dispose_draft is called by **comp** and **repl** when there is a draft that has not been sent.

dispose_draft uses a **select** list to present the user with the list of permitted responses. The user can reply by name or number.

```
function dispose_draft  # draft
{
  typeset draft=${1-$MhPath/draft}
  print -rn "Draft \"$draft\" exists ( "
  print -r - $(wc -c < $draft) bytes\).
  select disp in quit replace use list refile
  do   case $REPLY in
      [a-z]*)
          disp=$REPLY;;
      esac
      case $disp in
      q|quit)
          exit
          ;;
      rep|replace)
          ${MhRm-rm} "$draft"
          break
          ;;
      u|use)
           break
          ;;
      l|list)
          ${MhList-cat} "$draft"
          ;;
      ref|refile)
          read -r "fold?Folder? "
          if    refile "$draft" "+$fold"
          then  break
          fi
          ;;
      r|re)
          print -rn - "$i: ambiguous. "
          print "It matches\n\t-replace\n\t-refile"
          ;;
      esac
  done
}
```

form_letter *template file*

form_letter uses the *template* file to construct *file*.

form_letter generates a script in a temporary file that uses the contents of template as a here-document to the **cat** command. After it executes the temporary script it removes it.

```
function form_letter      # infile outfile
{
  typeset temp=/tmp/Mh$$
  if     test X"$message"
  then   print -r "cat > $2 <<!EOF!" > $temp
         cat "$1" >> $temp
         print -r  '!EOF!' >> $temp
  fi
  . $temp
  \rm -f $temp
}
```

what_now [*file*]

what_now presents the user with a choice of actions to take after the user has finished editing a draft.

```
function what_now      # file
{
  typeset i ifs file="${1-$MhPath/draft}" \
      nomail="no mail sent"
  if     test ! -r "$file"
  then   form_letter "$formfile" "$file"
  fi
  "${editor?No editor}" "$file"
  select i in edit list refile quit send
  do   case  $REPLY in
       [a-z]*)
            i=$REPLY;;
       esac
       case $i in
       e|edit)
            "${editor?No editor}" "$file"
            ;;
       l|list)
            ${MhList-cat} "$file"
            ;;
       r|ref|refile)
            read -r "i?MhFolder? "
            if      refile "$file" "+$i"
```

```
            then    break
            fi
            ;;
    q|quit)
        print -r "draft left on $file"
        return
        ;;
    s|send)
        read_header "$file"
        IFS='    ,:' ifs=$IFS
        set -- $To $Cc
        IFS=$ifs
        if    test ! "$To"
        then  err_exit "no addressees, $nomail"
        fi
        print - "\n$MhSignature" >> $file
        if    mail $* < $file
        then  \rm -f "$file"
              break
        else  print "$MhCommand: mail failed, $nomail"
        fi
        ;;
    *)  print -r - "$i unknown. Hit <CR> for help."
        ;;
    esac
  done
}
```

inc [+*folder*] [−**audit** *auditfile*]

inc reads your **MAIL** file and creates a file for each message in an MH folder. If you do not specify +*folder*, then MH uses the +**inbox** folder.

If specified, **inc** will use the **MhFile_protect** variable to set the permission on each message. Otherwise, the MH default of 644 will be used.

If you specify *auditfile*, then **inc** appends a scan message to this file for each message. This is useful for keeping track of the volume and source of incoming mail.

The new messages being incorporated are assigned numbers starting with the next highest number in the folder. As the messages are processed, **inc** displays a scan listing (in the same format as **scan**) of the new mail.

```
# inc - incorporate new mail
set -o noglob
MhCommand=${0##*}
typeset -fx check_args || . mh_init
```

```
trap   restore_env EXIT INT
check_setup
auditfile=$MhAuditfile \
      MhFolder=inbox \
      MhSwitches='-audit=auditfile'
check_args "$@"
MAIL=${MAIL-/usr/spool/mail/${HOME##*/}}
# see if there is any mail to incorporate
if     test ! -s "$MAIL"
then   err_exit "no mail to incorporate"
fi
# check validity
dir=$MhPath/$MhFolder
if     test "x$MAIL" = x -o ! -f "$MAIL"
then   err_exit "no mail file"
fi
# construct auditfile name
case $auditfile in
/*|"")
      ;;
*)  auditfile=$MhPath/$auditfile
     ;;
esac
check_folder
set_folder
MhCurmsg=MhLastmsg+1
# process each mail message
print "Incorporating mail into +$MhFolder"
while test -s "$MAIL"
do     let MhLastmsg=MhLastmsg+1
       mail -f ${MAIL} > /dev/null <<-!
       s $dir/$MhLastmsg
       !
       chmod ${MhFile_protect-644} "$dir/$MhLastmsg"
       scan_msg "$dir/$MhLastmsg" "$auditfile"
done
```

show [+*folder*] [*msgs*] [**−draft**]
prev [+*folder*] [*msgs*]
next [+*folder*] [*msgs*]

show displays each of the *msgs* you specify on standard output. The
messages are displayed exactly as they are, with no reformatting. **show**
displays the current message if you do not specify *msgs*.

If you specify the **MhList** variable in your Mh profile, it uses it instead of
cat to display the messages.

prev is equivalent to **show prev**. **next** is equivalent to **show next**.

If you specify +*folder*, it displays messages from this folder and then makes this the current folder. The last message displayed becomes the current message.

If you specify **–draft** with **show**, then the current draft is displayed.

```
# show - show mail message
set -o noglob
MhCommand=${0##*/}
typeset -fx check_args || . mh_init
trap   restore_env EXIT
function print_msg # message
{
   if    test ! -r $1
   then  err_exit "$MhMsg: no such message"
   else  print "(Message $MhFolder:$1)"
         ${MhList-cat} $1
   fi
}
check_setup
MhFolder=${MhCurfolder:-inbox}
case $MhCommand in
prev|next)
      MhMsg=$MhCommand
      ;;
*)
      MhMsg=cur;;
esac
if    test show = "$MhCommand"
then  MhSwitches='-draft'
fi
check_args "$@"
# check validity
if    test "$MhList" -a ! -x "$MhList"
then  err_exit "$MhList: No such executable"
fi
if    test "$draft"
then  if    test -r "$MhPath/draft"
      then  ${MhList-cat} "$MhPath/draft"
      else  err_exit "$MhPath/draft: No such file" \
            "or directory"
      fi
fi
set_folder
trap restore_env INT
message_list print_msg ${MhMsgs-$MhMsg}
MhCurmsg=MhLast
```

scan [*+folder*] [*msgs*] [**−**[**no**]**header**]

scan displays a one-line-per-message listing of the specified messages. Each scan line contains the message number, the date, the "From" field, the "Subject" field, and, if room allows, some of the body of the message.

If you specify **−header**, then **scan** displays a header containing the names of each of the fields.

```
# scan - produce a one-line-per-message scan listing
set -o noglob
MhCommand=${0##*/}
typeset -fx check_args || . mh_init
trap  restore_env EXIT
check_setup
MhFolder=$MhCurfolder MhMsg=all MhSwitches=-header-
check_args "$@"
# check validity
set_folder
if    test "$header"
then  print "Folder $MhFolder\t\t\t\t$(date)\n"
fi
message_list scan_msg ${MhMsgs-all}
```

rmm [*+folder*] [*msgs*]

rmm removes the messages specified by *msgs*. **rmm** does not change the current message.

If you specify *+folder*, it removes messages from this folder and then makes this the current folder.

```
# rmm - remove messages
set -o noglob
MhCommand=${0##*/}
typeset -fx check_args || . mh_init
trap  restore_env EXIT
function rm_msg # message
{
  if    test ! -r $1
  then  err_exit "$MhMsg: no such message"
  else  ${MhRm-rm} -f $1
  fi
}
check_setup
MhFolder=inbox MhMsg=cur
check_args "$@"
```

```
# check validity
set_folder
message_list rm_msg ${MhMsgs-cur}
```

comp [−**editor** *editor*] [−**form** *formfile*] [−[**no**]**use**]

comp creates a new message to be mailed.

The file *formfile* can be used to override the default skeleton formfile
.std_form. This also overrides the **MhStdform** variable, if any, in your
MH profile file.

If a draft of the message already exists, **comp** asks if you want to delete it
before continuing.

```
# comp - compose mail
set -o noglob
MhCommand=${0##*/}
typeset -fx check_args || . mh_init
trap  restore_env EXIT INT
check_setup
MhFolder=$MhCurfolder MhMsg=cur
formfile=${MhStdform-$MhPath/.std_form}
editor=${MhEditor-${VISUAL-${EDITOR-ed}}}
MhSwitches="-draft=folder -form=formfile \
            -editor=editor -use-"
check_args "$@"
# check validity
set_folder
set_message
draft=$MhPath/draft
PS3=Disposition?
if    test -r "$draft" -a ! "$use"
then  dispose_draft "$draft"
fi
PS3="What now? "
what_now "$draft"
```

repl [+*folder*] [*msg*] [−**editor** *editor*]

repl aids a user in producing a reply to an existing message. If you do not
specify arguments, it sets up a message form skeleton in reply to the
current message in the current folder, invokes an editor on the message,
and sends the composed message if so directed.

If you specify +*folder*, it replies to a message from this folder and then
makes this the current folder.

If you specify *msg*, it replies to this message and then makes this the current message.

```
# repl - reply to mail
set -o noglob
MhCommand=${0##*/}
typeset -fx check_args || . mh_init
trap  restore_env EXIT
check_setup
MhFolder=$MhCurfolder MhMsg=cur
formfile=${MhStdform-$MhPath/.std_form}
editor=${MhEditor-${VISUAL-${EDITOR-ed}}}
MhSwitches='-draft=folder -form=formfile -editor=editor'
check_args "$@"
# check validity
set_folder
print -r - "$MhPath/$MhCurfolder/$MhCurmsg"
draft=$MhPath/draft
PS3=Disposition?
if    test -r "$draft"
then  dispose_draft "$draft"
fi
PS3="What now? "
read_header "$MhPath/$MhCurfolder/$MhCurmsg"
what_now "$draft"
```

folder [*+folder*] [*msg*] [−[**no**]**pack**] [−[**no**]**header**]
folders [*+folder*] [*msg*] [−[**no**]**pack**] [−[**no**]**header**]

folder displays the current folder, the number of messages in it, the range of messages (low-high), and the current message within the current folder.

If you specify *+folder* and/or *msg*, they become the current folder and/or message.

The **−pack** switch compresses the message numbers in a folder, removing holes in the message numbering.

```
# folder - set or print information about folder
integer tfolder=0 tmsg=0
set -o noglob
MhCommand=${0##*/}
typeset -fx check_args || . mh_init
check_setup
MhFolder=$MhCurfolder MhMsg=$MhCurmsg
MhSwitches='-all -fast- -header- -pack- -recurse'
# check validity
check_args "$@"
```

```
if     test "$MhFolder" != "$MhCurfolder"
then   set_folder
fi
set_message
restore_env
if     test "$MhCommand" = folders -o "$header"
then   print -n "\t\tFolder      # of messages "
       print "range  ); cur  msg  (other files)"
fi
if     test "$MhCommand" = folders
then   cd "$MhPath" || err_exit "no $MhPath folder"
       set +o noglob
       for i in *
       do     if     test -d "$i"
              then   cd "$i"
                     folder_walk "$i"
                     cd ..
              fi
       done
       print -n "\n\t\t   TOTAL= $tmsg messages "
       print -r "in $tfolder folders."
else   if     cd "$MhPath/$MhFolder"
       then   folder_walk "$MhCurfolder"
       else   err_exit "$MhFolder: no such folder"
       fi
fi
```

refile [**–src** +*folder*] +*folder*... [*msgs*] [**–**[**no**]**link**]

refile moves or copies messages from a source folder into one or more destination folders.

If the destination folder doesn't exist, refile asks you if you want to create one. **refile** exits if you specify a negative response.

If you specify **–src** +*folder*, then it becomes the current folder for future MH commands.

```
# refile - file messages
set -o noglob
MhCommand=${0##*/}
typeset -fx check_args || . mh_init
function file_msg # message
{
   if     test ! -r "$1"
   then   err_exit "$MhMsg: no such message"
   fi
   for MhFolder in $folders
   do if    check_folder && test -r "$MhPath/$MhFolder/.cur"
```

```
        then  .  "$MhPath/$MhFolder/.cur"
              MhLastmsg=MhLastmsg+1
        fi
        while test -f $MhPath/$MhFolder/$MhLastmsg
        do    MhLastmsg=MhLastmsg+1
        done
        ${MhLink-ln} "$1" "$MhPath/$MhFolder/$MhLastmsg" ||
              cp "$1" "$MhPath/$MhFolder/$MhLastmsg"
    done
    test  "$link" || ${MhRm-rm} "$1"
}
check_setup
MhMsg=cur MhMany=yes
MhSwitches='-src=folder -draft -link-'
check_args "$@"
folders=$MhFolder
test    "$folders"  ||  err_exit "no folder specified"
if      test "$folder"
then    MhFolder=${folder#+}
        set_folder
fi
restore_env
message_list file_msg ${MhMsgs-cur}
```

.std_form

This is a copy of the form that is used with **comp** to compose mail, and
with **repl** to reply to messages. Note that this file is a form letter and is
processed as a here-document.

```
To: ${From}
cc: ${Cc}
Subject: ${Subject+Re:}${Subject}
--------
```

mh_init

The following code is in the common function file with the other function
definitions. It declares some global integer variables, and also declares all
the functions.

```
# This code gets executed first
typeset -ix MhCurmsg MhLastmsg MhFirst MhLast
typeset -fx err_exit check_setup check_args restore_env\
        read_header scan_msg message_range set_message \
        set_folder check_folder message_list folder_walk \
        skip_to_next back_to_prev what_now form_letter \
        dispose_draft
```

.Mhprofile

The following code is an example of an MH profile. It defines variables used by the MH programs.

```
# profile for ksh version of MH
MhPath=$HOME/mailbag
MhFolder_protect=711
MhMessage_protect=600
MhSignature="David Korn\nulysses!dgk"
MhAuditfile=$MhPath/.auditfile
MhList=/usr/ucb/more
```

EXERCISES

1. Modify the MH application in each of the following ways:
    a. Use new features in the 11/16/88 version of **ksh** to allow message numbers greater than 9999.
    b. Change **rmm** so that it moves each message to a subdirectory named **.trashcan**. Add an **unrmm** command to restore messages from **.trashcan**. Add an option to **folders** to remove all messages in each **.trashcan** directory that is more than a day old.
    c. Allow the "To address" field to also be the name of a file containing a distribution list. Send the mail to everyone on the distribution list. Allow a distribution list to contain distribution lists.
    d. Add an option to include the original letter, without the header, as part of the reply template. The original message should have > prepended to each line.
    e. Add an option to **refile** that allows you to annotate a message, using your editor, before you file it. The annotation should be appended to the message.
    f. Write a script that produces a scan listing of all messages in a given folder, or all folders that contain a given keyword. The match for the keyword should be case insensitive.
    g. Add the ability to send form letters to a distribution list, with fields such as the user's name different for each letter.

2. Write a program to archive files so that they can be restored or moved to a new location. The program should create a file that contains the contents of files in the specified directories and its subdirectories. The file should be in the format of a **ksh** script so that when the script is run, it recreates the directory hierarchy. The program should preserve the access permissions on all files. There should be an option to archive only those files newer than a specified file.

3. Write software to conduct an electronic survey. Assume that each recipient runs **ksh**. The program should take a file containing questions and choices for answers, and construct a **ksh** script and form letter to mail to each recipient. The form letter should instruct the recipient to run the generated script . The generated script should ask the user each of the questions, gather the results, and send the results back. The generated script should allow the recipient to use the built-in editors while answering questions. It should also allow the user to add comments using the editor defined by the value of the user's **VISUAL** or **EDITOR** variable. Also, write a script that reads and processes the return mail and produces a summary of responses for each question.

4. Write a system for distributing software electronically with the following features:
    a. There is a database with an account for each potential recipient. The database should contain a variable amount of information about each user, including the user's name, electronic address, telephone number, etc. Write a program to add, delete, and change entries in this database.
    b. The software should bundle all the files, including a script that builds and installs the software, into a single file using the archive program of exercise 2 or a similar program.
    c. The program should generate a form letter to send to the recipient explaining the contents of the shipment and instructions for unbundling it.
    d. The software should run the script to build the software, send a message back to the sender that indicates whether the software build was successful, and that reports any problems it encountered.
    e. Include the program that bundles and sends the software as part of the distribution. Allow recipients to forward the software to other users. The program should send a carbon copy of the completion message to the originator of the software.

5. Write a program that plays draw poker. Your program must be able to shuffle cards, deal cards, handle betting, determine winning hands, and keep track of bets.

PART VI

APPENDIX

19 GLOSSARY

Alias. A name used as an abbreviation for one or more commands. An alias enables you to replace a command name with any desired character sequence.

- *Exported alias*. An alias that does not get removed when **ksh** runs a script by name.
- *Preset alias*. An alias that is already defined by **ksh** itself whenever it is invoked.
- *Tracked alias*. Not really an alias. Its value gets set to the pathname of a program the first time the program is run. It is used to reduce the time **ksh** spends locating a program on subsequent requests.

Array. A variable indexed by a subscript.

Attribute. Characteristics optionally associated with a variable, such as readonly or uppercase.

Built-in command. A command processed by **ksh** itself. Its code is internal to **ksh**.

Built-in editor. Command line editors that are part of **ksh** itself. There are two of them, **emacs** and **vi**.

Command. An action for **ksh** to perform. A command can be a:
- *Simple command*.
  - Variable assignment.
  - I/O redirection.
  - Built-in command.
  - ((...)) Arithmetic evaluation.
  - Function.
  - Program.
- *Compound command*.
  - Pipeline.
  - Iteration command.
  - Conditional command.

Command substitution. A word or part of a word can be replaced by the output of a command.

Delimiter-word. The word that defines the string that ends a here-document.

Directive. A command processed by the **emacs** or **vi** built-in editor.

Directory. A file that contains filenames or directory names.
- Bin directory. A directory where programs are stored.
- Home directory. Your working directory when you log in.
- Root directory. The top level directory, named **/**.
- Subdirectory. A directory that exists in another directory.
- Working directory. Each pathname that does not begin with a **/** is defined relative to this directory. Each process has a working directory.

Environment. The state of a process, including such information as its open files, working directory, file creation mask, and local and global variables.
- *Child environment*. The environment of a child process.
- *Current environment*. The environment of the current process.
- *Parent environment*. The environment of the parent process.
- *Subshell environment*. The environment of a subshell.

Environment file. A script that gets read and executed whenever **ksh** begins execution.

Export. To pass a variable to a child process.

File. An object that can be read from and/or written to, and/or executed.

File creation mask. A number that represents which permissions should be denied whenever a user creates a file.

File descriptor. A small number associated with an open file.

Filter. A command that reads from its standard input and writes to its standard output.

Flag. A command option, usually indicated by a single letter preceded by a −.

Function. A command that consists of a list of **ksh** commands. Once a function is defined, it is executed when its name is referenced.

Group id. Each user is a member of one or more groups, each of which is identified by a number called the group id.
- *Effective group id*. Each process has an id which defines its permissions with respect to group access of files.
- *Real group id*. Each process has the group id of the actual user.

Here-document. Lines of a script that represent the standard input of a command in the script itself.

History file. The file in which **ksh** saves each command that you enter interactively. You can edit and reenter commands in the history file.

Identifier. A string of characters starting with a letter or an underscore, and containing only letters, digits, or underscores.

Interpreter. A program that reads commands from a terminal or a file, and executes them.

Interrupt. A signal, typically generated by the keyboard. It causes the current executing process to terminate unless a trap was specified to handle the signal.

I/O redirection. The process of changing the file associated with one or more file descriptors.

Job. A synonym for a pipeline initiated by an interactive shell.
- *Background job*. A job running in a process group not associated with your terminal.
- *Foreground job*. A job running in the process group associated with your terminal.
- *Job control*. The ability to stop jobs and switch them from foreground to background and vice-versa.

Link. Each directory entry is called a link. A file may have several links to it.

Option. A setting that affects the behavior of **ksh**.

Parameter. An entity that holds a value in the **ksh** language. Also see variable.
- *Named parameter*. A parameter denoted by an identifier. A shell variable.
- *Parameter expansion*. Replacing the parameter with its value.
- *Parameter modifier*. An operation which is applied while expanding a parameter.
- *Positional parameter*. A parameter designated by a number.
- *Special parameter*. A parameter whose name is **$, #, @, !, –,** or **∗**.

Path search. The means of finding the pathname of a program that corresponds to the program name.

Pathname. A string that is used to identify a file.

Pathname completion. The means of generating all the pathnames that match a given pattern.

Pathname expansion. The means of replacing a pattern with the list of pathnames that match the pattern.

Pattern. A string of characters that consists of literal characters that match only themselves, and pattern characters that match one or more characters.

Permission. The rights that you have to read, write, and/or execute a file, or to read, write, and/or search a directory.

Permission string. A string of 10 characters that is used to represent access permissions.

Pipe. A conduit in which a stream of characters can pass from one process to another. Each end of a pipe is associated with a file descriptor. A process will stop and wait for input if it reads from an empty pipe or writes to a full pipe.

Pipeline. One or more processes connected together by pipes.

Process. A single thread of execution that consists of a program and an execution environment.
- *Child process*. The new process created by a process.
- *Co-process*. A process created by **ksh** that has its input and output connected to **ksh** by pipes.
- *Parent process*. A process that creates a child process.
- *Process group*. Each active process is a member of a group identified by the process group id.
- *Process group id*. The process group id of the first process that starts a new process group.
- *Process id*. Each active process is uniquely identified with a positive integer called the process id.

Profile. A file containing shell commands. The file is executed when you log into the system.

Prompt. A message that an interactive **ksh** displays when it is ready to read input.

Protective mode. An option that is set when **ksh** runs with its real user id not equal to its effective user id, or with its real group id not equal to its effective group id.

Quoting. A mechanism to enable special characters to take their literal meaning.

Reserved word. A word that is reserved as part of the **ksh** grammar. Reserved words are recognized as reserved words only in certain contexts.

Restricted shell. An option which when set, limits the set of commands that can be executed.

Return value. A number from 0 to 255 that is returned by each command. A value of zero represents a True (successful) exit.

Script. A program written in the **ksh** language. A dot script is a script that is read and executed in the current environment.

Signal. An asynchronous message that consists of a number that can be sent from one process to another. It can also be sent from the operating system to a process when the user presses certain keys, or when an exceptional condition arises.

Standard error. The file associated with file descriptor 2. By convention, programs display all error messages on this descriptor.

Standard input. The file associated with file descriptor 0. Programs usually read their input from this descriptor.

Standard output. The file associated with file descriptor 1. Programs often write their output to this descriptor.

Subscript. An arithmetic expression contained in brackets after a variable name that evaluates to an index.

Subshell. A child shell that initially contains a copy of the parent shell environment.

Superuser. A user id that is not restricted by file permissions.

Terminal control characters. Keyboard characters that are processed specially by the system to erase input, to stop and restart output, and to send signals. The terminal control characters and their defaults are listed on page 11.

Tilde expansion. **ksh** expands certain words that begin with a ~.

Token. **ksh** splits its input into units called tokens.

Trap. A specification for an action for **ksh** to perform when a given condition occurs. An example of a condition is the receipt of a signal.

User id. Each user is identified by an integer called the user id.
- *Effective user id*. Each process has an id which defines its rights to access files and to send signals to other processes.
- *Real user id*. Each process remembers the id of the actual user.

Variable. A shell parameter denoted by an identifier.
- *Array variable*. A variable that is indexed by a subscript.
- *Variable assignment*. A command that assigns a value to a variable.

Word. A word is any token that is not one of the operators defined on page 124, a here-document, or a Newline.

Word splitting. After parameter expansion and command substitution, **ksh** splits words into command arguments.

---

20 QUICK REFERENCE

Page references to the book are at the right.

emacs *BUILT-IN EDITOR*		
√ means directive can be preceded by $\boxed{\text{ESCAPE}}$ *n*, where *n* is a number.		
Moving the Cursor		
√ $\boxed{\text{CONTROL}}$ **f**	(forward) Moves cursor right 1 (*n*) character(s).	92
√ $\boxed{\text{CONTROL}}$ **b**	(back) Moves cursor left 1 (*n*) character(s).	92
√ $\boxed{\text{ESCAPE}}$ **f**	(forward) Moves cursor right to 1st character past end of current (*n*th) word.	92
√ $\boxed{\text{ESCAPE}}$ **b**	(back) Moves cursor left to start of (*n*th) word.	92
$\boxed{\text{CONTROL}}$ **a**	Moves cursor to start of line.	93
$\boxed{\text{CONTROL}}$ **e**	(end) Moves cursor to end of line.	93
$\boxed{\text{CONTROL}}$ **]** *c*	Moves cursor to next character *c* on current line.	93
Deleting		
√ *Erase*	Deletes preceding 1 (*n*) character(s).	93
Kill	Deletes entire line. Subsequent *Kills* move cursor to start of next line.	94
$\boxed{\text{CONTROL}}$ **k**	(kill) Deletes from cursor to end of current line.	94
$\boxed{\text{ESCAPE}}$ *n* $\boxed{\text{CONTROL}}$ **k**	(kill) Deletes if *n* is to left or right of cursor: Left, from *n* up to, but not including, cursor. Right, from cursor up to, but not including, *n*.	94
√ $\boxed{\text{CONTROL}}$ **d**	(delete) Deletes 1 (*n*) character(s).	94
√ $\boxed{\text{ESCAPE}}$ **d**	(delete) Deletes from cursor to end of current (to right) 1 (*n*) word(s).	94
√ $\boxed{\text{ESCAPE}}$ $\boxed{\text{CONTROL}}$ **h** or $\boxed{\text{ESCAPE}}$ $\boxed{\text{CONTROL}}$ **?** or $\boxed{\text{ESCAPE}}$ **h**	Deletes from current cursor to back to start of current (to left) 1 (*n*) word(s).	95
$\boxed{\text{CONTROL}}$ **w**	(wipe out) Deletes line, from cursor to mark.	95
Marking, Yanking, and Putting		
$\boxed{\text{ESCAPE}}$ $\boxed{\text{SPACE}}$	Sets mark at location of cursor.	95
$\boxed{\text{ESCAPE}}$ **p**	(push) Saves region from cursor to mark, and "pushes" into buffer for use with $\boxed{\text{CONTROL}}$ **y**.	96
$\boxed{\text{CONTROL}}$ **y**	Restores last text deleted from line at cursor.	96
$\boxed{\text{CONTROL}}$ **x** $\boxed{\text{CONTROL}}$ **x**	(exchange) Interchanges cursor and mark.	95

Miscellaneous

	CONTROL t	(transpose) **emacs** transposes current with next character; **gmacs**, with 2 previous characters.	96
√	CONTROL c	(change) Changes current (*n*) character to uppercase; moves cursor to right 1 (*n*) characters.	96
√	ESCAPE c	Changes from current cursor to end of current (*n*th) word to uppercase. Moves cursor to next (*n*th) word.	97
√	ESCAPE l	(lowercase) Changes from cursor to end of current (*n*th) word to lowercase. Moves cursor to next (*n*th) word.	97
	CONTROL l	(line redraw) Moves to next line; displays current line. Use to redraw current line if screen garbled.	97
	End-of-file	End of file only if 1st character on line.	97
	CONTROL j or CONTROL m	Executes current line.	98
	ESCAPE =	Lists pathnames matching current word as if * appended to current word.	98
	ESCAPE *	Pathname expansion.	98
	ESCAPE ESCAPE	Pathname completion.	98
	CONTROL u	Multiplies count of next directive by **4**.	99
	\	Escapes next character.	99
	CONTROL v	(version) Displays version date of **ksh**. Press any key to resume entering commands.	99
	ESCAPE *letter*	(macro expander) Searches alias list for alias _*letter*. *letter* must not be **f**, **b**, **d**, **p**, **l**, **c**, or **h**.	99
√	ESCAPE . or ESCAPE _	(dot or underscore). Inserts on line, last (*n*th) word of previous **ksh** command.	100

History Directives

√	CONTROL p	(previous) Fetches previous (*n*th) line back in history file. Each time you press CONTROL p, the previous line is accessed.	100
	CONTROL o	(operate) Processes current line; fetches next line from history file. Repeat for multiline commands.	101
	ESCAPE <	Fetches least recent (oldest) history file line. Cannot go back more commands than defined by **HISTSIZE**.	100
	ESCAPE >	Fetches most recent (one you input last) line.	100
√	CONTROL n	(next) Moves down (forward) in history file. Fetches next 1 (*n*th) line forward from most recent line fetched.	101
√	CONTROL r [[^] *string*] RETURN	Searches backwards in history file for 1st occurrence of command line with *string*. Specifying ^ requires command line to begin with *string*. If *string* is omitted, fetches next command line with most recent *string*. Specifying *n* reverses the direction of the search.	101

vi *BUILT-IN EDITOR*		
√ means directive can be preceded by a number *n*.		

Input Mode

Erase	Deletes preceding character.	106
Kill	Deletes line.	106
`CONTROL` v	Next character processed with literal meaning.	106
\	*Erase* and *Kill* processed with literal meaning.	106
`CONTROL` w	(word) Deletes previous input vi-word.	107
End-of-file	Returns end of file only if 1st character on line.	106

Control Directives

`RETURN`	Executes **ksh** current line.	107
`CONTROL` l	(line redraw) Moves to next line. Displays current line.	107
#	Inserts # and enters command as a comment.	108
=	Lists pathnames that match current word.	108
\	Pathname completion.	108
*	Pathname expansion.	109
@*letter*	Macro substitution of alias named _*letter*.	109
√ ~	Upper/lowercase. Moves 1 (*n*) character(s) right.	109
√ .	Repeats 1 (*n*) time(s), most recent **vi** directive that changed current or previous command.	109
√ v	Invokes **vi** program with designated command.	109

Control Mode — Moving the Cursor

√ l or `SPACE`	Moves right 1 (*n*) character(s).	110
√ w	(word) Moves right to start of next (*n*th) vi-word.	110
√ W	(Word) Moves right to start of next (*n*th) vi-WORD.	110
√ e	(end) Moves right to next (*n*th) end of vi-word.	110
√ E	(End) Moves right to next (*n*th) end of vi-WORD.	110
√ h	Moves left 1 (*n*) character(s).	111
√ b	(back) Moves left to preceding (*n*th) start of vi-word.	111
√ B	(Back) Moves left to preceding (*n*th) start of vi-WORD.	111
^	Moves left to 1st character on line not Space or Tab.	111
0	(zero) Moves left to 1st character on line.	111
$	Moves right to last character on line.	112
√ |	Moves to next (*n*th) character on line. Default is 1.	112

Control Mode — Moving to Character

√ **f***c*	(find) Moves right to next (*n*th) *c*.	112
√ **F***c*	(Find) Moves left to preceding (*n*th) *c*.	112
√ **t***c*	(to) Moves right to character before next (*n*th next) *c*.	112
√ **T***c*	(Back **T**o) Moves left to character after preceding (*n*th preceding) *c*.	113
√ ;	Repeats most recent **f**, **F**, **t**, or **T** directive once (or *n* times).	113
√ ,	As above, but reverses direction to original directive.	113

Control Mode — Adding and Changing Text

Type directive (puts you into input mode) and type text to append or insert.
Press ⎡ESCAPE⎤ to return to control mode or ⎡RETURN⎤ to execute command.
motion consists of the text from the current cursor position to the cursor
position defined by **Moving the Cursor** or **Moving to Character** directives.

	a	(**append**) Appends to right of cursor.	113
	A	(**Append**) Appends to end of current line.	114
	i	(**insert**) Inserts to left of cursor.	114
	I	(**Insert**) Inserts to left of 1st character not Space or Tab.	114
	R	(**Replace**) Replaces.	114
√	**c***motion*	(**change**) Changes to the text you type, characters starting at cursor up to other end of specified *motion*. You can put *n* before or after **c**.	114
	C	(**Change**) Deletes current character through end of line, and enters input mode. Same as **c$**.	115
	S	(**Substitute**) Deletes entire line and enters input mode. Same as **cc**.	115

Control Mode — Replace

√	**r***c*	(**replace**) Replaces with *c*, 1 (*n*) character(s) starting at cursor. Cursor positioned on last character changed.	115
√	**_**	(**underscore**) Appends last word (or *n*th) vi-WORD from previous command, and enters input mode.	116

Control Mode — X/Delete

motion consists of the text from the current cursor position to the cursor
position defined by **Moving the Cursor** or **Moving to Character** directives.

√	**x**	(**x-ing out**) Deletes 1 (*n*) character(s) at cursor.	116
√	**X**	(**X-ing out**) Deletes 1 (*n*) character(s) to left of cursor.	116
√	**d***motion*	(**delete**) Deletes 1 (*n*) character starting at cursor up to and including other end specified by *motion*. Saves characters in buffer. Retrieve with **u**ndo or **p**ut. You can put *n* before or after **d**.	116
	D	(**Delete**) Deletes from cursor to end of line.	117
	dd	(**delete**) Deletes entire command, no matter where cursor is on line.	117

		Control Mode — Yank/Put	

motion consists of the text from the current cursor position to the cursor position defined by **Moving the Cursor** or **Moving to Character** directives.

√	y*motion*	(**y**ank) Yanks current character through character that *n motion* would move cursor to; stores characters in buffer for subsequent use with **p** or **P**. Text and cursor not changed. You can put *n* before or after **y**.	117
	Y	(**Y**ank) Yanks from cursor to end of line. Same as y$.	117
	yy	(**y**ank) Yanks (copies) entire current line into buffer, no matter where cursor is on line.	117
√	**p**	(**p**ut) Puts previously yanked or deleted text (or *n* copies of yanked text) to right of cursor.	117
√	**P**	(**P**ut) Same as above, but to left.	118

Control Mode — Undo

	u	(**u**ndo) Undoes preceding text-modifying directive.	118
	U	(**U**ndo line) Undoes all text modifying directives made on current line. Use **u** to undo **U**.	118

Fetching Previous Commands

√	**k** or **–**	(minus) Moves up (back) to fetch (*n*th) preceding command. Each time you enter **k**, preceding command back is fetched.	119
√	**j** or **+**	(plus) Moves down (forward) to fetch (*n*th) next command. Each time you enter **j**, next command forward is fetched.	119
√	**G**	(**G**o back) Fetches oldest accessible command, or command *n* from start of history file.	119
	/*string* `RETURN`	Moves left and up (back) through history file to search for most recent occurrence of *string*. Null *string*: Previous string specified is used.	119
	/^*string* `RETURN`	Same as /*string*, except matches *string* only if it is at beginning of line.	119
	?*string* `RETURN`	Same as above, but searches in reverse direction, right and down (forward).	120
	?^*string* `RETURN`	Same as ?*string*, except matches *string* only if it is at beginning of line.	120
	n	Repeats most recent / or ? directive.	120
	N	As above, but in reverse direction.	120

SPECIAL CHARACTERS

| & ; < > ( ) $ ` \ " ' Space Tab Newline
When patterns are processed * ? [ ]
When they begin a new word # ~
When variable assignments are processed = [ ]   124

COMMENTS

Begin with unquoted # sign, and go to next Newline.
Legal anywhere token may begin.   124

IDENTIFIERS

a-z A-Z 0-9 _ (underscore)
First character cannot be a digit.
No limit on number of characters.
Uppercase and lowercase characters are distinct.   125

ALIAS NAMES

First character is any non-special printable character.
Other characters are same as for identifiers (see above).
Aliases whose names are of form _letter_ define macros for **emacs** and **vi**
built-in editors.
See aliases, and **alias**.   126

VARIABLE ASSIGNMENTS

identifier=value
identifier[expression]=value   126

OPERATORS

I/O redirection operators: > >> >& >| < << <<- <& < >
Control operators: | & ; ( ) || && ;; (( )) |&   124

RESERVED WORDS

{ } case do done elif else esac fi for function if in select
then time until while [[ ]]
ksh recognizes only:
    As first word on line.
    After operators ; | || & && |& ( ).
    As 1st word after reserved word, except after **case**, **for**, **in**, **select**, [[.
    As second word after **case**, **for**, **select**. However, **in** is the only legal
    reserved word in this case.   125

PATTERNS
Regular Characters

Regular characters are all those characters that are not pattern characters.
Regular characters match themselves.
Quote with a \ any special characters to use them as regular characters.   126

Pattern Characters

[...]	Delimits set of characters.	127
	– (minus) Within [], indicates range of characters. Stands for itself after opening [, after ! following [, or before closing].	
	! Immediately after opening [, reverses the match.	
	] Stands for itself after opening [, or after ! following opening [.	
	\ Removes special meaning of –,], !, and \.	
?	Matches any single character.	127
*	Matches zero or more occurrences of any and all characters.	128
?(*pattern* [|*pattern*])		
	Optionally matches any *pattern* between ( ).	128
*(*pattern* [|*pattern*])		
	Matches zero or more occurrences of any *pattern* between ( ).	128
+(*pattern* [|*pattern*])		
	Matches one or more occurrences of any *pattern* between ( ).	128
!(*pattern* [|*pattern*])		
	Matches averything except any *pattern* between ( ).	128

QUOTING/GROUPING

\	Escape Character	133
\Newline	Line Continuation	133
'...'	Literal (Single) Quotes	133
"..."	Grouping (Double) Quotes	134
`...`	Old Command Substitution	134
$(...)	New Command Substitution	135
${...}	Parameter Expansion	135
((...))	Arithmetic Evaluation	135
identifier[...]=	Array Variable Assignment	135

I/O REDIRECTION

Operator can be preceded by 0-9, with no intervening Space or Tab.			136
Standard input	File descriptor 0 open for reading.		
Standard output	File descriptor 1 open for writing.		
Standard error	File descriptor 2 open for reading or writing.		18
< word		Reading	136
> word	*>	word*	Writing	138
<< word	*<<– word*	Here-Document	137
<& word	*>& word*	Duplicating Input/Output	138, 139
<> word		Reading/Writing	138
>> word		Appending	139

SIGNALS

Always needed:	Supported for job control:
Interrupt (**INT**)	Keyboard stop (**TSTP**)
Quit (**QUIT**)	Tty input (**TTIN**)
Hangup (**HUP**)	Continue (**CONT**)
Termination (**TERM**)	Stop (**STOP**)
Kill (**KILL**)	21

PERMISSIONS

File can have these permissions:
   Read, Write, and/or Execute, by owner, group, and/or others.
   Setuid and/or setgid
Specify with 4-digit octal number:
   1st: Setuid and/or setgid
   2nd: Owner
   3rd: Group
   4th: Other
Each octal digit is sum of values corresponding to permissions of owner, group, and/or others:
   Read: 4
   Write: 2
   Execute or Search: 1   17

Permission string is 10 characters. First is **d** for directory; – for file. Other 9, in groups of 3, are owner, group, and other: **r** read; **w** write; **s** setuid or setgid; **x** execute/search. – in any location indicates it lacks that permission.   18

CONDITIONAL EXPRESSION PRIMITIVES

-r *file*	True if *file* exists and is readable.
-w *file*	True if *file* exists and is writable.
-x *file*	True if *file* exists and is executable.
-f *file*	True if *file* exists and is a regular file.
-d *file*	True if *file* exists and is a directory.
-c *file*	True if *file* exists and is a character special file.
-b *file*	True if *file* exists and is a block special file.
-p *file*	True if *file* exists and is a named pipe (fifo).
-u *file*	True if *file* exists and its set-user-id bit is set.
-g *file*	True if *file* exists and its set-group-id bit is set.
-k *file*	True if *file* exists and its sticky bit is set.
-s *file*	True if *file* exists and it has a size greater than zero.
-L *file*	True if *file* exists and is a symbolic link.
-O *file*	True if *file* exists and its owner is the effective user id.
-G *file*	True if *file* exists and its group is the effective group id.
-S *file*	True if *file* exists and it is a special file of type socket. 131

Primitive can be any of following unary expressions:

-t [*fildes*]	True if file whose file descriptor number is *fildes* (default 1) is open and is associated with a terminal device.
-o *option*	True if *option* is on.
-z *string*	True if length of *string* is zero.
-n *string*	True if length of *string* is non-zero. 131

With **test** and **[**, primitive can be any of these binary string expressions:

string1 = *string2*	True if *string1* is equal to *string2*.
string1 != *string2*	True if *string1* is not equal to *string2*. 132

With **[[...]]**, primitive can be any of these binary string expressions:

string = *pattern*	True if *string* matches pattern *pattern*.
string != *pattern*	True if *string* does not match pattern *pattern*.
string1 < *string2*	True if *string1* comes before *string2* .
string1 > *string 2*	True if *string1* comes after *string2*. 132

Primitive can be any of these binary file expressions:

file1 **-nt** *file2*	True if file *file1* is newer than file *file2*.
file1 **-ot** *file2*	True if file *file1* is older than file *file2*.
file1 **-ef** *file2*	True if *file1* is another name for file *file2*. 132

Primitive can be any of these expressions comparing 2 arithmetic expressions:

exp1 **-eq** *exp2*	True if value of *exp1* and *exp2* are equal.
exp1 **-ne** *exp2*	True if value of *exp1* and *exp2* are not equal.
exp1 **-gt** *exp2*	True if value of *exp1* is greater than value of *exp2*.
exp1 **-ge** *exp2*	True if value of *exp1* is greater than or equal to value of *exp2*.
exp1 **-lt** *exp2*	True if value of *exp1* is less than value of *exp2*.
exp1 **-le** *exp2*	True if value of *exp1* less than or equal to value of *exp2*.132

With **test** and **[**, a primitive can be a string by itself. In this case the primary is True if the string is not Null.   132

ARITHMETIC EXPRESSIONS	

Use arithmetic expressions:
    As array subscript.
    For each argument in **let**.
    Inside ((...)). ((...)) is same as **let** "...".
    As shift count in **shift**.
    For arithmetic comparison operators of **test**, [, or [[...]].
    As resource limits in **ulimit**.
    As right-hand side of variable assignment to an integer variable.
Calculations use longest integer arithmetic type.
No check for overflow.
	129

Associativity is left to right, except = is right to left.
Precedence:
    Operators in top box are highest precedence.
    Operators within a box are of equal precedence.
	129

(*expression*) Overrides precedence rules	129
–*expression* Unary minus	129
!*expression* Logical negation ~*expression* Bitwise negation	130
* Multiplication / Division % Remainder of 1st expression modulo 2nd expression	130
+ Addition – Subtraction	130
<< Left shift >> Right shift	130
<= Less than or equal to >= Greater than or equal to < Less than > Greater than	130
== Equal to != Not equal to	130
& Bitwise and	130
^ Bitwise exclusive or	130
| Bitwise or	130
&& Logical and	130
|| Logical or	130
identifier = expression Assignment *identifier op= expression* Compound assignment	130

Constant   [*base#*] *number*
    base   Decimal integer 2-36. Default base 10.
    number   Any non-negative number
	129

identifier Variable	129

PARAMETER EXPANSION		
Basic		
${*parameter*}		171
Modifiers		
${*parameter*:–*word*}	Using default values	172
${*parameter*:=*word*}	Assigning default values	172
${*parameter*:?*word*}	Displaying error if Null or unset	172
${*parameter*:+*word*}	Using alternate value	173
Substrings		
${*parameter#pattern*}	Remove small left pattern	173
${*parameter##pattern*}	Remove large left pattern	173
${*parameter%pattern*}	Remove small right pattern	173
${*parameter%%pattern*}	Remove large right pattern	174
Other		
${#*parameter*}	String length	174
${#*identifier*[*]}	Number of elements of an array	174
${#*identifier*[@]}	Number of elements of an array	174

ATTRIBUTES		
Use **typeset** to set and unset attributes.		193
–u	Uppercase	165
–l	Lowercase	166
–i or **–i***base*	Integer	166
–L or **–L***width*	Left-justified	166
–LZ or **–LZ***width*	Strip leading zeroes	167
–R or **–R***width*	Right-justified	167
–Z or **–Z***width*	Zero-filled	168
–RZ or **–RZ***width*	Zero-filled	168
–r	Read-only	168
–x	Exported	168
–H	Host operating system pathname mapping	169
–t	Tagged	169

PARAMETERS AND VARIABLES		
Special Parameters Set by ksh		
@	Positional parameters	175
*	Positional parameters	175
#	Number of positional parameters	176
–	Option flags	176
?	Return value	176
$	Process id of this shell	177
!	Background process id	177

Variables Set by ksh		
_	Temporary Variable	178
ERRNO	System Error Number	178
LINENO	Current Line Number	178
OLDPWD	Last Working Directory	179
OPTARG	Option Argument	179
OPTIND	Option Index	179
PPID	Parent Process Id	180
PWD	Working Directory	180
RANDOM	Random Number Generator	180
REPLY	Reply Variable	181
SECONDS	Elapsed Time and Seconds	181

Variables Used by ksh			
		Default	
CDPATH	Search Path for **cd** Built-in	None	182
COLUMNS	Number of Columns on Terminal	Implicit: 80	182
EDITOR	Pathname for Your Editor	Implicit: **/bin/ed**	182
ENV	User Environment File	None	182
FCEDIT	Editor for **fc** Built-in	Implicit: **/bin/ed**	183
FPATH	Search Path Auto-load Functions	None	183
HISTFILE	History Pathname	Note 1	183
HISTSIZE	Number of History Commands	Implicit: 128	184
HOME	Your Home Directory	Note 2	184
IFS	Internal Field Separator	Space-Tab-Newline	184
LINES	Number of Lines on Terminal	Implicit: 24	185
MAIL	Name of Your Mail File	Note 2	185
MAILCHECK	Frequency of Mail Check	600	185
MAILPATH	List of Mail Files	None	185
PATH	Path Search Directories	**/bin:/usr/bin:**	186
PS1	Primary Prompt String	$	186
PS2	Secondary Prompt String	>	186
PS3	Select Command Prompt	**#?**	187
PS4	Debug Prompt String	+	187
SHELL	Pathname of the Shell	Note 3	187
TERM	Terminal Type	None	188
TMOUT	Timeout Variable	Note 4	188
VISUAL	Visual Editor	None	188
Note 1: Implicit: **$HOME/.sh_history**			
Note 2: Set by system administrator.			
Note 3: May be set to pathname for **ksh** during login.			
Note 4: Zero (unlimited), or set by system administrator.			

KornShell LANGUAGE GRAMMAR		
newline	Newline character.	
name	Syntax of an identifier.	
test-primary	Conditional test expression.	131
string	Any sequence of non-special characters.	
digit	0–9	
expression	Syntax of an arithmetic expression.	129
complete-command		
	list newline	
list		
	term...	
	[*term...*] *and-or*	154
term		
	and-or newline	
	and-or ;	155
	and-or **&**	155
	and-or **|&**	156
and-or		
	pipe	153
	pipe **&&** [*newline...*] *pipe*	155
	pipe **||** [*newline...*] *pipe*	155
pipe		
	[**time**] *pipeline*	154
pipeline		
	command	
	pipeline **|** [*newline...*] *command*	
command		
	simple-command	144
	compound-command [*io-redirect...*]	153
compound-command		
	(*compound-list*)	161
	brace-group	161
	[[*test-expr*]]	156
	for *name* [**in** *word...*] *separator group*	158
	select *name* [**in** *word...*] *separator group*	158
	while *compound-list separator group*	160
	until *compound-list separator group*	160
	if *compound-list* **then** *compound-list else-part* **fi**	157
	case *word* **in** [*case-body*] **esac**	157
	function-def [*newline...*] *brace-group*	162
compound-list		
	[*newline...*] *list* [*newline... list*]... [*newline...*]	

group	
	brace-group
	do-group
brace-group	
	{ *compound-list* **}**
do-group	
	do *compound-list* **done**
else-part	
	[**elif** *compound-list*]... [**else** *compound-list*]
case-body	
	case-item... [*newline*...]
case-item	
	[*newline*...] [**(**] *pattern* **)** [*compound-list*] **;;**
pattern	
	word [**|** *word*]...
function-def	
	name **()**
	function *name*
simple-command	
	cmd-word...
	((*expression* **))**
cmd-word	
	assignment
	io-redirect
	word
assignment	
	name [**[** *expression* **]]** **=** *word* 126
io-redirect	
	[*digit*]*io-operator* *word* 136
io-operator	
	< or **<<** or **<<–** or **<&** or **<>**
	> or **>|** or **>>** or **>&**
word	
	string
	name
separator	
	;
	newline...
test-expr	
	test-primary
	(*test-expr* **)**
	! *test-expr*
	test-expr **||** *test-primary*
	test-expr **&&** *test-primary*

BUILT-IN COMMANDS

If return value is not shown, it is True.

† Dagger designates built-ins treated differently: **ksh** processes variable assignment lists specified with command before I/O redirection. Assignments remain in effect when the command completes. Errors in these built-ins cause the script that contains them to terminate.   191

Note: **bg**, **fg**, **kill**, and **wait** take arguments called a *job*. *job* can be specified as a process id. When the **interactive** option is on, *job* can also be specified as one of the following:

%number	To refer to the job by *number*.
%% or *%+*	Current job.
%−	Previous job.
%string	Job whose name begins with *string*.
%?string	Job whose name contains *string*. 44

† **:** [*arg...*]
         Null Command. *args* are expanded.   214

† **.** *file* [*arg...*]   Dot Command
         Reads complete *file* (dot script) and executes commands.
         Return value: Return value of last command executed.   201

† **alias** [**−tx**] [*name* [*=value*] ...]
         −t   Use to set and/or list tracked aliases.
         −x   Use to set and/or display exported aliases.
         Return value: **False** if all *name*(s) not aliases.
         Value is the number of *name*s that are not aliases.   191

bg [*job...*]
         Resumes stopped *job* and runs in background.
         Return value: **False** if **monitor** option is off.   211

† **break** [*n*]
         Exits smallest (or *n*th) enclosing **for**, **while**, **until**, **select** loop.   201

cd [*directory*]   208
         Changes working directory.
         Return value: **False** if change not successful.
cd *oldstring newstring*
         Substitutes *newstring* for *oldstring*.
         Return value: As above.   209

† **continue** [*n*]
         Continues smallest (or *n*th) enclosing **for**, **while**, **until**,
         or **select** loop.   202

echo [*arg...*]
         Echoes *arg*(s) on standard output. Also see **print**, below.   205

† **eval** [*arg...*]

> Reads arguments and executes resulting commands.
> Return value: Value of command as determined by *arg*s.   202

† **exec** [*command*] [*arg...*]

> Opens, closes, and/or copies file descriptors.
> Replaces **ksh** with *command*, without creating a new process.
> *arg*(s) are arguments to command.
> Return value: If *command* specified, command does not return.
> Otherwise, True.   205

† **exit** [*n*]

> Exits. If this is the login shell, logs you out.
> Return value: *n*, if specified. Otherwise, value of preceding
> command.   203

† **export** [*name* [*=value*]] ...

> Sets export attribute.   192

fc [**−e** *editor*] [**−nlr**] [*first* [*last*]]

> Displays, edits, and/or reexecutes commands from history file.
> **−n**   Suppresses command numbers when displayed.
> **−l**   Displays commands. Or use preset alias **history**.
> **−r**   Reverses order of commands.
> *first*   If *last* not specified, default is −16 if **−l**. Or −1 if no **−l**.
> *last*   Default is *first* if *first* specified. Otherwise, −1.
> Return value: False if invalid arguments. If **−l** not specified, value
> of last command is reexecuted.   214

fc −e − [*old=new*] [*command*]

> Reexecutes previous entered command. Or use preset alias **r**.
> Return value: Value of reexecuted command.   215

fg [*job...*]

> Moves background *jobs* into foreground.
> Return value: False if **monitor** option off.   211

getopts *optstring name* [*arg...*]

> Checks *arg* for legal options as specified in *optstring*. Option letter
> is saved in *name*. If no *arg*, processes positional parameters.
> Return value: True until **getopts** encounters the end of options.   216

jobs [**−lp**] [*job...*]

> Displays *job*s (or all active jobc), with process id if **−l** specified.
> Displays only process ids if **p** specified   212

kill [*−signal*] *job...*

> Sends signal to jobs or processes.
> Return value: Number of processes **kill** not able to send signal to. 212

kill −l

> Displays signal names and numbers.   213

let *arg...*

> Evaluates one or more arithmetic expressions.
> Return value: False if value of last expression is zero.   217

---

† **newgrp** [*group*] [*arg...*]
    Equivalent to **exec /bin/newgrp** *arg....*
    Return value: None.   217

---

print [**–Rnprsu**[*n*]] [*arg...*]
  –R Doesn't use \ conventions. Processes all but **–n** as *arg*.
  –n Doesn't add trailing Newline to output.
  –p Redirects *arg*(s) onto co-process.
  –r Doesn't use \ conventions.
  –s Redirects *arg*(s) to history file.
  –u Redirects arg(s) to file descriptor *n*. Default is 1.
  Unless you specify **–r** or **–R** , **print** uses escapes:
  \a Alert character (bell).
  \b Backspace.
  \c Print line without adding Newline.
  \f Formfeed.
  \n Newline.
  \r Return.
  \t Tab.
  \v Vertical Tab.
  **** Backslash.
  \0*x* 8-bit character, ASCII code is 1-, 2-, or 3-digit octal
      number *x*.   206

---

pwd
    Displays working directory.   209

---

read [**–prsu**[*n*]] [*name*?*prompt*] [*name...*]
  –p Reads input line from co-process.
  –r A \ at end of line doesn't signify line continuation.
  –s Saves copy of input line as command in history file.
  –u Reads from file descriptor *n*. Default is 0.
  name
    If omitted, default is **REPLY**.
  name?*prompt* If **interactive** on, displays *prompt* on
    standard error.
  Return value: True, unless *End-of-file* encountered.   207

---

† **readonly** [[*name*[=*value*]]...
    Sets readonly attribute.   193

---

† **return** [*n*]
    Causes function to return to invoking shell script.
    Return value: *n*, if specified. Otherwise, value of preceding
    command.   203

set [±**aefhkmnopstuvx**−] [±**o** *option*]... [±**A** *name*] [*arg*...]
Set options. Specify − and option letter, or −**o** *option*.
Unset options. Specify + and option letter, or +**o** *option*.
Set positional parameters. Specify *arg*(s).
Set array values. Specify ±**A** *name* and *arg*(s).
Sort positional parameters or *arg*. Specify −**s**.
Unset positional parameters. Specify −− and do not specify *arg*.

allexport (**a**)	Sets export attribute for subsequent assignments.
bgnice	Runs background jobs at lower priority.
emacs	Puts you in **emacs** built-in editor.
errexit (**e**)	If False return value, executes **ERR** trap if set.
(**f**)	See **noglob**, below.
gmacs	Puts you in **gmacs** built-in editor.
(**h**)	See **trackall**, below.
ignoreeof	If **interactive** set, doesn't exit on *End-of-File*.
keyword (**k**)	Places words in variable assignment list.
markdirs	Appends **/** to directory names.
monitor (**m**)	Runs background job in separate process group.
noclobber	Will not overwrite an existing file with > redirection operator. Specify >| to overwrite an existing file.
noexec (**n**)	Reads commands but doesn't execute them.
noglob (**f**)	Disables pathname expansion.
nolog	Doesn't store function definitions in history file.
nounset (**u**)	Error message when tries to expand unset variable.
privileged (**p**)	On when effective and real ids differ.
(**t**)	Reads and executes one command, then exits.
trackall (**h**)	Commands with alias name syntax become tracked.
(**u**)	See **nounset**, above.
verbose (**v**)	Displays input on standard error as it is read.
vi	Puts you in **vi** input mode.
viraw	Specifies **vi** character-at-a-time input.
xtrace (**x**)	Expands **PS4** and displays on standard error.
−−	No more option arguments 197

⁺ **shift** [*n*]
Shifts positional parameters left by *n*.   201

test [*expression*]
[[*expression*] **]** Left Bracket Command
Note: The [[...]] command (page 156) makes **test** and **[** obsolescent.
Checks type of a file, if two pathnames are same file, permissions, etc.
Return value: False if value of *expression* is not True. Also False
if *expression* is not specified.   218

---

† **times**
Displays time consumed by current **ksh** and child processes.   209

---

† **trap** [*action*] [*condition...*]
Specifies action when *condition*(s) arise.
Displays list of *action*(s) and *condition*(s) for trap settings.   204

---

† **typeset** ±**f**[**tux**] [*name...*]
  −t   Turns on **xtrace** option for specified function(s).
  −u   *name* refers to function that has not yet been defined.
  −x   Allows function definitions to remain in effect.
Return value: **False** if all *name*(s) not functions, unless **u**.
Value is number of *name*s not functions.   193

---

† **typeset** [±**HLRZilrtux**[*n*]] [*name*[=*value*]]...
Turns on/off and displays attributes for variables. See meaning
of attributes on page 308.   194

---

ulimit [−**acdfmpst**] [*n*]
Sets or displays system resource limits on some systems.
  −a   All current resource limits.
  −c   Size limit of *n* blocks on size of core dumps.
  −d   Size limit of *n* kilobytes on size of data area.
  −f   Size limit of *n* blocks on files written by child processes.
  −m   Size limit of *n* kilobytes on physical memory.
  −s   Size limit of *n* kilobytes on stack area.
  −t   Time limit of *n* seconds to be used by each process.
  n   Sets specified resource limit to *n*. Otherwise displays limit.   210

---

umask [*mask*]
Sets or displays file creation mask.   211

---

unalias *name...*
Removes each alias *name*.   196

---

unset [−**f**] *name...*
Unsets value(s) and attributes.
  −f   Causes name to refer to a function instead of a variable.
Return value: **False** if all *name*(s) not functions or variables.
Value is number of *name*s not functions or variables.   196

---

† **wait** [*job...*]
Waits for *job*s (or all processes) to terminate.
Return value: Termination status of last process waited for.   213

---

whence [−**v**] *name...*
Finds absolute pathname of each *name* when *name* is a program.
  −v   Finds type of item each name is. Or use preset alias **type**.
Return value: **False** if any *name*(s) not found.   219

PRESET ALIASES

```
autoload='typeset -fu'
false='let 0'
functions='typeset -f'
hash='alias -t'
history='fc -l'
integer='typeset -i'
nohup='nohup '
r='fc -e -'
true=:
type='whence -v'                                              146
```

OTHER COMMANDS

```
┌──────────────────────────────────────────────────────┐
│                                                        │
│                                                        │
│          21   PORTABILITY                              │
│                                                        │
│                                                        │
└──────────────────────────────────────────────────────┘
```

ksh code has been installed on many diverse computers and operating systems. However, **ksh** is not yet as widely available as is the Bourne Shell. In addition, there are several versions of **ksh** and the Bourne shell. This chapter summarizes the differences between versions of the Bourne shell and versions of **ksh** that you need to know if you plan to write scripts that run with more than one shell and/or on more than one system.

One aspect to portability is the ability to write scripts that run on different systems. Shell scripts rely on commands that are built into the language and on programs that are available on the operating system. While some programs may not be present on all systems, the command language and built-in commands of a given shell will always behave the same no matter what system the shell is running on. Because so many of the features of **ksh** are built in, it is possible to write **ksh** programs that do not rely heavily on the underlying operating system. This makes them easy to port to other systems running the same version of **ksh**.

The other aspect of writing portable scripts is writing them to run on systems that do not have **ksh**, or that don't have the latest version. In this case you have to restrict the features you use to those found in all versions of the shell you wish to run it with. However, scripts will not be completely portable if they rely on other programs.

This chapter summarizes most of the differences between the original version of the Bourne shell, the System V Release 3 Bourne shell, the 06/03/86 version of **ksh**, and the 11/16/88 version of **ksh**.

FEATURES OF ksh NOT IN BOURNE SHELL

The following features are not in the early version of the Bourne shell. Therefore, for maximal portability, avoid using these **ksh** features:
- # for comment. (Use : instead.)
- ! for negation within a character class.
- : within parameter expansions.
- Redirection with built-in commands.
- Shell functions.

test and **echo** were not built-ins on early versions of the Bourne shell and thus their behavior is system dependent.

FEATURES OF ksh *NOT IN SYSTEM V SHELL*

This section lists features that are part of **ksh,** but not part of the System V Release 3 Bourne shell. This list is not complete. There are additions to some built-in commands that are not noted.

The following are features of the 11/16/88 version of **ksh** not in the System V Release 3 Bourne shell:
- Attributes for variables, array variables, arithmetic, aliases, tilde expansion, and co-processes.
- Operators ((...)) **| & >| <>.**
- Reserved words **function, time, select,** [[and]].
- Substring expansions ${*name#pattern*} ${*name%pattern*} ${*name##pattern*} ${*name%%pattern*}
- Expansion of positional parameters greater than 9, ${*digits*}.
- String length expansion ${#*name*}.
- Command substitution syntax $(*command*).
- Pattern matching *(*pattern*), ?(*pattern*), +(*pattern*), and !(*pattern*).
- The variables **_, ENV, ERRNO, FCEDIT, FPATH, HISTFILE, HISTSIZE, LINENO, OLDPWD, PPID, PS3, PS4, PWD, RANDOM, REPLY, SECONDS, TMOUT.**
- Built-in commands **alias, bg, fc, fg, jobs, let, print, typeset, unalias,** and **whence.**
- **test** operators **−nt, −ot, −ef, −O, −G, −S.**
- **cd −** and **cd** with two arguments.
- Assigning **values** with **readonly** and **export.**
- Symbolic names for signals and traps.
- Names for options and **set −o.**

COMPATIBILITY OF ksh *WITH SYSTEM V SHELL*

This section lists the incompatibilities known to exist between the 11/16/88 version of **ksh** and the System V Release 3 version of the Bourne shell. *Note*: For conciseness, we refer to the System V, Release 3 version of the Bourne shell here as **bsh.**

In addition to the incompatibilities listed here, the output of built-in commands and error messages sometimes differs between **ksh** and **bsh** in a few cases. For instance, **times** produces two lines of output in **ksh** and only one line in **bsh.**

Character **^**:
  ksh Is not special.
  bsh Is an archaic synonym for **|.**

IFS variable:
> **ksh** Is only effective for **read**, and the results of parameter expansion and command substitution. **ksh** always initializes **IFS**.
>
> **bsh** Is effective for all words. Thus, for instance, **IFS=x; exit** executes **e** with argument **it**.

If an environment variable is modified:
> **ksh** New value is passed to the child processes.
>
> **bsh** You must export the variable for this to happen.

time:
> **ksh** Is a reserved word. Thus **time a | b** times the pipeline in **ksh**, while only **a** is timed in **bsh**. You can also **time** built-in commands and functions.
>
> **bsh** Is not a reserved word. You cannot **time** built-in commands or functions.

select and **function**:
> **ksh** Are reserved words.
>
> **bsh** Are not reserved words.

Scope of variable assignments on command lines:
> **ksh** Except for a subset of built-in commands, denoted with † in the ***Built-In Commands*** chapter, the scope of variable assignments is only for the command or function they precede.
>
> **bsh** All built-in commands and functions treat variable assignments as globals.

for, **while**, and **until** loops with I/O redirection:
> **ksh** Are executed in the current process environment. Assignments made within loops remain in effect after the loop completes.
>
> **bsh** Executes in a separate process environment. No side effects are possible.

Semantics of functions:
> **ksh** You can specify local variables, and you can write recursive functions. Errors in functions abort the function, but not the script that they are in. Parameter **0** expands to the function name. Traps defined in functions are local. **ksh** allows function names to be the same as variable names; therefore, **unset** requires you to specify **–f** when the name refers to a function.
>
> **bsh** All variables are global. You cannot write recursive functions. Errors in functions abort the script that calls them. Parameter **0** is unchanged inside a function. Traps are global. Functions and variables must have distinct names.

Words that begin with **~**:
> **ksh** May be expanded by tilde expansion.
>
> **bsh** Does not have this feature.

When '((' occurs where a command name is valid:
  ksh Assumes that an arithmetic expression follows.
  bsh Means nested (...).

Two adjacent **IFS** delimiters, other than Space or Tab, used with **read**:
  ksh Generates a Null input argument. Therefore, you can use **IFS=:**
    and correctly read the **/etc/profile** file even when fields are omitted.
  bsh Multiple delimiters count as a single delimiter.

Arithmetic test comparison operators (**–gt**, **–eq**, **–lt**, ...):
  ksh Allows any arithmetic expressions as operands.
  bsh Allows only constants.
  Note: If you say **test x –eq 0** in **bsh** (which is meaningless), it returns
    True. In **ksh**, it depends on the value of the variable **x**. If there is no
    variable **x** or if **x** does not evaluate to a number, then **ksh** produces an
    error message.

Environment handed down to a program:
  ksh Is not sorted.
  bsh Is sorted.
  Note: No program should ever rely on the environment variables being
    sorted since any program can modify the environment.

hash command:
  ksh Has a preset alias **hash** that does most of what the **bsh** built-in
    hash command does, except for the **–r** option. In **ksh**, you must
    specify **PATH=$PATH** to achieve the same result as **–r** in **bsh**.
  bsh Has a built-in **hash** command.

set – – with no arguments:
  ksh Unsets the positional parameter list.
  bsh Sets parameter **1** to Null, and unsets the other positional parameters.

Specification of command line options:
  ksh Accepts options of the form **–x –v** as well as **–xv** both for
    invocation and for **set**.
  bsh Only allows one option argument.

Unbalanced quotes:
  ksh Does not allow unbalanced quotes with any script. *Note*: **ksh**
    behaves like **bsh** for **eval** statements.
  bsh If the end-of-file is reached before a balancing quote in **bsh**, it
    quietly inserts the balancing quote.

Failures of any built-in command:
  ksh Except for built-ins denoted with † in the *Built-In Commands*
    chapter, failures cause a return value of False, but do not cause the
    script that contains them to abort. In this respect, **ksh** treats most
    built-in commands semantically the same as non-built-in commands.
  bsh Causes a script that contains the built-in to abort.

Sequence $(:
> **ksh** Is special. When used within grouping (double) quotes, $(must be preceded by \ to remove its special meaning.
> **bsh** Sequence is illegal outside of grouping (double) quotes. Processed literally inside grouping quotes.

exec, when used without arguments (for I/O redirection):
> **ksh** Sets close-on-exec on each file descriptor greater than 2.
> **bsh** Does not set close-on-exec on any files.

When the real user id is not equal to the effective user id, or the real group id is not equal to the effective group id:
> **ksh** Resets the effective user and group ids to the real user and group ids unless the **privileged** option (**-p**) is on.
> **bsh** Does not do this.

NEW FEATURES IN 11/16/88 VERSION OF ksh

New Pattern Matching Capabilities

The following pattern matching capabilities (page 128) have been added:
> **?**(*pattern* [|*pattern*] ...) optionally matches any *pattern*.
> *****(*pattern* [|*pattern*] ...) matches zero or more instances of any *pattern*.
> **+**(*pattern* [|*pattern*] ...) matches one or more instances of any *pattern*.
> **@**(*pattern* [|*pattern*] ...) matches one instance of any *pattern*.
> **!**(*pattern* [|*pattern*] ...) matches anything except any of *pattern*.

New test Compound Command

A new compound command beginning with the new reserved word [[and ending with the new reserved word]] has been added (page 156). This compound command is intended to replace both **test** and [. The operators **&&** and | | replace **-a** and **-o**. Unquoted parentheses are used for grouping. The words between [[and]] are not expanded for word splitting and pathname expansion. The operators = and != allow the right-hand side to be a pattern. You can also specify < and > within [[ ]] to compare two strings.

New Arithmetic Operators

The arithmetic operators |, &, | |, &&, ^, <<, >> and ~ (page 130) have been added. Use them in any arithmetic expression.

All of the assignment operators, +=, etc. (page 130) are now recognized by **ksh**. The precedences and associativity of **ksh** arithmetic operators are the same as those of the C programming language.

Changes to Variables

Six new variables have been added:

ERRNO   (page 178) is set to the value of the error number after each system call.

FPATH   (page 183) is used to search for function definitions. The declaration **typeset –fu** *name* causes *name* to be searched for in **FPATH** directories. A preset alias has been added, **autoload='typeset –fu'**.

LINENO   (page 178) is set to the line number of the current command.

OPTARG   (page 179) is set with the new **getopts** command.

OPTIND   (page 179) is set with the new **getopts** command.

PS4   (page 187) evaluates to the prompt used with **set –x**. The default is + .

The attributes for exported variables (page 168) are now passed to separate invocations of **ksh**. Thus, setting a variable readonly and exporting it causes it to be readonly whenever **ksh** is invoked.

The **IFS** parameter (page 184) is reset to the default value after reading the environment file, even if you export **IFS**.

Editing Changes and Additions

The following changes and additions have been made to the built-in editors:

- Searches starting with a ^ (pages 101 and 119) now match only at the beginning of the line in both **emacs** and **vi**.
- The new **vi** directive \ (page 108) causes the current word to be extended as far as possible as long as it matches a unique pathname.
- The **emacs** directive ESCAPE ESCAPE (page 98) now behaves like the **vi** directive \, above.
- The directive | (page 112) has been added to **vi**.
- The **vi** directive **r** (page 115) can now be preceded by a count.

Changes to Reading and Expanding

To conform with the proposed IEEE POSIX 1003.2 shell standard, variable assignment lists are expanded from left-to-right (see page 150).

Each pattern in a **case** statement (page 157) now allows an optional (. The (is required when a **case** statement is part of a $() command substitution.

The previously unadvertised <> redirection operator (page 138) now works. This operator causes a file to be opened for read and write. The file is not truncated.

Aliases can now be expanded inside other aliases (page 145). Thus, if you alias **foo=bar bar=bam**, then **foo** expands to **bam**. However, an alias will not reexpand within its own expansion, so that you can define alias, **alias ls='ls –l'**. If you alias **foo=bar bar=foo**, then **foo** expands to **foo** and **bar** expands to **bar**.

The expansions for **~+** and **~–** have been changed to expand to **$PWD** and **$OLDPWD**, respectively (page 146). Previously, they returned the value of the present working directory and the previous working directory at the time they were read. This caused surprising results when used within scripts or functions. Also, **~** is no longer recognized as special after a **:** within a variable assignment (page 146).

ksh now reads to the matching unquoted **}** when it encounters **${** (page 135). Earlier versions of **ksh** tokenized words between **${** and **}** when reading them.

ksh reads and expands arguments for the built-in commands **alias**, **export**, **readonly**, and **typeset** that are in the format of a variable assignment specially (page 191). They are processed for **~** substitution and do not undergo parameter expansion or word splitting.

If the last element of a pipeline (page 190) is a built-in, a compound command, or a function, it now runs in the current process environment. Previously, it ran in a subshell. If you require the previous semantics, use parentheses. All of the other elements of a pipeline continue to be run in a subshell. This remains a caveat and you should use parentheses if you require that pipeline elements be carried out in a subshell environment.

Changes to Built-in Commands

The **alias** (page 191) and **typeset** (page 193) built-ins now allow option arguments as separate words, rather than all in one word; for example, **typeset –ux** and **typeset –u –x**. Also, commands that allow multiple options, now allow you to specify **––** as an indicator that there are no more options. This is needed in case the next argument starts with a **–**.

The alert character escape sequence **\a** (page 206) has been added to the **echo** and **print** built-in commands. The sequence **\a** expands to the Bell character.

The built-in commands **break** (page 201), **continue** (page 202), and **exit** (page 203) now behave like special built-ins and have a dagger in front of them.

Several options have been added to **test [,** and **[[...]]** (page 131).
  –O *file* returns True if file is owned by real user.
  –G *file* returns True if file is owned by real group.
  –S *file* returns True if file is of type socket.

You can now assign values to an array variable with **set –A** *name value* (page 200).

A **DEBUG** trap (pages 64 and 204) has been added to aid debugging. This trap is executed after each statement. Also, an execution trace now displays I/O redirections.

The **getopts** built-in (page 216) has been added.

typeset –p has been removed (page 193).

New Options to Built-in Commands

The **nolog** option (page 198) has been added to the **set** built-in command to disable the saving of the source for functions in the history file.

The **noclobber** option (page 198) has been added. With **noclobber** on, > *file* produces an error if *file* already exists. Use >|*file* to write to a file when **noclobber** is on.

The meaning of the **–p** option (page 199) has been changed, as well as its name. Previously, **–p** caused the path to be reset to a default value and the shell not to run your personal **.profile** and **$ENV** files. Instead, the shell executed a file named **/etc/suid_exec**. The **–p** option was automatically enabled whenever the real and effective user or group id were not equal. This was called the **protected** option. In the 11/16/88 version, the **–p** no longer resets the path to a default value. In addition, the effective user id and group id are set to the real user id and group id unless **ksh** has been invoked with the **–p** option, which is now called **privileged**. In addition, turning off **privileged**, (**set +p**), sets the effective ids to their real values. On some systems, **set –p** restores the permissions to what that they were before the **set +p**.

set –o bgnice (page 197) is now the default mode.

The declaration **typeset –fu** *name* causes *name* to be searched for in **FPATH** directories (page 70). A preset alias has been added, **autoload='typeset –fu'**.

Change to Co-processes

You can now move the file descriptors for a co-process (a job followed by |&) to a numbered file descriptor. Do this by using **exec** *n*<&p for moving the read descriptor (page 138) and **exec** *n*>&p for moving the write descriptor (page 139), where *n* is a digit. Once you move this descriptor, you can close it or redirect any command to or from it (page 66).

Change to Job Control

You can now refer to jobs as *%?string* (page 211) to match a job that contains *string* as part of its name. The **wait** command now allows you to specify a job to wait for. Earlier versions only allowed process ids.

OBSOLESCENT FEATURES

Caution: The following features are currently supported by **ksh** for backward compatibility only. Their use is strongly discouraged. These features may be removed from **ksh** at some point in the future.

- The **–k** and **–t** options to **set**.
- **echo** as a built-in command. (Use **print** instead.)
- **test** and [as built -in commands. (Use [[...]] instead.)
- The `...` command substitution. (Use **$(...)** instead.)
- The *identifier*( ) function definition syntax. (Use **function** *identifier* instead.)

POSSIBLE EXTENSIONS

Process Substitution

This is available only on versions of the UNIX system that support the **/dev/fd** directory for naming open files. Each command argument of the form <(*list*) or >(*list*) runs process *list* asynchronously connected to some file in the **/dev/fd** directory. The name of this file becomes the argument to the command. If the form with > is selected, then writing on this file provides input for *list*. If < is used , then the file passed as an argument will receive the output of the *list* process.

The following example cuts fields 1 and 3 from files fi1 and fi2 respectively, pastes the results together, and sends the results to the processes pro1 and pro2, as well as putting them onto standard output. Note that the file that is passed as an argument to the command is a UNIX system pipe, so that the programs that expect to seek on the file will not work.

Example

```
paste <(cut -f1 fi1) <(cut -f3 fi2) | tee >(pro1) >(pro2)
```

Floating Point Arithmetic

The attributes **exponential** (**–E**) and **float** (**–F**) are reserved for real valued variables. Each can be specified with a number that specifies:

–E The number of significant figures to use when the number is expanded.

–F The number of places after the decimal when the number is expanded.

22 CHARACTER SET

This table may be useful when you specify ranges of characters in character classes, or when you read a printout that shows non-printing characters in their octal representation, or when you use **print** or **echo** with the \\ı option, etc.

ksh displays letters, digits, and punctuation characters as you would expect. For instance, **ksh** displays control characters as ^A (octal 001), ^B (octal 002), etc.

The character set shown here may differ slightly on different terminals and different systems.

CONTROL CHARACTERS

Dec	Octal	Hex	ASCII	Explanation
0	000	00	^@	NUL (Null)
1	001	01	^A	SOH (Start of heading)
2	002	02	^B	STX (Start text)
3	003	03	^C	ETX (End text)
4	004	04	^D	EOT (End of transmission)
5	005	05	^E	ENQ (Enquiry)
6	006	06	^F	ACK (Acknowledge)
7	007	07	^G	BEL (Bell)
8	010	08	^H	BS (Backspace)
9	011	09	^I	TAB (Tab)
10	012	0A	^J	LF (Linefeed, Newline)
11	013	0B	^K	VT (Vertical Tab)
12	014	0C	^L	FF (Formfeed)
13	015	0D	^M	CR (Carriage return)
14	016	0E	^N	SO (Shift out)
15	017	0F	^O	SI (Shift in)

Dec	Octal	Hex	ASCII	Explanation
16	020	10	^P	DLE (Data link escape)
17	021	11	^Q	DC1 (X-ON)
18	022	12	^R	DC2
19	023	13	^S	DC3 (X-OFF)
20	024	14	^T	DC4
21	025	15	^U	NAK (Negative acknowledge)
22	026	16	^V	SYN (Synchronous idle)
23	027	17	^W	ETB (End transmission blocks)
24	030	18	^X	CAN (Cancel)
25	031	19	^Y	EM (End of medium)
26	032	1A	^Z	SUB (Substitute)
27	033	1B	^[	ESC (Escape)
28	034	1C	^\	FS (File separator)
29	035	1D	^]	GS (Group separator)
30	036	1E	^^	RS (Record separator)
31	037	1F	^_	US (Unit separator)

SPACE

Dec	Octal	Hex	ASCII	Explanation
32	040	20		SPACEBAR SP (Space)

PRINTING CHARACTERS

Dec	Octal	Hex	ASCII	Explanation
33	041	21	!	Expands to command number in **PS1**
34	042	22	"	Grouping quoting
35	043	23	#	Comment character
				Substring operator, left truncate
				Default primary prompt for superuser
36	044	24	$	Default prompt
				Parameter expansion
				Special parameter
37	045	25	%	Substring operator, right truncate
				Job identifier
38	046	26	&	Asynchronous execution
39	047	27	'	Single quote
				Literal quoting
40	050	28	(	Subshell grouping
41	051	29	)	
42	052	2A	*	Wildcard match in patterns
43	053	2B	+	
44	054	2C	,	
45	055	2D	–	
46	056	2E	.	(dot) Working directory
				Built-in command
47	057	2F	/	Name of root directory
				Pathname separator
48	060	30	0	
49	061	31	1	
50	062	32	2	
51	063	33	3	
52	064	34	4	
53	065	35	5	
54	066	36	6	
55	067	37	7	
56	070	38	8	
57	071	39	9	
58	072	3A	:	Null built-in command
59	073	3B	;	Command separator
60	074	3C	<	Redirects command input

Dec	*Octal*	*Hex*	*ASCII*	*Explanation*
61	075	3D	=	Used in variable assignments
62	076	3E	>	Redirects command output
				Default secondary prompt
63	077	3F	?	Single character match in patterns
64	100	40	@	
65	101	41	A	
66	102	42	B	
67	103	43	C	
68	104	44	D	
69	105	45	E	
70	106	46	F	
71	107	47	G	
72	110	48	H	
73	111	49	I	
74	112	4A	J	
75	113	4B	K	
76	114	4C	L	
77	115	4D	M	
78	116	4E	N	
79	117	4F	O	
80	120	50	P	
81	121	51	Q	
82	122	52	R	
83	123	53	S	
84	124	54	T	
85	125	55	U	
86	126	56	V	
87	127	57	W	
88	130	58	X	
89	131	59	Y	
90	132	5A	Z	

Dec	*Octal*	*Hex*	*ASCII*	*Explanation*
91	133	5B	[	
92	134	5C	\	Escape quoting
93	135	5D	]	
94	136	5E	^	
95	137	5F	_	(underscore)
96	140	60	`	Backquote (grave accent) Used for old command substitution
97	141	61	a	
98	142	62	b	
99	143	63	c	
100	144	64	d	
101	145	65	e	
102	146	66	f	
103	147	67	g	
104	150	68	h	
105	151	69	i	
106	152	6A	j	
107	153	6B	k	
108	154	6C	l	
109	155	6D	m	
110	156	6E	n	
111	157	6F	o	
112	160	70	p	
113	161	71	q	
114	162	72	r	
115	163	73	s	
116	164	74	t	
117	165	75	u	
118	166	76	v	
119	167	77	w	
120	170	78	x	

Dec	Octal	Hex	ASCII	Explanation
121	171	79	y	
122	172	7A	z	
123	173	7B	{	Command grouping
124	174	7C	|	Pipe command output
125	175	7D	}	
126	176	7E	~	Tilde substitution

DELETE, RUBOUT

Dec	Octal	Hex	ASCII	Explanation
127	177	7F		DEL, RUB (Delete, rubout)

INDEX

334 *Index*

A

a directive, in **vi**, definition 113
A directive, in **vi**, definition 114
aborting programs 27
access,
  permissions,
    as component of long file listing 28
    specifying 18
  rights,
    inherited by child process 234
    to files and processes as component of environment 233
addition, arithmetic expression 130
alias, declaration command, format 191
aliases,
  as component of environment 233
  creating with **alias** 145
  defining 30
  definitions,
    inheritance rules for 145
    not inherited by child process 234
  displaying 31, 145
  as **emacs** macros 99
  ending is Space or Tab 145
  exported,
    glossary definition 293
    managing with **alias** 191
    testing a name for 219
  glossary definition 293
  informal definition of 30
  interaction with command processing 141
  preset 145
  preventing from being recognized 132
  processing of 192
  quick reference 303
  removing a name from 145, 196
  shared by a function and its invoking script 151
  substitution, processing of 145
  syntax of 126, 191
  testing a name for 219
  tracked,
    characteristics and processing 151
    managing with **alias** 191
    testing a name for 219
    using 199
  use with functions 71
  as **vi** macros 109
allexport (**–a**), set option, definition 197
and,
  bitwise, arithmetic expression 130
  conditional primitive connector 156, 218
  logical, arithmetic expression 130

and list command, format 155
Apollo Computer, as vendor of **ksh** 4
appending,
  to files 139
  standard output 34, 139
  text, in **vi** 113, 114, 116
Apple Computer, as vendor of **ksh** 4
application programming 239
architecture, design spec for MH 264
arguments,
  echoing 205, 206
  incorrect,
    as trigger for False return value 189
    number of as trigger for False return values 189
  Null, how processed 149
  processing 64, 216
    of built-in commands 190
arithmetic,
  base of variables, specifying 129, 195
  comparison operators, use of arithmetic expressions in 129, 130
  constants, format of 129
  evaluation syntax 135, 217
  expressions,
    comparing 130, 132
    evaluating 217
    quick reference 307
    syntax of 129
    use as array subscripts 170
    use of integer attribute with 129, 166
    where used 129
  floating point, as possible extension to **ksh** 326
  integer, concepts of 60
arrays,
  assigning values to 200
  assignment, syntax 135
  concepts of 61, 170
  determining number of elements in 174
  element zero, obtaining 170
  parameters for 170
  referencing all elements of 170
  specified 170
  subscript expansion in 129, 171
  unsetting 196
  variables,
    assignment syntax 135
    assigning values to 197
    and attributes as component of the KornShell 6
ASCII,
  character set 327

NOTES

NOTES

NOTES

NOTES

NOTES

NOTES

NOTES

NOTES

NOTES

NOTES